MASTERING THE MOUNTAIN

THE NEW AMERICAN TEACHING METHOD TO DOWNHILL SKIING

by Walt Snellman

Drawings by Kim Jackson Snellman and Erick Ingraham

Ziff-Davis Publishing Company·New York

Copyright © 1980 by Ziff-Davis Publishing Company
All rights reserved.
No part of this book may be reproduced in any form without permission in writing from the publisher.
All photographs by Walter Snellman and Kimberly Jackson Snellman.
Manufactured in the United States of America.
First printing, 1980.
Library of Congress Catalog Card Number: 80-51123
ISBN: 0-87165-084-3 (hardcover)
      0-87165-085-1 (paperback)

Ziff-Davis Publishing Company
One Park Avenue
New York, N.Y. 10016

MASTERING THE MOUNTAIN

Acknowledgments

My deep-felt thanks to Kim Jackson Snellman for her moral support, her critique, her long hours spent drawing and typing, and her remarkably good humor, especially when I'd change some detail just after she had completed an illustration. I'd also like to thank Garmont USA for supplying ski boots and White Stag for supplying the skiwear worn in many of the photographs. Finally, my thanks to the thousands of students I've instructed who unknowingly taught me a great deal about skiing and ski teaching.

CONTENTS

Introduction: What—Another "How to Ski" Book?   xi

Section I: Your Equipment and Environment   1
1. An Equipment Primer   3
2. Appropriate Apparel and Accessories   16
3. Skis—More Than Just Boards   20
4. The Care and Feeding of Your Skis   27
5. All Feet are not Created Equal   33
6. Coping with Cold and Altitude   37
7. Surmounting Adverse Weather   42
8. Choosing a Ski Area   45
9. Shopping for a Ski School   48

Section II: First Motions on Skis   51
10. Will I be Able to Ski?   53
11. Getting to the Slopes   55
12. Where Pointeth the Feet, So Goeth the Skis   58
13. The Wedge   68
14. Steering Turns   73
15. Lifts   78
16. Skier Safety and Courtesy   83

Section III: Knee Movements Left and Right   85
17. Weight Transfer and Edging   87

18	The Traverse	94
19	About Face	99
20	The Sideslip	102
21	Uphill Stem Turns	109
22	Slowing Down	115
23	A Basic Skidded Turn	119
24	Upper Body Position	123
25	Downstem Turns	128

Section IV: Knee Movements Up and Down — 133

26	The Hockey Stop	135
27	Vertical Knee Action	140
28	Parallel Weight Transfer Turn	144
29	Mogul Mastery	151
30	Active Unweighting	157
31	Speedy Skiing	165

Section V: Dynamic Actions — 173

32	Anticipation and Rebound Unweighting	175
33	Anticipation in the Bumps	183
34	Weight Distribution and "Sitting Back"	188
35	Avalement	196
36	Carving	203
37	Lateral Projection	210
38	Powder Passion	217
39	Intrigue on Ice	227
	Epilogue	233
	Glossary	235

MASTERING THE MOUNTAIN

INTRODUCTION

WHAT—ANOTHER "HOW TO SKI" BOOK?

Skiing is unique. No other sport offers as many variables in equipment, terrain, weather, surface conditions, technique, personal style, and speed. Because of this, skiing poses a continual mental and physical challenge to its participants. This challenge is evident as skiers always push themselves that extra bit, skiing just a little faster, seeking out harder slopes, racing against others, or braving the cold for one more run. Whether as a first timer or a seasoned racer, each skier experiences a thrill of challenge as he places ever more exacting demands on his body. This seeking for perfection makes each skier never completely content with his ability. Ask one hundred skiers why they ski, and you'll receive one hundred different reasons, such as "For fun," "It's thrilling," or "For the sunshine and the exercise." Ask the same people what their goal is, and they'll all reply they want to ski better. This might be phrased as "Looking more graceful," "Handling moguls smoothly," "Skiing as well as my husband," or "Winning a NASTAR gold."

In recent years a rash of mind improvement ski books have been published. I thoroughly agree with the inner skiing premise, that a positive mental attitude improves your learning capacity. But, if I decided to take up a new sport, such as skydiving, you'd need three men and a boy to drag me anywhere near an airplane if all I had read was "Think light" and "Float free." I'd first want to know all the details of wearing the chute, pulling the cord, etc., and I'd want to practice each step until I could do it without thinking. Most people feel the same way about skiing. They want to know how to ski better, which is why I have written a technique book.

While growing up, we lose much of our childlike openness and simplicity. As adults (and that includes most teenagers) we often learn new sports with difficulty. We have matured into rational, problem-solving beings who want to understand how to do something before we physically do it. I taught myself to ski by the trial-and-error method as a young adult, and it was a struggle. A logical, step-by-step approach helps us to achieve our goals, whether they be making a fortune in the market, cooking a Chinese meal, or racing in the Olympics. This book will show you the steps needed to reach your own personal ski goal.

Not too long ago ski instruction was confusing. Each country taught a different technique, yet, when you analyzed the top skiers of each nation, they all skied the same way. The Professional Ski Instructors of America have been world leaders in simplifying ski teaching, thanks to their skill concept. This book follows the outlines of the new American Teaching Method, which recognizes that each step in the learning process is only a refinement of the basic skills you'll learn your first days on skis. It's a well-tested method for rapid improvement.

Each ski school and each instructor modifies the general teaching outline. Based on my teaching experience in Aspen, Jackson Hole, and Lake Tahoe, I've included what I have found works best for most skiers. I've presented a standard learning sequence and commonly accepted terminology so that you can easily relate this book to ski school lessons, magazine instructional articles, and other skiers. We learn best by actual experience, so I've included numerous "on the snow" exercises. These are the same ones I'd give you in lessons on the hill. Wherever a photograph might be too vague, I've included an illustration to more clearly define a concept. You have in your hands the same ideas and maneuvers I'd teach you in several years of private lessons.

There is more than one way to skin a cat and also to learn skill improvement. I frequently give several approaches to achieve the same skill level. This recognizes that you, as an individual, may respond better to one method than to another. It also gives you a more total ski experience, as you should be aware of different ways to turn skis, and not be confined to one method. The ultimate result is a versatile skier, one who can use various techniques to handle any terrain, someone who is master of the mountain.

Section I of the book contains general background information. You may want to refer to specific chapters as the need arises, when you are about to purchase equipment, ski in stormy weather, wax skis, or choose where to ski. Section II is aimed at a beginner's first days on skis. Sections III, IV, and V correspond roughly to ski school class levels C, D, and E/F. So you don't stereotype yourself as a certain alphabetical level skier, I've labeled these sections to correspond with the controlling body motions that are emphasized in each section. Beginners will naturally start with the first technique chapter and progress onward. If you are a more experienced skier and want to improve, don't automatically open to an advanced chapter. Try the exercises in progression the first time. These consist of basic skills required at every level of the sport. If you can truly accomplish each exercise, then it should only take an hour or two

HOW TO USE THIS BOOK

until you are up to a new one. But there's a very good chance that one of them will stump you, and it may just well be the reason you are stuck on a plateau at what you thought was a more "advanced" level.

Look at each exercise as a way to improve your skills, and not as a goal of a specific way to ski. A parallel turn shouldn't be any better than a stem turn; it's simply a different use of the same principles. Relate each exercise to a refinement of the basic skills. These are *steering,* which is a pivoting action applied to the skis; *edging,* which is a lateral motion to tip a ski on its side; and *pressure,* which is the amount of weight applied (or not applied) to a ski. Along with these technical skills you'll refine your innate ability to balance, as you learn to stay upright over your feet by *balancing.*

Whatever skill level you fit into, let your learning experience be fun. If you force yourself to do something, or get frustrated and try too hard, you won't improve. Don't worry about striving to perfect each exercise. If you find you can't do one, skip it and come back and try it again later. Meanwhile, additional mileage or another exercise may have provided the clues you needed to do the "hard" one. Whenever you read an exercise, I suggest you visualize yourself in the illustration, doing the maneuver. Imagine yourself performing the action, "feeling" all your muscles move for you at the right time. On the snow, accomplish the whole sequence first in your mind, then immediately do it while moving.

Remember that there is no "right" or "wrong" way to ski. There are simply efficient or inefficient ways to get down the hill. Use the ideas in this book as a guide to an efficient method of skiing. Your body likes to work smoothly, so when something feels graceful or good, keep doing it. Enjoy yourself, and don't get too caught up in technique or terminology. After all, everything boils down to the reality that skiers flow with gravity and turn only two ways—left or right. The way you do this will develop your individual skiing style.

Section 1

YOUR EQUIPMENT AND ENVIRONMENT

Your equipment and its condition greatly affect how well you ski, as do the weather, temperature, and snow quality. In this section you'll learn the finer points of selecting gear suited for your ability, and maintaining that equipment for maximum performance. You'll discover ways to stay warm in the cold and to ski comfortably in nasty weather. Finally, you'll find some clues to aid you in your choice of ski areas and ski schools.

1
AN EQUIPMENT PRIMER

Without equipment, a skier is only a walker and talker. Modern skiing technique has evolved mainly because of improvements in equipment. Space-age materials for boots and skis, combined with safer release bindings, have recently made the sport easier and hence more enjoyable. Knowing this, every skier is somewhat of an equipment "nut," always seeking out better gear for maximum performance. Whenever two skiers get together, their talk turns eventually to what they're skiing on. To non-skiers, the vocabulary sounds exotic, as the skiers mention flex, cants, slalom cuts, anti-shock and the like. In this chapter we'll examine the basic function and features of equipment. This will give you a better idea of what to look for when you buy, and also help you interpret the unique terminology.

While poking around in grandma's attic, you may come across some leather lace boots and seven-foot skis with metal edges attached by screws. Have fun with them in your backyard or use them for den decorations. However, for your own safety and pleasure on the slopes, use modern equipment. It doesn't have to be this year's most expensive models, but it should be in good shape and reasonably new. Generally, skis, boots, or bindings more than four years old have been superseded by equipment which is lighter, more responsive, and safer.

If you have not been on skis before, I recommend that you rent equipment your first couple outings. During the beginning stage you'll use special short learning skis, which will be different from the ones you'll soon want to buy. Try to rent your gear at a time when the shop is least busy (that's *not* at 9 A.M. on a sunny Saturday morning). Renting from a local ski shop near your home saves hassle at the ski area, and allows you to play with the equipment in the privacy of your living room ahead of time. If you'll be at a resort area for several days, you should rent from a shop there. This gives you the availability of quick adjustments or exchanges near the slopes. Before leaving any shop, be certain the binding release has been checked and that you understand how to put on the bindings, and how to adjust them if necessary. They're your legs, so ask the shop all the questions you want.

When you are ready to buy your own equipment, and are looking for advice, go to a reputable sporting goods store which specializes in ski gear. (With very few exceptions discount, mail order, or department stores don't have the trained personnel or shop facilities you'll need.) Visit several stores to get various opinions and to be aware of all of the varieties available. Collect manufacturers' literature and stay current by reading the skiing magazines. Ski gear changes rapidly—what was "hot gear" four years ago may today be as obsolete as tail fins on cars.

Here are a few pointers on what to look for in equipment.

BOOTS

Although skis are the glamour item when buying, I'll discuss boots first because they are just as important. It's essential that a boot fit your foot snugly, but comfortably. When you rotate your foot, the boot transfers this turning movement to the skis. Any free play in the boot causing your foot to move inside delays a turn and may even raise blisters. The boot must also instantly transfer knee motions left or right (called edging or lateral motions) to the skis. This means that the boots must be rigid enough that when you move a knee left the boot angles that way immediately, without sideways bend in the ankle. However, a boot must still allow a normal forward ankle movement, or "flex." Finally, boots must keep your feet warm and dry.

Shop for boot models suited to your skiing ability. Manufacturers frequently designate boots as recreational, advanced recreational (or sport) and racing. Their literature or a ski shop can tell you what models are intended for easy cruising, turning in the bumps, or running gates.

Let's get down to the physical makeup of the boot. The outer shell consists of one to four separate pieces of special plastics. The forward flex is accomplished by either the use of a freely moving hinge near the ankle or the bending of the shell material. Padding on the tongue cushions your shin as you flex forward. A very easy flexing, or "soft," boot requires large forward and backward movements to affect the pressure applied to the tips or tails of the skis. These boots are known as "forgiving" of errors, and are generally built for beginners. Very stiff flexing boots are extremely responsive but need precise movements, and are for experts and racers. The stiffness is designed to vary throughout the range of ankle flex. A popular compromise flex is soft at its midrange of travel, but stiffens rapidly at the ends. This "freestyle" or sport flex provides good bump absorption and control. Some boots will have adjustable springs, clips, or rubber blocks built in, enabling you to vary the flex.

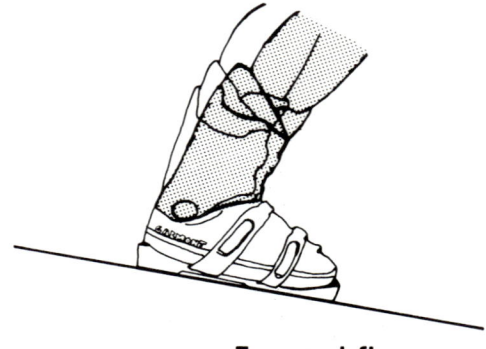

Forward flex

4

The buckle system opens for easy entry, and tightens the shell for a firm fit. More expensive boots often have a micro-adjustment buckle, which allows tightness levels between the large notch positions.

Inner boots nest within the outer shells. These "liners" or "bladders" of molded foam give warmth and padding, and accommodate variations in foot shapes. Thick padding on the cuff cushions the leg and also allows limited ankle movement sideways. Frequently a "flow" material is enclosed in pockets in the liner at critical fit areas, especially ankles and heels. This semiliquid gunk molds itself to your foot for a precise fit. "Memory foam" also flows and retains its shape inbetween wearings. Liners are removable, which lets you more effectively dry out a wet boot, or modify their fit by attaching additional padding. In most designs you'll need a friend to hold open the rigid plastic shell while you remove or insert the liner.

Most boots force you to stand with your ankles flexed forward, and hence your knees must be bent for balance. This stance doesn't sound like much fun, as your thigh muscles will tire more easily, but you'll soon find that it's the only way to ski. This "forward lean" is caused by a combination of the forward angle of the upper shell and the footbed angle, which raises your heel higher than the toes. The more advanced you become, the greater the lean angle you'll need. Some boots allow you to adjust this angle, from an upright position for standing around to a deep forward angle for racing.

Forward lean angle

Most people's legs angle outward from the ankles, and many boots accommodate this structure with an outward lean built into them, known as a "cant angle." Ask your shop salesperson about this to decide how much it will affect you. (If you are knock-kneed you would not want this built-in cant angle.) Some boots have an adjustable cant angle. See the chapter "All Feet are Not Created Equal" for further information on matching foot and leg structure to the boots.

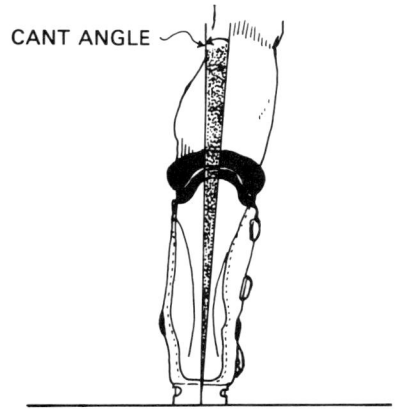

Cant angle

Although boots are basically unisex, models are frequently classified as "men's" and "women's." Be open-minded about trying the type that suits your needs. What are called "men's models" are usually a medium width in the larger sizes. "Women's models" are a narrow width in smaller sizes, with an especially low soft cuff to fit the calf better. Some women's models cater to fashion also, with stylish shells and pile lining. Specialized boots are even made for women who frequently wear high-heeled shoes, which reduces their ankle flexibility. If you have small feet for your weight, ask the salesperson to verify that the boot will stiffen up enough with maximum forward ankle bend to release your bindings. A boot too soft for your weight could lead to a tendon injury. This is especially critical in women's boots. If you're extremely light or have very large feet for your size, the salesperson should check that the boot is soft enough to flex for skiing comfort and control. If you are an aggressive female skier you may find women's boots too soft in general.

The primary consideration in a boot is a comfortable fit. If the boot color clashes with your parka you can still ski. If the boot hurts, you can't. Any pain or pressure points in the shop will be magnified by a factor of ten on the slopes. Try on many brands and various sizes. The size stamped on a boot doesn't mean anything when compared to your shoe size. To ensure a proper fit, keep in mind the points listed below.

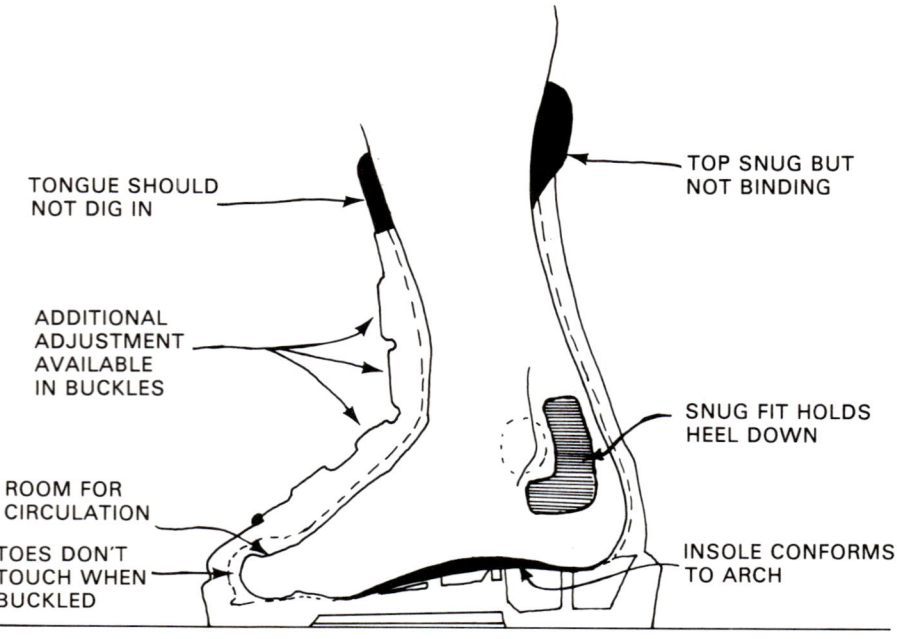

Boot fit

1. Wear thin ski socks. Every boot liner will "give" somewhat and you can change to thicker socks when it does. If you wear pants with an inner stirrup you may want to wear them when trying boots, as they will take up extra room.

2. When the boot is unbuckled, your toes should just touch the front, with no more than one-half inch from the heel to the back of the heel cup.

3. Tap the heel on the floor to seat it into the heel cup. With the heel on the floor and toes raised, start buckling from the toes upward. Before fastening the top buckles stand up and flex forward at the ankle to ensure the heel is back.

4. Make sure all the buckles will fasten and still have plenty of adjustment left, as you will probably tighten them more when you get used to them.

5. If your boot has a flow liner, allow a few minutes for it to conform to your foot.

6. The boot should grip tightly at the ankle, heel, instep, and ball of the foot, but must not be painful. Flex your knees up and down while standing to verify this. A too tight boot will reduce warmth; a too loose boot will be sloppy and abrade your skin.

7. With someone holding down the back of the boot, try to raise your heel. Ideally there should be no upward movement at the heel, as this would rub while skiing. With removable liners padding can be inserted to "hug" the heel and prevent free play.

8. You should be able to wiggle your toes so they have adequate blood circulation for warmth.

9. Press the boot toe-first into the floor, trying to stand up on tiptoes. If the toes press hard against the front of the boot, it is too short.

10. Flex forward several times to make sure a buckle or tongue crease won't dig into the front of the foot. Pressure should be distributed evenly on the shin, and not concentrated in one spot.

11. Standing with weight pressed back on the heels, the ball of the foot should not lift off the insole.

Once you have selected the best fitting boot, the ski shop can custom fit it to your foot by expanding the plastic shell, removing or adding padding in the liner, and modifying the footbed. After wearing them on the slopes you'll probably want to return to the ski shop for a fine-tuning of their fit.

An old song says "These boots were made for walkin'," but ski boots aren't. Their heels will wear down, affecting the binding release. For long distances get a boot carrier and wear after-ski boots. Boots don't require much care, but they should be thoroughly dried indoors in the evening so they will be flexible, warm, and dry when you put them on the next time. Plastic can take a "set," so once dry it's a good idea to buckle them up to make your next buckling on the slopes easier. Be good to your boots and in return they'll be good to your feet.

SKIS

Thankfully, the good old days are gone, at least in regard to skis. Years ago, you'd choose your wooden slats by stretching an arm above your head and finding a ski that reached your palm. Nowadays, modern plastics, adhesives, and metals plus design refinements have produced lighter, shorter, and more responsive skis. However, with over 300 models on the market, many of them new each year, the choice of what to buy often seems overwhelming. Ski engineering has created a wealth of terms used to describe how skis perform on the snow. For these details on ski design, refer to the chapter "More Than Just Boards."

You'd like your skis to turn quickly and with little effort, which is what short skis do best. However, you'd also like your skis to be stable with speed and to hold well on hard snow, which is what long skis do best. As you can see, any length ski is going to be a compromise. Skis are measured in centimeters, abbreviated cm, so you'll have to think metric. One inch equals 2.54 cm (if you want to be exact), or two inches are approximately 5 cm. Ideally, you should go by your weight to find a ski size, but most manufacturers assume you're the mythical normally proportioned person, and relate ski size to your height. Therefore you'll need to know your height in centimeters. To save you some multiplying, a 5'3" tall person is 160 cm, a 5'7" person is 170 cm, and a 5'11" person is 180 cm. You can guesstimate inbetween. Remember this figure, since it will determine what length ski you will buy.

Don't worry about what brand to buy. Despite manufacturers' claims, performance varies little from brand to brand if you compare the same model type. The important decision you face is what type ski to buy and in what length. Then you can choose among manufacturers for the color, availability, guarantee, and price you like.

No uniform system exists to classify ski types. Your best bet is to read the skiing magazines and manufacturers' literature, and to talk to ski shops to find the skis suited for you. As a generality, we can divide skis into three overlapping categories: recreational, sport, and racing. This excludes the specialized short ski you may rent your first couple times, known as a teaching or a GLM (graduated length method) ski.

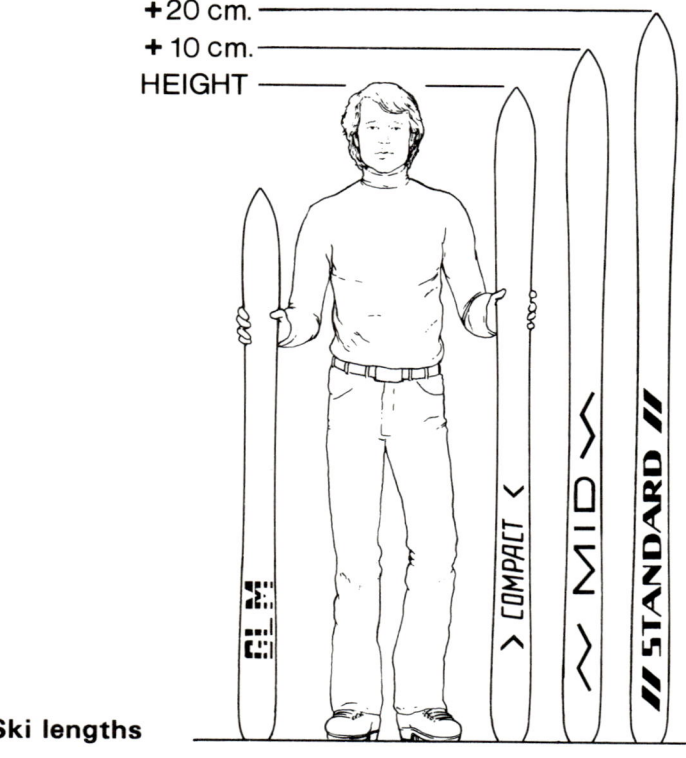

Ski lengths

Recreational skis are made for relaxing, fun skiing. If you're a new skier, this may be your choice. They turn easily by foot steering and work best at slower speeds in skidded turns. This group is designed to be skied in short or "compact" lengths, from head height to 10 cm above head height.

Sport skis, sometimes called advanced recreational skis, cover a broad range of skier abilities, from athletic intermediate to expert. These skis work best with a combination of skidded and carved turns at slow to medium speeds (10–25 m.p.h.). This group includes high performance mid-length skis, generally 10 to 15 cm above head height. The mid-length offers a good choice between ease of turning and stability. Another division in this sport group is the long and soft full-length ski, generally 15 to 20 cm above head height. These skis offer good stability at speed while softening reactions to bumps and ruts, in what's called a "smooth" ride. Specialized skis such as those made especially for moguls or for mountaineering also fall into the sport category.

Racing skis, sometimes called high performance or competition, are full length skis designed for stability at medium to high speed (20+ m.p.h.). They respond best to carved turns on any terrain. Some of them are true racing skis, but some are "detuned" racing skis. This means they will still cruise with the best of them, but are designed to be more responsive, smoother, and more forgiving of technical errors. Some long and soft skis could be included in this category also. The racing skis are generally skied 20 cm or more above head height. In this category (and in some sport skis) you may run into the distinction between slalom and giant slalom styles. A slalom ski makes the quickest turns. A giant slalom ski won't turn as quickly but it carves better in wide radius turns, and it is more stable at higher speeds. Being softer at the tips and tails, the giant slalom usually handles moguls and powder better than the slalom model.

In all categories, the lengths given are approximate and should be verified with the ski shop and the technical brochures. If you're heavy for your height or especially aggressive you might go 5 cm longer than recommended. Conversely, if you're light for your height or especially cautious, you might go 5 cm shorter.

Most ski shops have demo skis for rent, so you can try several pairs before you buy. Sometimes the rental fee can be applied toward the purchase price. Once you own your skis you'll want to keep them performing like new ones. The chapter "The Care and Feeding of Your Skis" will show you how to do that.

BINDINGS

Binding design effectively combines two opposite desires. Your first desire is for the boots to attach rigidly to your skis so any leg or foot motions are instantly transmitted to the skis. Your second desire is for the boots to be completely free of your skis the instant you lose control and take a spill, as this prevents snow from twisting the skis and injuring your legs. Amazingly, modern bindings do just this, as evidenced by the reduced number of lower leg injuries in recent years. Even more amazingly, the bindings also distinguish between actual spills and momentary large shocks, such as hitting a bump at high speed, when you don't want them to release. Bindings may cost half of what your skis cost, and they're worth every penny. Just as with boots and skis, binding design is changing rapidly. To be fully informed, talk to ski shop personnel and instructors, and read the skiing magazines and manufacturers' brochures.

Be certain the binding you choose is recommended for your

weight and skiing ability. A European standard, known as DIN, applies to most ski bindings. It assigns the numbers 1 to 10 (plus R for heavy racers) to binding release settings. Thus the amount of force needed to release a binding set at a certain DIN number will be the same for any manufacturer. (A word of caution: older bindings and some non-European manufacturers do not conform to these standards.) You can determine what DIN number you require by referring to a chart of your weight and ability; use this number to aid your selection. For instance, as a 120-pound beginner, your DIN number is 5. Say the manufacturer you like has two models, one adjusting from DIN 2 to 5, and one from DIN 4 to 8. The latter is a better choice as it will still be appropriate when you improve.

Bindings should always be mounted and adjusted in a reputable ski shop. Even with DIN numbers, the settings must still be tailored to your particular boots and skiing style. The shop will accurately set and test the release force with a special machine. Ask for the directions that come with the bindings. Yes, they are full of small print and many diagrams with arrows. Spend twenty minutes to understand what they say so you know how to put on and how to adjust your binding (should it be necessary), and what lubrication or maintenance should be done. If you don't understand the directions, a ski shop mechanic will gladly explain them to you. You wouldn't risk life and limb in a car without knowing the basics of operating it, so apply the same rule to your bindings.

Separate toe and heel units from the European manufacturers

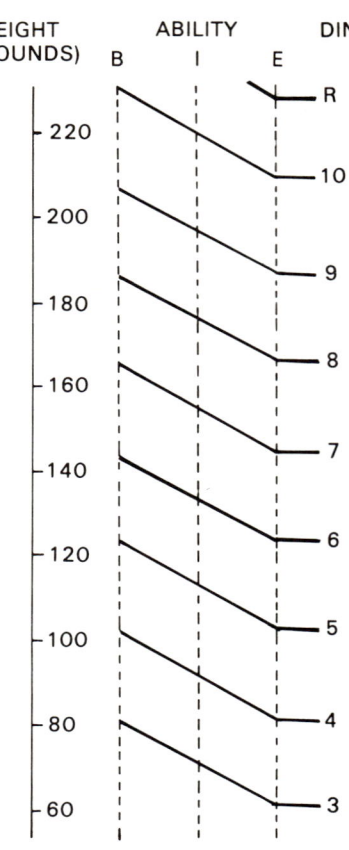

DIN binding numbers
Read horizontally from your weight to your ability level—beginner, intermediate, or expert. The nearest solid line is your proper DIN number.

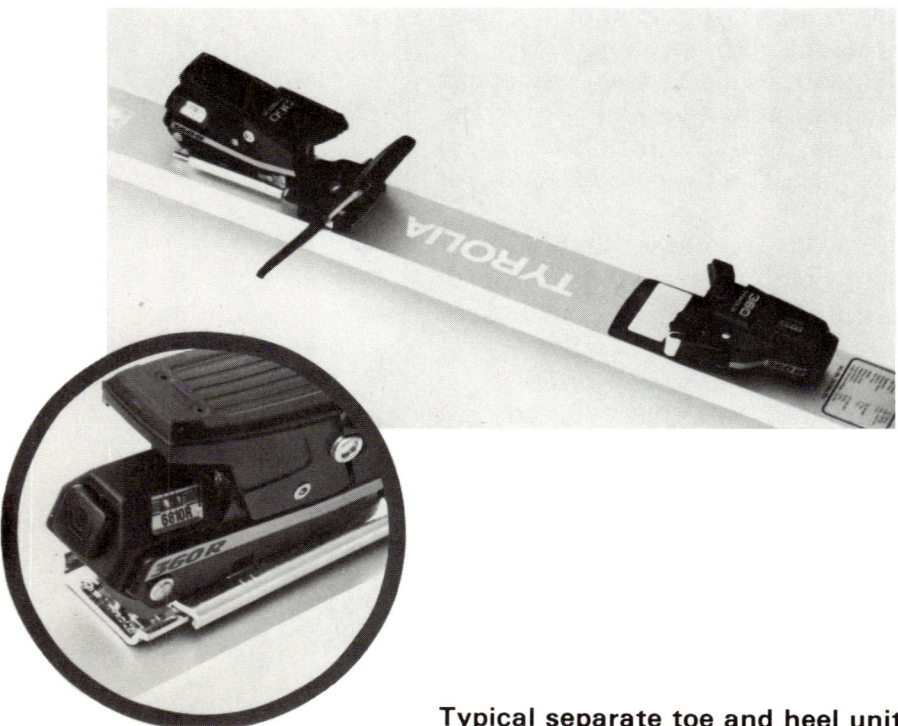

Typical separate toe and heel unit

are by far the most popular type of binding. They are sometimes called *step-ins,* since after cocking the heel unit they latch closed on a boot as you step into them. These bindings allow the toe to release laterally (left or right) and the heel to release upward. These release angles cover the majority of falls in which the ski could exert damaging force to the leg. One manufacturer also incorporates a diagonal release in his heel unit.

The toe unit has a screw to adjust for the boot sole thickness, and a screw to vary the release setting. This setting is calibrated on a visual scale in DIN numbers. An *anti-friction pad,* made of Teflon, sits on the ski in the boot sole area to ensure smooth, frictionless lateral release at the toe.

The heel unit contains a screw to adjust the upward release setting, as displayed on a calibrated scale. Another adjustment varies the unit's location forward and backward, which changes the *forward pressure.* This is the force which the heel unit exerts against the boot to press it firmly into the toe cup. A correct setting is indicated by a small scale, frequently an arrow which lines up with an engraved line. The boot must be in the binding for the setting to register. Some heel units may have a screw to adjust the hold-down lug height to various boot thicknesses. If not, they are "self adjusting." Another type of heel unit has a turntable incorporated in it. This is designed to reduce heel friction when the toe release functions, putting less twisting force onto the leg.

Turntable heel

With separate toe and heel units, you should keep the boot sole as free of grit as possible, and avoid wearing down the sole by excessive walking. The anti-friction pad should be replaced when it becomes scratched up.

Plate bindings from American manufacturers are designed to keep boot friction or sole warping from affecting the release setting. The boot is attached to a metal or plastic plate which then snaps

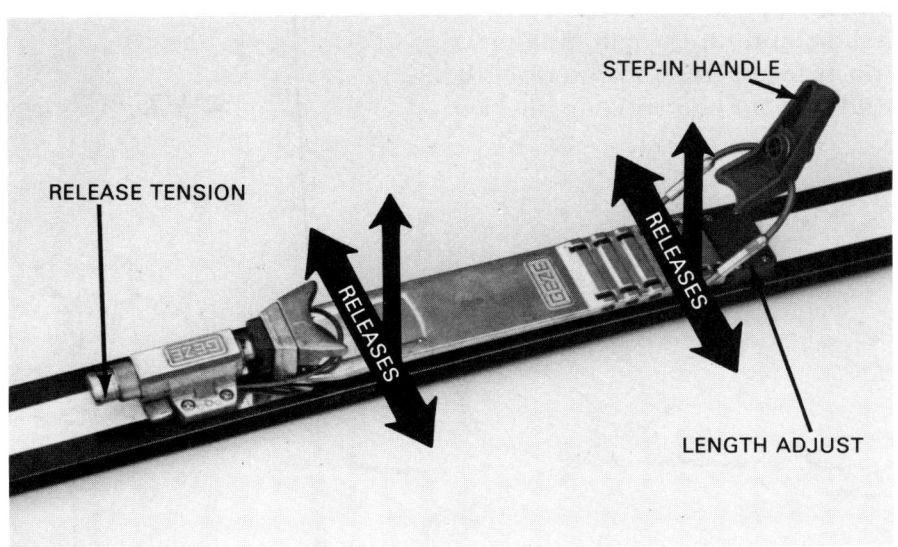

Plate binding

11

into the release mechanism mounted permanently on the ski. The plate remains attached to the boot in a release, but is easily detachable for walking. Plate bindings offer additional angles of release, usually left, right and up at both heel and toe. One popular semi-plate binding mounts a small metal plate permanently onto the boot sole. This toeless style also gives a release straight forward. In yet another variation, one manufacturer attaches the plate to a complicated pulley cable system, so that after a fall the ski snaps back onto the plate automatically.

Release settings on plate bindings are adjusted by a single spring-loaded screw. For this reason, some models are not suited for certain skiers. As an example, if a skier leans against the boot back to recover balance, the toe could release upward. When the skier tightens the adjustment to prevent this unwanted release, he may find that the other release angles are now tightened beyond a safe range. Your ski shop can help determine which plate binding is appropriate for you.

All bindings have some elasticity, called *anti-shock*, built in. If you twist your foot as in a fall, the toe binding starts to release sideways. However, if you stop this twist, as in a recovery, the toe unit's "return to center" force snaps the boot back to its normal position. This feature is especially useful when you hit a rut or bump which deflects your ski tip. Instead of releasing, the binding absorbs the momentary shock. You'd like to have your boot recentered back in the binding rapidly, so a short "return time" is a desirable feature. Heel units have a similar anti-shock feature in the vertical direction.

A ski shop check once or twice a year is the best indicator of proper binding function. Their performance on the slopes will give you an indication of correct operation. They should release during most falls, but not before. However, also recognize that not every fall requires a release. You should perform a go or no-go test once in a while between shop checks. Buckle up your boots and stand in one binding at a time. Have a friend stand on the tail of your ski. Then rapidly flex forward (using poles for balance so you don't fall over), lifting the heel, which should release before your heel ten-

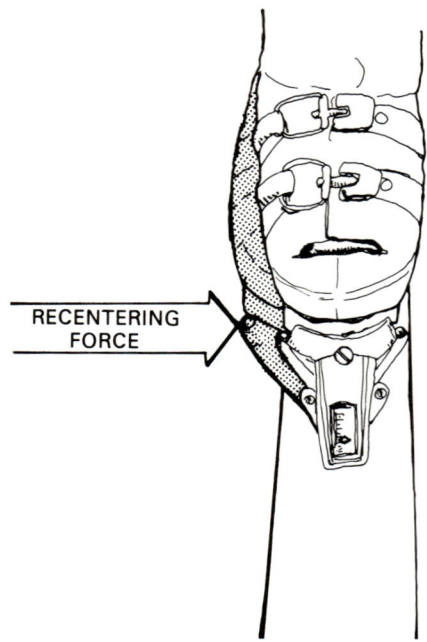

Anti-shock in a binding

Binding release checks

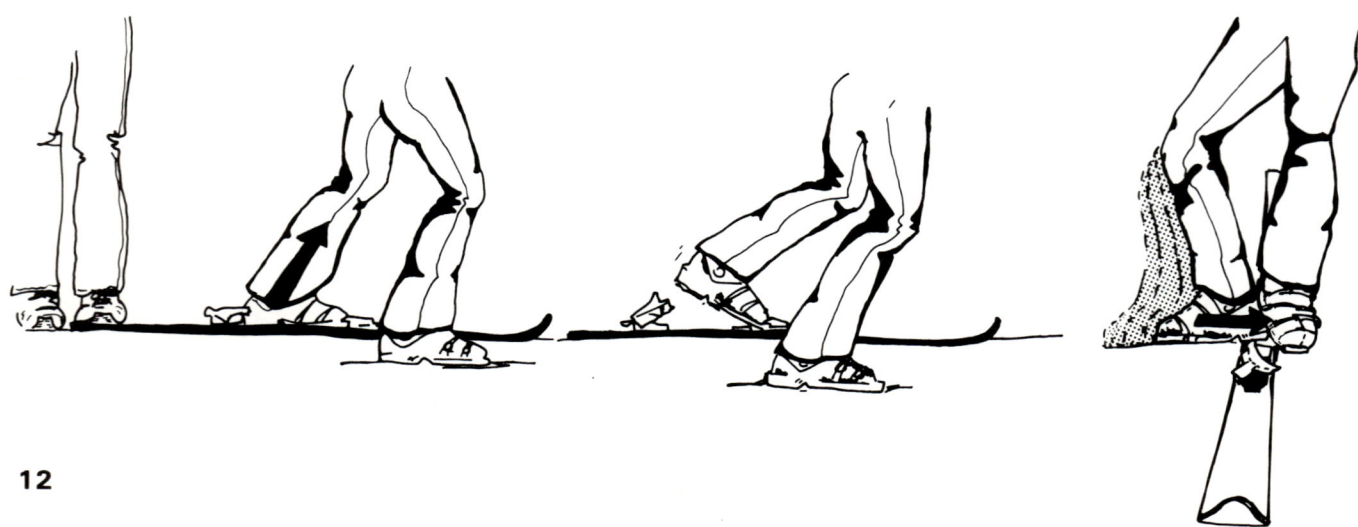

dons hurt. To check the toe piece function, kick one boot toe with the heel of the other. A good sharp kick should release it.

Whatever bindings you select, take care of them. Lubricate with the recommended oil or spray. When they're on top of a car, keep salt and dirt out of them by covering the binding area. Check frequently for loose screws, worn parts, or changes in the release settings. Keep your boots, ski surfaces, and bindings free of grit. Your legs will thank you.

Whenever you do take a spill, you don't want your ski to continue on down to the base lodge by itself. The traditional way of preventing a runaway ski is by wearing a *retention strap*. Sometimes known as a "safety strap," it fastens permanently to the heel binding and snaps closed around your boot or lower leg. A strap's main advantage is that it keeps your skis with you, so you don't have to climb up or down a hill retrieving them. The strap does have a major disadvantage: dragging along an attached ski in a nasty fall invites cuts or bruises. If you've never seen the medieval weapon known as a mace, you can just watch a windmilling ski to understand the principle. This is why ski brakes were invented.

RUNAWAY PREVENTION

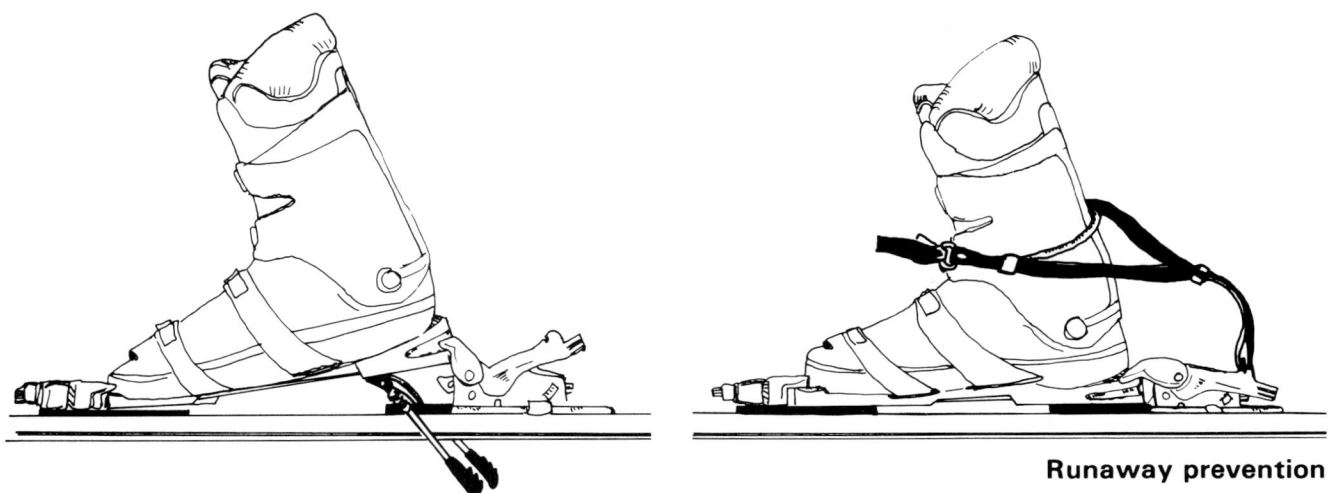

Runaway prevention

Ski brakes fold up when your boot is in the binding, and extend two arms to stop the ski when you release. These ski stoppers are supplied as an integral unit of many bindings. Their only disadvantage is that the ski almost never ends up within reach of your body, and you have to walk uphill to reclaim it, not always an easy task. If you venture into deep powder, you should also attach some sort of leash from your leg to the ski. It's amazing how many skiers with only ski brakes spend an hour digging holes looking for a released ski lost under a foot of fluff.

As a beginner, the type of pole you choose will not be too important. When you reach the intermediate or better stage you may want a more expensive model. It should balance well and be light

SKI POLES

and strong. The length, however, is important to every level of skier. A pole approximately 70 percent of your height is a good size to buy. Test the length in a store with your boots on (or equivalent sole height shoes). Turn the pole upside down, and grip it just below the basket. Keep your elbow directly below the shoulder and close to the body. If your forearm is parallel to the floor, the pole is right. Gripping below the basket allows length for the point of the pole to sink into the snow when you use it. Shops will cut down a pole if it is too long, so if you're between sizes, choose the longer one. Basket style is not especially important, although larger baskets give better support in soft snow. One thing to notice is the point. Inexpensive poles will have a tapered point shaped from the same tube of metal which makes up the shaft. Quality poles have a separate tempered point pressed into the shaft. This point can be replaced when it gets dull. Some types of tips can be sharpened.

Proper pole length

The grips come in two types, traditional straps and the newer strapless. With either type, try them with gloves or mittens if possible. The strap grips have a slight advantage in cushioning the wrist when skiing on ice or extremely hard pack. They also allow the palm to slip easily to the top of the pole to provide support when needed, as in a herringbone or in spurting out of the starting gate in a race. Look for adjustable straps which will fit various size gloves. The strapless hand grips have a left and a right hand. They are extremely quick to put on and take off. Since the hand can slide out easily, they can prevent a dislocated shoulder in case the basket snags on anything.

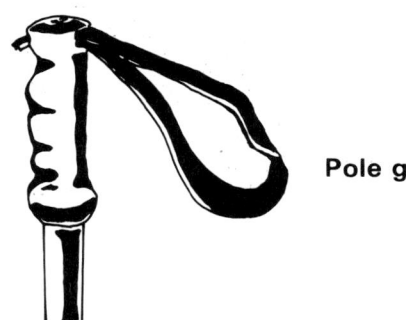

Pole grips

KEEPING YOUR GEAR YOURS

It's a sad commentary on our society that ski theft has become a real problem. The vast majority of skiers you'll encounter are great people who respect your property. Unfortunately, there is sometimes a person, perhaps a non-skier, who may look at your equipment and envision a stack of dollars sitting there on the snow. Occasionally someone may mistake your gear for his, pick up the skis, and not discover until the next ski trip he has the wrong skis (after all, if you've seen one ski, you've seen them all). At a restaurant on top of a mountain, ski disappearance is rare, but watch out near a parking lot! Record the serial numbers of your skis and keep these numbers with other important information. When renting equipment, take a minute to jot down your serial number so you can find your skis among the dozens of similar ones. Having your name engraved on your skis can act as a deterrent to theft—it can also decrease the resale value. If your local ski area or police department offers a registration program for skis, take advantage of it. This is usually a recording of your serial numbers and the issuance of a sticker to place on your skis.

Your best protection is to keep the skis and poles in sight. As areas don't have ski-in restaurants or rest rooms, locking them up is next best when you must take them off. There are coin operated racks at many areas, or skis can be locked anywhere with a short cable lock available at all ski shops. The lock can be carried around your neck or waist when not in use. As a minimum precaution, separate your skis by placing one ski and pole in one rack, and the other ski and pole some distance away. This makes it difficult to locate a pair. Just remember where you put them!

2

APPROPRIATE APPAREL AND ACCESSORIES

From your experience in winter weather, you know that your body temperature varies greatly. You can be freezing cold while standing around, or dripping with perspiration when very active. A wise choice of clothing must keep you warm while riding lifts in a snow storm and also prevent you from overheating while you're actively moving on the hill. Additional hints on staying warm will be found in the chapter "Coping with Cold and Altitude."

Choose clothes that retain body heat while still allowing freedom of movement. Dressing in layers traps insulating air spaces and lets you remove or add garments to control your temperature. Name brand skiwear generally assures you of quality apparel suited to the rigors of downhill skiing at an affordable price. However, if you want to economize, there is no need to buy the latest fashionable outfits. They won't help your skiing technique, although they may very well enhance your après ski activities. Ski shop sales, ski swaps and thrift shops all sell inexpensive clothing. If you don't have a ski outfit, wear as much wool as possible. It will keep you warm even when it's wet.

Long underwear is a basic starting point for cold days. It's relatively inexpensive, even for a good quality double layer type consisting of an outer wool layer for warmth and an inner cotton layer for comfort. Single layer styles frequently have a thermal weave which traps air for warmth. For women, panty hose provide extra insulation on days that are nippy but not quite long underwear weather.

Generally, one pair of medium-weight wool blend ski socks provides all the warmth and moisture absorption needed in a modern boot. These socks have a terry-like inside and a smooth outside. For extra warmth you may wear a silk liner inner sock; with snug boots you can sneak by with just the thin silk sock.

On your top, a cotton turtleneck is standard equipment. Its elasticized knit cuffs and neck keep out the cold wind, and the neck band can be turned up for extra protection. A wool or wool blend sweater goes over the turtleneck. A windshirt is a light-weight nylon shirt which can be worn either under or over the sweater. It'll do marvels, keeping you warmer by blocking out wind and retaining your body heat while moving. The windshirt is especially handy on days warm enough to ski without a parka.

A parka is essential for the majority of the winter. It should provide warmth, be water-resistant, windproof, and of a nonskid material (never a slippery shiny finish that will slide all the way down the hill). Look for large, strong plastic zippers with a pull tab you can grasp while wearing mittens. Several outer and inner pockets with zipper or Velcro closures will come in handy. Knit cuffs on the sleeves and a cuff or snug fit at the parka's bottom will keep out snow and cold drafts. Look for features such as a tuckaway hood, sewn-on lift ticket ring, or machine washability. For extremely cold climates, down insulation will be the warmest, although somewhat bulky in style. Down parkas are often quilted to hold the feathers in place. Polyester synthetics are almost as warm as down, and are also washable. Available under many trade names, they are particularly useful in damp climates, as they retain loft (and hence warmth) when wet. The polyesters come in a batting, so they don't require quilting and can be easily tailored to a form-fitting style.

On warmer days you can wear an unlined windproof shell of heavy fabric. This can zip up the front or pull over your head (an anorak). A down vest on these sunny days gives you arm freedom but still provides chest warmth.

I especially recommend insulated ski pants for cold or snowy weather. Also known as powder pants or warmups, they will keep your thigh muscles warm for more responsive skiing. The lining is usually a lighter weight polyester, bonded to tricot. An unlined style made of nylon or poplin comes in handy for wind or water protection in warmer weather. Traditional stretch pants conform to your body shape; they are either all synthetic or a blend of wool and synthetic.

Whatever style pants you choose, look for useful features. A snow-cuff sewn inside the leg will stretch over your boot and keep out (that's right) snow. A pocket or two will hold needed small items. Stretch inserts along the sides or at the hips will allow for lots of movement while still looking sleek. Some pants may zip to the jacket; others have built-in suspenders while still others will need suspenders or a belt. The bib style provides extra warmth for your torso and positively prevents snow from sneaking into your midriff. In normal waisted pants you may want a high back area, to provide extra warmth to the kidney region. I have found that when this section of my lower back gets chilly I'm cold all over (and also require frequent pit stops).

In a pinch, even old wool pants will work fine. Avoid jeans. Even on a warm day they will soak up water and give you cold legs, leading to stiffer skiing and more chance of injury.

Hand protection is essential. Mittens are the warmest, as your fingers are together. However, gloves provide dexterity for adjusting boot buckles or zippers and making more precise pole plants. In either style, down or polyester filling preserves warmth. Extra warmth can be added with a pair of wool blend or silk liners worn underneath. Leather is the most common outer material, and its breathable properties keep your hands from getting clammy. Renew the leather once in a while with a leather oil or saddle soap to keep it supple and water-resistant. Your gloves or mittens should be just loose enough for movement and to trap an air layer next to your hand. The cuff area should be long enough to cover the exposed wrist and snug enough to keep out snow. Clips on the wrist will let you fasten the gloves to your parka, out of the way in the lunch line.

Hats should be large enough to cover the lower ear tips, but also snug enough not to blow off in the wind. Once again, wool provides warmth even when it gets wet.

For sunny or lightly overcast days don't go on the slopes without a quality pair of dark sunglasses. I'm partial to a large, somewhat curved style for maximum peripheral vision. They also keep my eyes from watering when I ski. A plastic polarized type cuts out reflected glare for squintless vision (nobody wants crow's feet). The silver mirrored type are darker than most, and also great for unobtrusive girl/guy watching. Some sun sensor types change shading density or even color with light variations. Clip on dark plastic lenses are sold to fit over prescription glasses. If you wear glass lenses you might consider a shatterproof variety. For those of you worried about "racoon eyes," take off your sunglasses and close your eyes while riding the chair lifts, or else suntan the eyelids at lunchtime.

For heavy overcast or snowy days goggles with yellow lenses improve vision. Some styles will fit easily over prescription glasses. The more expensive types are designed with a double sealed lens or a permanently treated lens surface to prevent fogging. On doubtful days when you're not sure whether or not it will snow, the goggles can always be worn on your forehead over the hat, or slung around the back of your neck.

If you are inclined to sunburn at the beach, you will be more inclined to burn while skiing, even in December. Carry a small tube of suntan lotion in a parka pocket. In that pocket also stash a stick-type lip balm containing a sunscreen.

Always carry a trail map of the area where you are skiing. It will come in handy to locate suitable trails for your ability, find patrol phones, rest rooms, etc. Ask for one when you buy your lift ticket and keep it in your pocket.

Snapshots are always fun to admire after a trip. If you carry a bulky camera, consider a special body fastening strap. You'd be surprised how high over your head a camera on a neck strap can bounce when you hit a bump. In cold weather, you should keep the camera, particularly the battery powered types, as warm as possible for proper shutter function. I like an automatic 110 pocket camera which I can zip into an inside parka pocket and can operate while wearing gloves.

Après ski wear at most resorts is casual, and anything goes. Jeans, sweater and a ski parka are typical. Consider the snow in your choice of footwear. Some people like hiking boots. I prefer "moon boots" with foam insulation for warmth, a nylon shell for water resistance, and a lug sole for slip prevention.

Some optional gear adds to a day's pleasure. These items may include a fanny pack or belt pack which can carry many items too bulky to fit in a parka pocket such as lunch, wax, extra windbreaker; a handful of tissues to handle the ever-present runny nose; a Bota bag—an animal skin slung over the shoulder that will hold a full day's supply of Gatorade; battery powered foot warmers to electrically heat your toes; a scarf or gator for extra neck warmth and a touch of class; a candy bar tucked in a pocket for extra quick energy and warmth when you tire; a small piece of moleskin in case the boots decide to act up; earphones with built-in radios or tape players that strap to your waist if you can't endure a day of just Mother Nature's sounds; a little change in the pocket for a hot drink or snack; a pen and paper to write down names and addresses of people you meet; a comb to straighten windblown hair; a binding tool for on-the-slope adjustments; airline schedules; a harmonica for the times you have to ride single. You can choose what is really valuable to you from this list and add some of your own. With planning, determination, and fortitude, you might even survive a day with only a couple of them.

3

SKIS—MORE THAN JUST BOARDS

Every pair of skis has its own unique handling characteristics. Some skis hold great when put into large high-speed turns on hardpack, but sink to the bottom in powder. Others may whip through the bumps, but bounce out your fillings on ice. What makes each pair different is an interrelated set of design characteristics. The variables in the design are sometimes determined by computer analysis, sometimes by trial and error testing. We'll explore the common terms used to describe how skis perform to give you a good idea of what to look for in your next pair.

As you pick up a pair of skis, you'll notice their most obvious features: length and weight. The two are related, with an average pair weighing in at around 3.4 kilograms. (To save you metric madness, that's 7½ pounds.) As mentioned in the chapter "An Equipment Primer," long skis are stable at high speeds, while short skis turn easier at more moderate speeds. The difference is due to several common physical factors. The first is the moment arm or the lever effect. Basically, the longer the ski, the more resistance exerted by snow at the tips and tails as you try to turn. (To misquote Archimedes, "Give me a ski long enough and I can move the world.") A second reason is the polar moment of inertia, sometimes called "swing weight." It simply means that the longer the ski the longer it takes to both start and stop moving the tip and tail areas (one of Isaac Newton's Laws). Imagine carrying a long piece of lumber under your arm and consider the length of time and force it takes to turn around 180 degrees with it. Compare this with the time it would take to turn around when carrying a short board, and you'll understand swing weight.

You can easily imagine the increased stability a long ski affords over a short one. With a longer ski your support base is increased and small bumps don't affect your balance as much. It's the difference between standing on tiptoes and standing on the whole of the foot. It is also the reason cars with a longer wheel base give a smoother ride.

Manufacturers measure length in two ways, either by the straight line distance from tip to tail, known as the *chord length,* or by the curved length along the entire bottom of the ski, known as the *surface length.* Thus, a ski measured in chord length by an American manufacturer will be about 2 cm longer than another ski called the same "size" but measured in surface length by a French manufacturer.

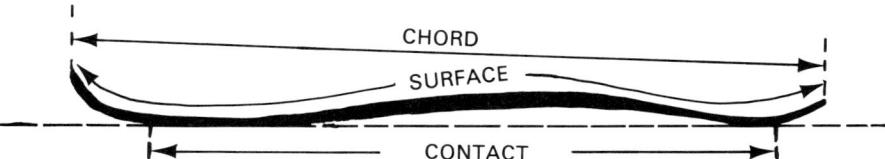

Measuring ski length

The running surface, or *contact length,* is the length of the ski which actually touches the snow when you are on it. It runs about 20 cm shorter than the total length. Bindings are mounted so the ball of your foot is over the center of this running surface. You can see the importance of standing balanced over your feet to use the whole running surface length. Leaning too far forward or back would only use part of the ski, and would be the same as having the bindings mounted in the wrong place.

The average *width* of a ski also affects performance. Some shorter length skis are made extra wide, which increases stability from side to side, and also the surface area for support in soft snow. A major effect of the width is the extra force required to edge it the same amount as a narrower ski. This can result in more time required to "change edges" to make a turn.

When you look at a ski bottom you'll first notice the *edges.* These narrow strips of hardened steel run the length of the ski and are necessary to bite into the snow to aid in turning. They should be sharp, flush with the bottom, and not nicked or rusty. Edges are of two types: a single piece or a segmented (or cracked) piece. A single-piece edge contributes to the rigidity of the ski, while the segmented edge is more flexible and independent of the ski's rigidity. Some manufacturers claim a segmented edge will "snake" (follow the terrain very closely) better than a ski with a single edge. Others claim a single edge has less drag and is more durable. "You pays your money and you takes your choice."

Your skis may have a *groove,* which runs right down the middle of the base of the ski. It is the only straight part of your ski. Sometimes it's useful for straight running in soft snow to keep a flat ski "tracking" straight. The shape of the groove, whether round or square, is not important. Skis without a groove obtain their tracking stability from the flared shape of the tail, which acts like feathers on an arrow.

Another noticeable characteristic of skis is their *camber.* This is the arched design which shows a gap when you place a pair of skis bottom to bottom. It functions to distribute your weight over the entire bottom of the ski so the whole ski length is used effectively. Skiing on a ski without camber, one which has "gone flat," is like skiing on a waxed boot, as the tip and tail are virtually useless. To feel the camber work, put a finger under the tip of a ski on the floor, then press down the center of the ski with your other hand— pressure immediately increases on the finger. When purchasing used skis, place them on a flat surface to verify that they have camber and aren't bent.

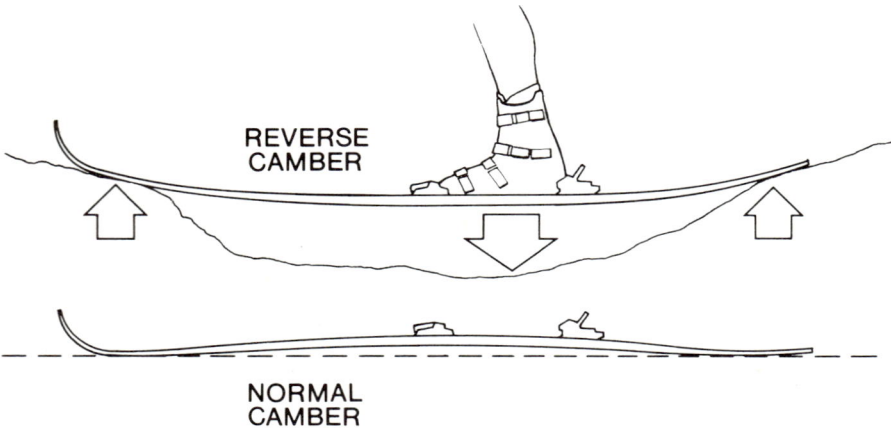

Camber

If the tip and tail of a ski are suspended, as on books in the living room or terrain on the mountain, and pressure is put on the center of the ski, it will go into *reverse camber.* That is, it will be bent opposite its original shape. When pressure is released, a ski in reverse camber springs back to normal camber, an effect called "rebound."

If we only skied straight downhill without turning we wouldn't need any more variables, but we also wouldn't have much fun. So the next noticeable feature on a ski is its *sidecut.* Skis don't have parallel sides, but rather are widest at the front (tip or shovel), narrow at the middle (waist), and moderately wide at the tail. Sidecut has several functions which come into play as soon as you move your knees laterally (left or right) to put the skis on an edge. On a skidding ski (one going sideways down the hill dragging an edge on the snow), the tip of the ski bites into the snow more deeply than the tail, as the latter is not as wide. This causes the tip to slow up while the tail tries to swing around to get ahead of the tip. This pivoting effect changes the ski's direction and makes a rough skidded turn.

Sidecut has another much more important function. If the ski were straight, like a ruler, when it was tipped at an angle the whole edge would touch the snow in a straight line. The ski would tend

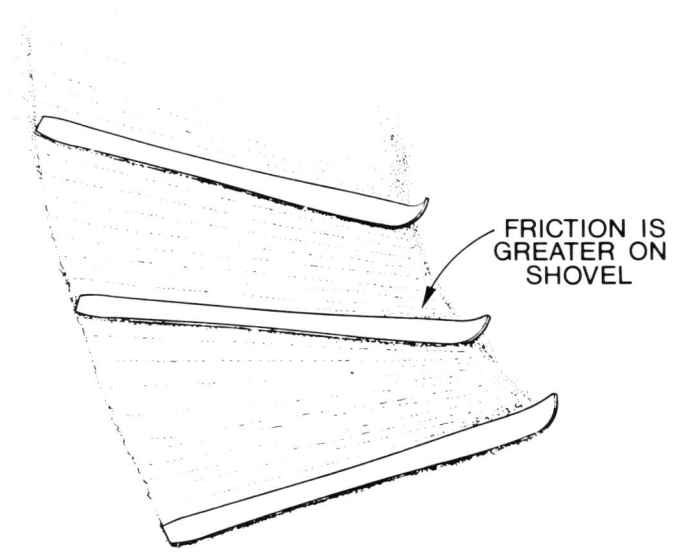

Sidecut aids skidded turns
Less friction on the tail causes it to rotate farther than the tip.

to travel in this straight line. However, due to the hourglass shape, when an unweighted ski is edged, only the tip and tail touch the snow. By standing on the ski in this position it is weighted and pushed into reverse camber until the whole edge touches the snow. Now the edge forms a curve on the snow, and the ski tries to travel (or "carve") along this arc to make a turn. The more extreme the hourglass shape, the sharper the turn a ski wants to make. Downhill skis have relatively straight sides or a low *sidecut angle*. Slalom skis don't run well straight downhill, as their high sidecut angle demands short turns. In between, giant slalom skis carve best with wide turns.

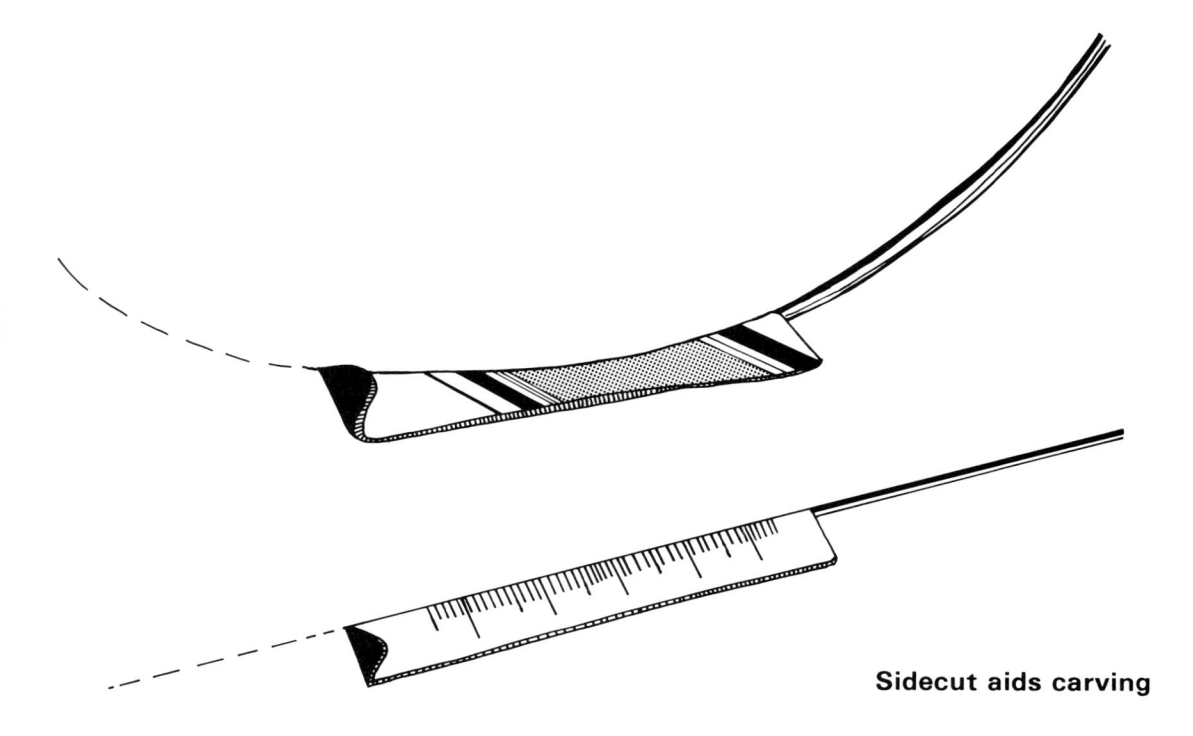

Sidecut aids carving

You're not at the mercy of a ski's particular sidecut, however. To see why, place a ski on a smooth floor. Tip it slightly on an edge and press in the boot area to remove camber. The whole edge touches the floor, making a slight arc. Now increase the edge angle and again press out the camber. The arc is now sharper, resulting in a tighter turn. Thus you can vary the carving radius of your ski by increasing edging. More tips will be found in the chapter titled "Carving."

Another easily discernible feature is the *flex,* or the amount a ski will bend with force applied against its bottom camber. When skiers walk into a ski shop and start testing skis by bending them, they are "flexing" the skis. A ski has an overall flex, found by pushing down in the boot area. It also has varying flex throughout its length, with the tip generally "softer" than the tail. An especially soft forebody ski floats well in powder. Skis which are soft in flex initiate turns easily, but won't hold in a high-speed turn. Sport and mogul skis fall in this category. The firmer flexing racing skis require more precision to start turns. They hold well at speed, but the stiffer shovel hits into moguls harder, making for a bumpy ride. When comparing flex you also must compare length, as a shorter ski can be stiffer than a longer one, yet still perform like a softer ski.

Longitudinal flex
Flexing a ski shows the softer tip, the overall flex, and the stiffer tail.

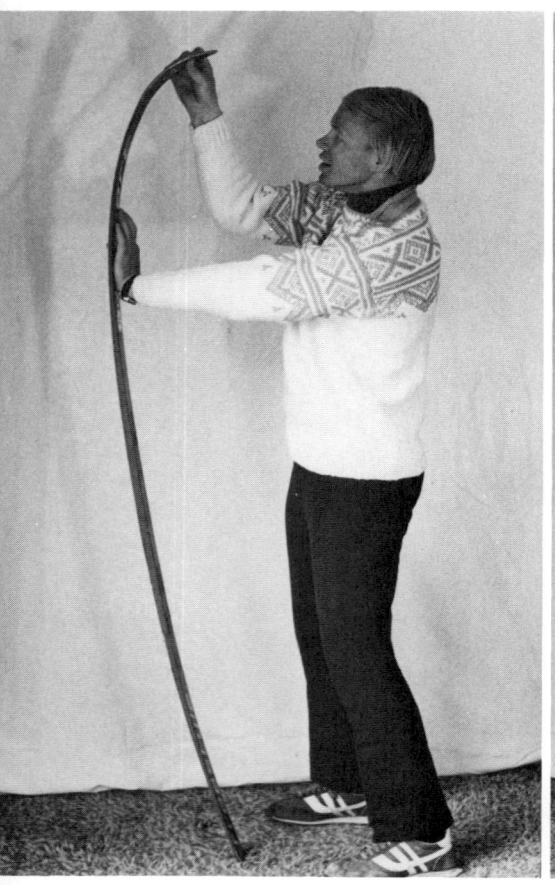

Torsional flex refers to the resistance a ski offers to a twisting force. Without some torsional rigidity, when you put a ski on its edge by tilting up your boot, the tip and tail sections would stay flat, like a long wet egg noodle, not helping you to turn. You can see the torsional resistance of a ski by placing it flat on the floor. Have someone stand on the tail while you take the tip and try to twist it. The tip will give somewhat to this force, but only slightly. A *torsionally soft* ski allows the tip to twist when hitting a bump or rut. Thus the tip deflects and follows the minor terrain change without throwing a skier's feet out of balance. This type of ski is called "forgiving." It will initiate turns easily, but with speed or on ice will be deflected out of its carved path. In a *torsionally stiff* ski the tips and tails retain their carving path despite deflections. Because they require more work to initiate turns and twist less in the bumps, they are called "demanding" or "precise." Torsion is frequently measured by how much force is needed to twist the tip and tail a certain amount while holding the center rigid. A ski can sometimes be bent inadvertently to a permanently twisted position called "warp." Check for warp by placing the ski on a perfectly flat floor and verify that it touches both edges at the tip and the tail.

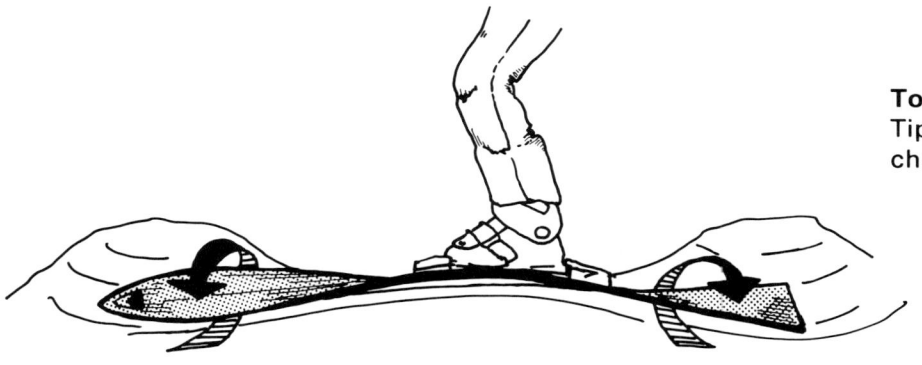

Torsional flex
Tips and tails twist with terrain changes.

Combining a ski's flexes, width, camber, and sidecut leads to the term *pressure distribution*. It defines how your weight is transferred to each part of the ski. Carving skis distribute much of your weight to the tip and tail. Recreational skis need to ski without tip and tail hang-up, so more of your weight is transferred to the pressure zone under your foot, minimizing pressure at the extremities of the skis.

Another factor is *damping,* or the ability of a ski to absorb vibrations. On soft snow it's not critical, as the snow softens shocks. But on ice the damping is necessary to keep the ski running quietly. If it vibrates it will lose contact with the snow surface, causing rapid changes between a skid and a carve. This is known as "chatter." A highly damped ski won't vibrate as easily, but it often feels somewhat dead underfoot. A lightly damped ski may vibrate on hard snow, but it feels lively and responsive.

Cutaway drawings will show you the internal construction of skis.

They are fun to look at and study, but don't mean much. Thanks to space-age technology there are dozens of construction methods and materials to achieve the same design parameters. Don't be swayed by the difference between "super activated boron fibers" versus "compressed sagebrush."

When choosing a ski, study the manufacturer's recommendations for the type of skier you are. Consider your skiing speed, the type of terrain you like, the size of your turns, the snow texture you generally encounter, and the methods you use to turn your skis. Ideally, try the skis out at the slopes. What matters most is performance and durability. All the technical factors work in combination with one another to make each ski model unique and suited to a different type skier. They really are a lot more than just boards.

4
THE CARE AND FEEDING OF YOUR SKIS

You certainly wouldn't drive a car without checking the oil and water now and then, or replacing worn parts. Similarly, skis need routine maintenance for best performance. They perform only as well as they are tuned. Don't expect good response from unwaxed skis with dull edges. Although ski shops can tune up skis for you, it's such a simple procedure that you can do it yourself whenever you want and save a high labor cost. The primary things to look for on a ski base are sharp edges filed to perfect right angles; a flat base area across the entire bottom, including the edges; and a smooth running surface with gouges filled in.

Bottom filing (flat filing). Abrasion with the snow causes the polyethylene base of the ski to wear away more quickly than the metal edges. Even in new skis on the rack the plastic base can be shaved lower than the edges during the final belt sanding at the

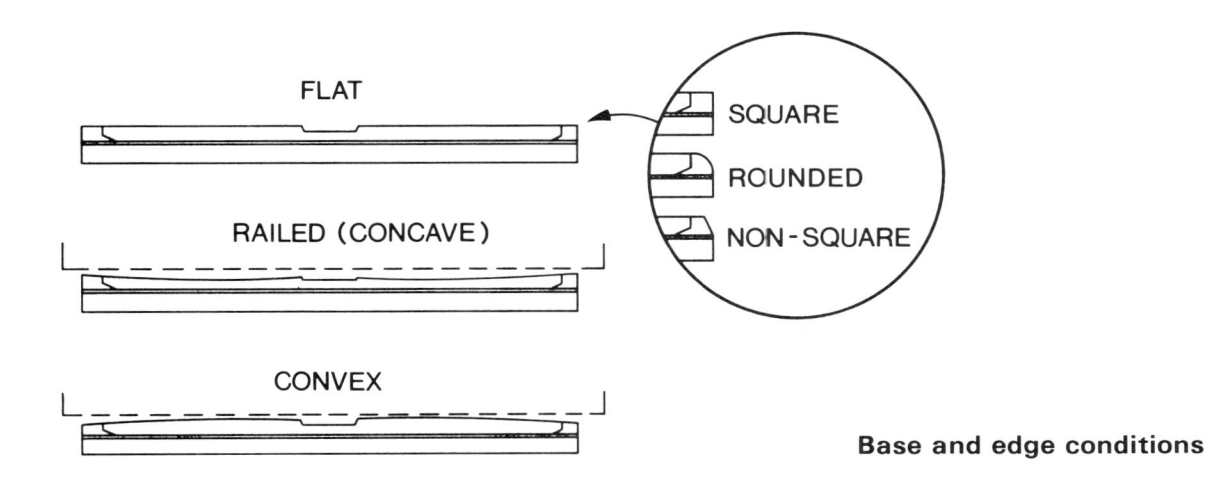

Base and edge conditions

factory. Skis in this condition are said to be "railed" and indeed you'll think you are skiing on rails; they will track well but will be difficult and jerky to turn. You can feel railed skis by putting them bottom to bottom, pressing at the centers to remove some camber, and sliding the ski tip bottoms back and forth width-wise against each other. Railed edges will catch as metal scrapes against metal. The best test is to put a straightedge across the ski in various places from tip to tail. A ruler will work, but you'll need a metal ski scraper anyway, so you might as well use it. If you can see light under the straightedge in the base area, the ski is railed. This is where bottom filing comes in handy to reduce the edge height.

An ideal work area for filing the bottom will have a large vise to hold the ski securely on a workbench. Lacking a vise, you will have to block the ski so it does not move. In a pinch, brace it against a kitchen countertop or table. Take a ten- or twelve-inch mill bastard file and hold it flat on the bottom of the ski at a 45 degree angle, with the right hand closer to the body than the left (reverse these directions if you are left-handed). The file grooves or "teeth" facing you will be lined up parallel to the ski edges. If you feel comfortable pulling the file toward your body, then the file handle must be in the left hand for the teeth to cut. If you will push the file away from your body, the handle must be in the right hand. Now draw the file along the ski, keeping the thumbs pressed flat on the file above each edge to prevent the file from bending and removing base unevenly. File in only one direction, lifting the file between long strokes; move down the ski, filing in sections. Clean the base frequently with a cloth to prevent filings from being ground in. On a railed ski you can feel the file cutting only the raised edges at first. As they are cut down, the file will move more smoothly and quietly when it is running on the plastic. Keep checking with the scraper for a flat bottom. A slight concavity remaining in the groove area will not affect performance.

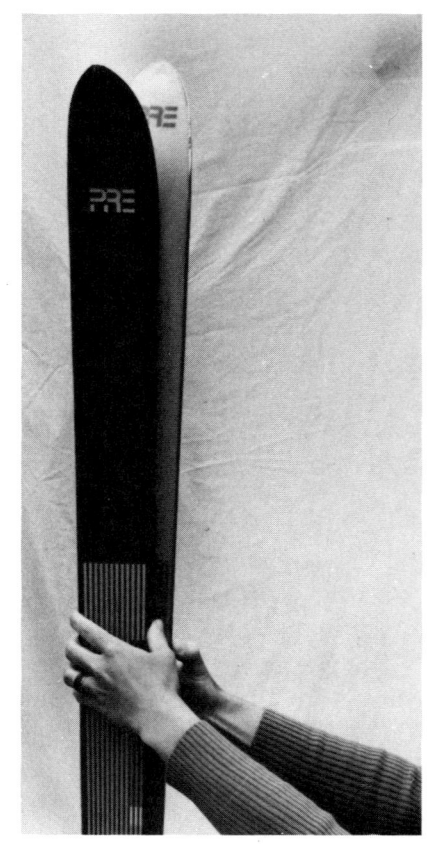

Feeling railed edges

Checking the base for flatness

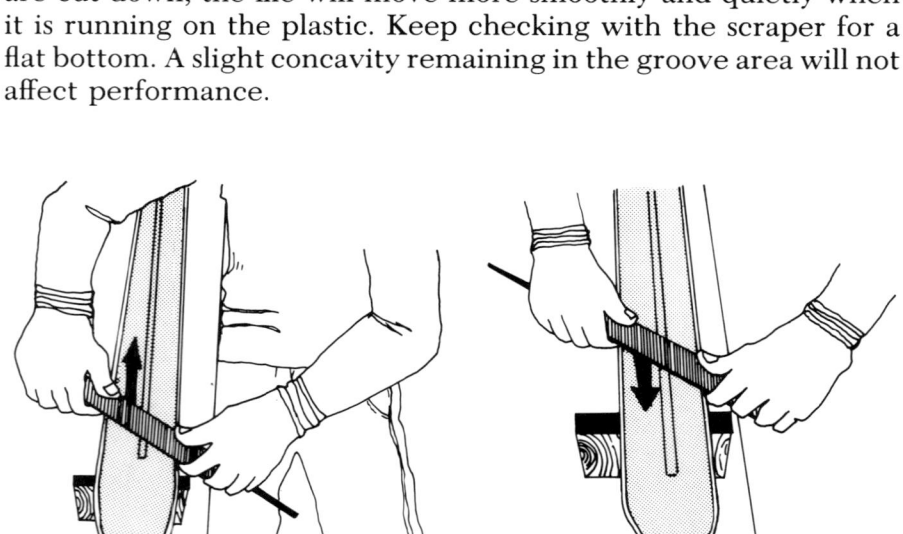

PULLING THE FILE

PUSHING THE FILE

Bottom filing

Clean the file frequently by running a file card or wire brush in the direction of the grooves. If wax or base material accumulates in the grooves, run the file under hot water to soften the wax and then brush it out. Edges are made of hard steel, so your file will get dull after a while, perhaps being good for ten or twelve complete sharpenings. The price of a new file is small compared with the great improvement in skiing it provides. If you buy any special type of ski file other than a mill bastard, be sure you know the correct way to hold and use it.

Side filing (edge filing). Flat filing sharpens the edges by removing material from the bottom. To finish the sharpening, the ski is turned up on its side and the edge is filed at right angles to the base. Side filing does not have to be as vigorous as bottom filing since its only purpose is to touch up the sharpness and not to level out a base. To avoid wearing away the edge, be judicious in the amount of metal you remove. When side filing, it is essential that the edge be filed at an exact right angle to the base. For best results, either purchase a device that will hold the file at a 90 degree angle to the base, or try a special ski edge file. These ride along with the base as a guide while filing the side edge and will ensure a perfect right angle.

With extensive practice you may be able to side file without a guide. Generally an eight- or ten-inch mill bastard is a good size for side filing. It can be held either at a 45 degree angle, as in bottom filing, or parallel to the ski. It works best when pushed away from the body, with the knuckles of one hand "riding" on the base as a guide. To eliminate a burred edge, file in a direction so the small metal filings end up on the sidewall of the ski. With a light at the proper angle you can see fresh metal glint as you file; this will help you judge the right angle.

Finishing touches to filing. If you can run a fingernail at right angles to the edge and get a white scraping, that edge is sharp. Run the fingers lightly down the edges. Any snags or burrs can be felt and removed by lightly running a sharpening stone or emery cloth on a wood block flat on the base and side. To prevent sharp tips and tails from hooking or catching, take the stone and lightly round off the edge at the extremities; that is, the six or seven inches back from the tip, and from the tail forward a couple of inches. The sharpening stone will come in handy on the slopes also, to remove burrs on your skis caused by scraping over rocks.

Convex bases. In some cases the polyethylene portion of the base may be higher than the edges, making the base a convex shape and causing the ski to act "squirrely" by tracking poorly. It is the reverse of railed skis. The problem can be easily detected with a metal scraper; the correction is easily made by using the scraper to remove the high sections of base.

Repairing gouges. Imperfections in the base surface cause irregularities in the way the ski runs. They can be repaired by filling in with a polyethylene candle, commonly called a P-tex candle,

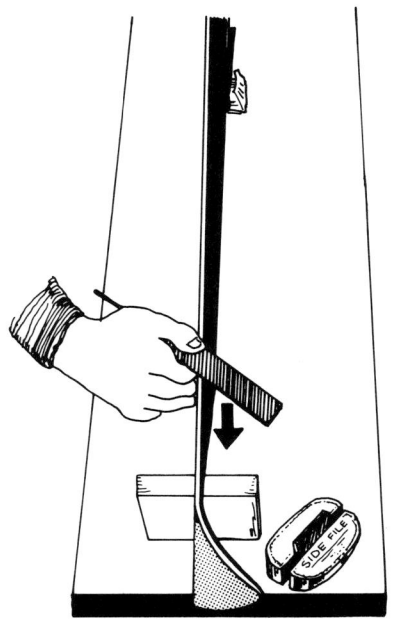

Side filing

available in colors to match the ski base. First, warm the ski to room temperature for proper adhesion. Clean off all dirt and metal filings. Light the P-tex candle, holding the lighted end downward. A butane lighter provides a hot flame for igniting the candle, thus preventing excessive carbon buildup. Let it drip for a while until it is burning well and any unburned carbon from lighting it has dropped off. (Be careful, as these flaming drips tend to set things on fire, are difficult to remove from rugs, and really smart when they land on your hand.) Now hold the burning end just above the gouges and let the drips fill them in higher than the base. Extinguish the candle when all the gouges are filled. The candle stays hot quite a while so dunking it in cold water is best. Using a single edge razor blade or a metal scraper, roughly level off the patched areas. For a final smoothing, use some fine steel wool. It will sand off the repaired area so well that it can't even be detected.

Filling gouges

Major repairs. After enough miles, any skis accumulate enough nicks and abrasions that it's time for a bigger repair job. Take your boards to your ski shop and request a wet belt sanding. They'll grind down the base to a smooth surface using a machine and also side file. This type of sanding can be done only several times before you're out of base, but each time it's like owning a new pair of skis.

Waxing. All ski bases need waxing! Wax makes a ski go faster and also makes it turn easier. Use it to fill in minor scratches until you get time to patch them. P-tex is somewhat porous; when you see a whitish color in the polyethylene, the base is long overdue for some wax.

Wax can be sprayed or rubbed on, but hot waxing is the most efficient and longest lasting method. Buy a secondhand iron at a thrift store—it won't be used for anything but waxing. Choose a block of alpine (not cross country) wax suitable for the type of snow you expect to be skiing. Most manufacturers use a color-coded wax, for example, red for above 32 degrees F., blue for 18–32 degrees F., and green for under 18 degrees F. Some waxes are general purpose, for a variety of temperatures. If you have brand-new skis, seal the base first with a soft wax, the same one you would use for above 32 degrees F. Set your iron on a "wool" temperature setting, which is enough to melt wax without burning it. While the iron is heating, clean the ski base thoroughly with a cloth. Hold the iron point down over the ski and press a corner of the wax block against it. Drip one stream of wax onto the ski on each side of the groove. Then iron on the wax, continually moving the iron to avoid damaging the ski from too much heat. It will glide easily and is much more fun than doing shirts. When the wax has cooled, run a plastic scraper along the base to leave only a thin coat. Next, if your ski has one, clean the groove. For rounded grooves a spoon works well. On square grooves a blunt screwdriver or a specially cut piece of plastic can be used.

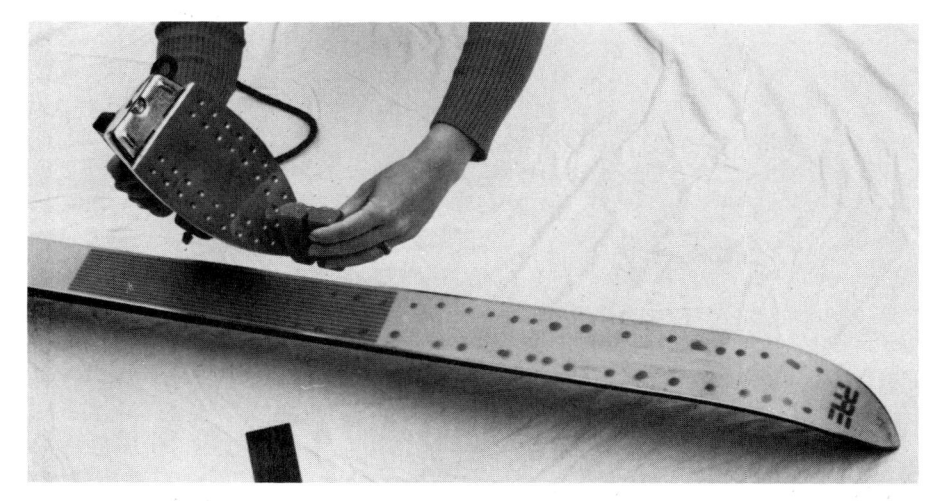

Hot waxing

Scraping wax

In spring slush a soft silver wax is almost essential to keep the skis from grabbing in the sticky snow. It is available in bar, paste tube or spray form; any of these can be applied over existing wax between runs.

While you are in a waxing mood, put some auto wax on the top surfaces of your skis. It will cover small scratches, protect against abrasion and paint fading, and allow snow to slide off easily. When you are putting up your boards for the summer, protect the entire edge from rust by running a bar of wax at an angle along the edges to coat them.

Keep your skis healthy and happy. They may not bring you your newspaper and slippers every evening, but they'll perform for you at their absolute best on the slopes.

5

ALL FEET ARE NOT CREATED EQUAL

All men are created equal, but all feet are different. The idealized perfectly structured skier never has any problems with edging. When he moves his knees laterally and twists his lower legs, the skis immediately edge equally and turn. Coming out of a turn he never catches an edge. His feet never hurt. He doesn't sound much like you or me, because there is no such person. Many of your problems in skiing could be caused not by a lack of technique, but rather by your unique bone structure.

Let's start with the feet. In theory, when you rotate your lower leg into a turn, your foot rotates also, turning the rigid boot which edges and turns the ski. In fact, many people have a misalignment of the lower leg and the heel bone. When they rotate the lower leg, their ankle bone moves inward and their toes move outward. The podiatrists call this *excessive pronation.* It's fairly common, but in excess causes skiing distress. The moment of a turn is when the foot should be rigid. All of a sudden, pronation "unlocks" the foot as the arch lowers and the ball of the foot widens. This results in foot motion inside the boot rather than boot motion to the ski.

How do you know if excessive pronation is your problem? First of all, have a friend look at the backs of your bare feet and lower legs as you stand normally. The bone alignment will either be ideal, a straight line, or pronated, with the ankle inward. Look at your street shoes. Wear on the inside of the heels is a symptom. As you step from a shower or swimming pool, look at your tracks. Although your arch may be normal, excessive pronation makes your footprints look as though you have no arch.

Excessive pronation deters edging
Knee movement results in inefficient leg and foot motions which do not edge a ski.

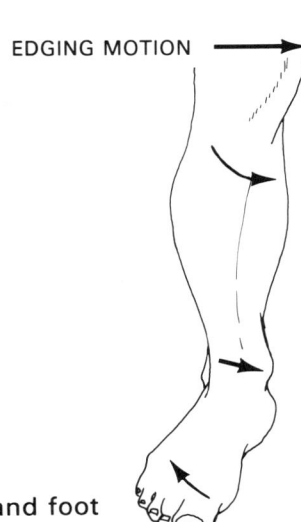

EDGING MOTION →

On the slopes, excessive pronation will cause difficulty in getting onto an edge. If you answer "yes" to any of the following questions, you may have this common foot problem. Do you continually skid and have difficulty in tracking? Do you need extreme knee or hip angulation or upper body contortion to get any edge at all? Do your ankles rub the insides of your boots? Do you wear a wider boot than your foot size would indicate, to avoid pain from your forefoot hitting the sides of your boots? Do you constantly try to tighten your boots over your instep for more support? After a short time on the slopes do your feet cramp, or perhaps become numb and cold?

That's a lot of nasty ailments. If you can't edge well, you can't ski well. Fortunately there's a solution, called an *orthotic device.* This is a footbed of semirigid material which supports your foot and holds the foot bones in correct alignment. Generally, it consists of a wedge which lifts the inside of the heel, a socket to cradle the heel, a support under the arch, and a support under the ball of the foot to keep it from twisting. The orthotic will allow you to edge rapidly and easily without foot muscle fatigue. As a side benefit, it may alleviate knee, ankle, and back ailments.

Extreme pronation may require a special orthotic made by a podiatrist. However, most cases can be cured with orthotics from up-to-date ski shops. Several methods are being used. The simplest are footbeds of a semisolid flow foam which molds to the shape of your foot bottom. Some methods custom mold a support as you stand on a warm pliable material which conforms to your foot. The most elaborate methods take a cast of your foot and mold an orthotic from that. Some boot manufacturers supply adjustable orthotics as an integral part of the boot. A boot fitting specialist at a ski shop can custom fit this for you. Another boot approach uses a movable footbed, allowing your foot to rock inside the boot rather than keeping it rigid.

Other foot problems may require special fitting devices. These difficulties can include *supination,* evidenced by an extremely high arch. Another problem could be caused by a correctly aligned heel, but with a twist in the forefoot.

Now that you have your feet corrected, let's look at your lower legs. When the mythical ideal person stands with his feet touching each other, his ankles, calves, and knees also touch. Since we're real people, it doesn't always work that way. Sometimes the knees will touch, while the feet and calves are apart. This is called knock-knee, and it can cause a skier to be stuck in a wedge. A fairly common situation is for the knees to be apart, in a bowlegged position. With this "cowboy stance" a skier tends to walk on the outside of his feet. When his feet are fastened rigidly to the skis, the skier stands on the two outside edges when schussing, instead of on a flat ski. In a turn, the skier's outside ski does not have enough edge, and the inside ski has too much. This leads to ski separation and dependence on the inside ski. Skiers needing leg compensation sometimes lift the inside ski or tuck the lower knee in the crook of the upper knee.

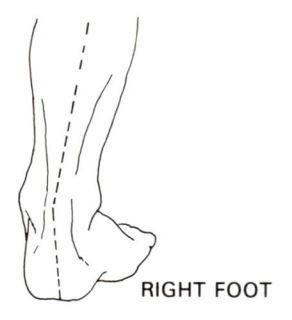

RIGHT FOOT

Heel bone misalignment

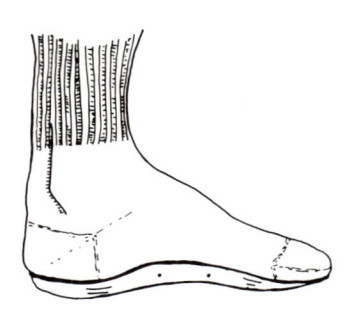

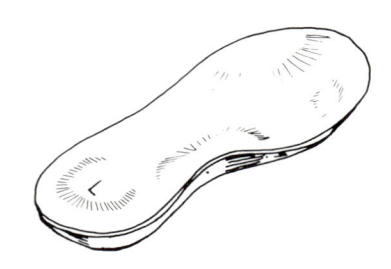

Orthotic device to correct excessive pronation

UNCOMPENSATED   CANTED

STRAIGHT RUNNING

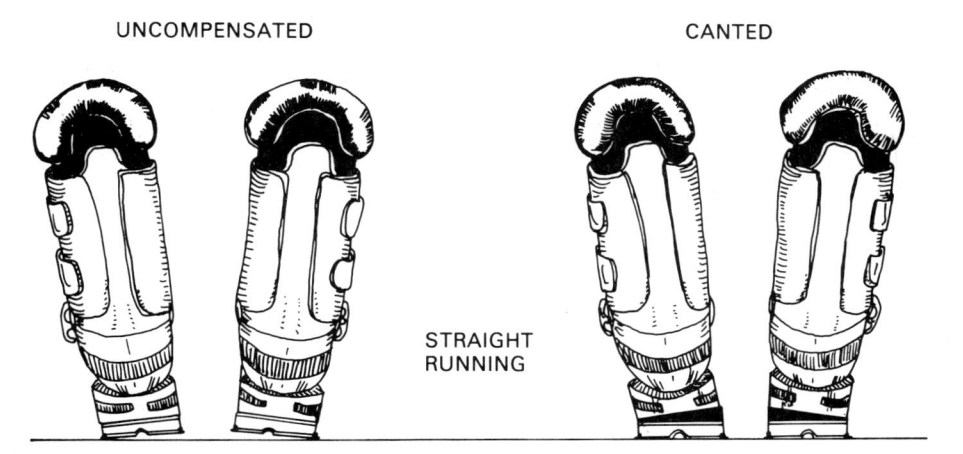

SKIS RIDE OUTSIDE EDGES   SKIS FLAT ON SNOW

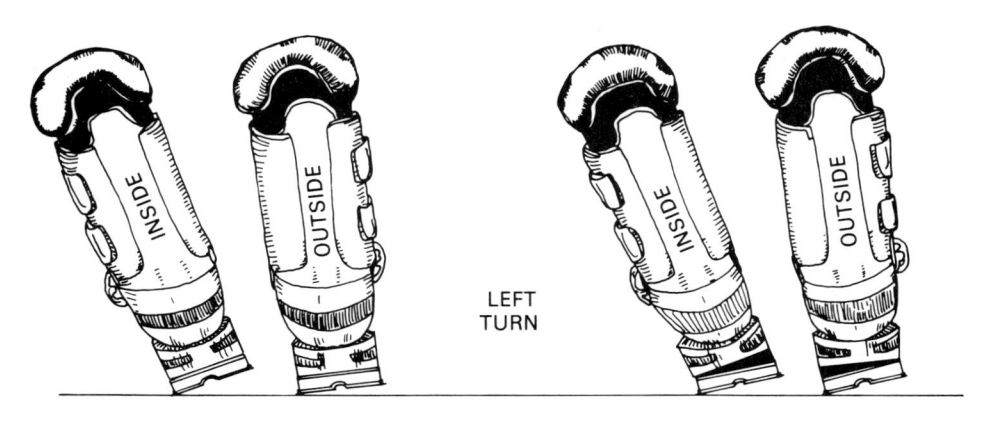

LEFT TURN

SKIS EDGE UNEQUALLY   SKIS EDGE EQUALLY   **Bowlegged stance**

How can you determine your leg structure? Look at the heels of your street shoes. Wear on the outside indicates a bowlegged stance. Stand without shoes in your normal straight running position. Have a friend run a straight line (a pendulum, such as a key tied to a string) from the center of your knee to your foot. If the center of each knee doesn't line up with the center of each foot (between the second and middle toe) your leg structure is off. Wearing completely buckled ski boots, stand on a hard floor in a stance you'd use on the slopes. Have a friend look at the tails of your skis to see if the whole ski is flat on the floor, rather than on an edge. Move both knees left an equal amount and have the friend measure at the ski tail to see if both ski edges are lifted off the floor by equal amounts, which is the case in ideal leg structure. Repeat to the right. Moving knees left to right, you should ideally feel both skis go flat on the floor at the same time. Ski straight down the fall line on a gentle slope. Look at the tracks on the snow to see if you were riding flat skis. If you were on outside (or inside) edges instead, it's due to bone structure. Stand across the hill in a traverse position. Both skis should be angled equally to the snow. If you must make uncomfortable movements to achieve the equal angles (maybe tucking in your downhill knee), you need compensation. Wearing ski boots, get measured on a canting machine at a ski shop.

Several solutions are available to the bowlegged stance. The easiest is to move your feet apart, or your knees closer together. This puts you on flat skis once again. Because almost everyone's lower legs flare outward, most boots have an outward lean angle of two or three degrees built into them. This accommodates the shape of your lower leg, but fills in the gap which would normally be on the inside of your feet. Essentially, the boots wedge, or raise up the inner part of your foot. This is known as a *cant*.

Some boots and plate bindings have built-in adjustments to dial in your own cant. Lacking these, wedge-shaped plastic cants can be attached underneath your bindings and boot area. These tilt your whole boot to the outside. Sometimes boot soles are ground down on the outside to cant. Of course, if you are knock-kneed, the corrections are just the opposite.

A good ski shop will be your best bet for correcting foot and leg problems. Get adjusted for orthotics first, then cants if necessary. Back on the slopes, you may need to become accustomed to your new edging capabilities as your skeletal structure works more efficiently. Once you discover the quick response and precise edging orthotics or cants supply, your skiing will become even more fun.

6
COPING WITH COLD AND ALTITUDE

You've probably discovered that becoming part of your environment is one of the joys of skiing. However, cold comprises a majority of this environment and can easily ruin a day on the slopes. When you're used to sitting in a 70 degree room, exposure to zero degrees removes all thoughts of technique or fun and reduces a ski day to one of survival. Let's find out cold's battle tactics so you can combat it.

First of all, the higher you go, the colder the air temperature. Dressing just warm enough for the valley temperature won't be adequate protection for the summit. As a rule of thumb, figure on at least a 4 degree F. temperature drop for every 1,000 feet of elevation gained. (For you metric buffs, that's 2 degrees C. for every 300 meters.) Don't be deceived by the sun. If you feel warm near the base lodge, maybe you're getting extra sunshine there. Up on those shady north-facing slopes you won't have that warmth to rely on.

Wind is your worst enemy, and it will be stronger higher up the mountain, or even higher above the ground in a chair lift. Just as in hot weather you feel cooler with a fan blowing on you, so in cold weather the wind will convince you to wear your longies next time. Moving air is extremely effective at taking away heat. Weather reports refer to this as the "wind chill factor." A 20 degree F. air temperature with a 20 mile per hour wind means you should dress as though it were minus 10 degrees F., because that's how cold it will feel. Don't forget that even on a calm day just riding the chair lift will give the equivalent of an 8 m.p.h. wind, reducing 20 degrees F. to an effective 2 degrees. Skiing downhill also creates warmth-robbing wind equal to the speed at which you're traveling. Since most of us don't carry wind chill charts in our parkas, you can estimate by adding 10 to the wind speed and subtracting that total

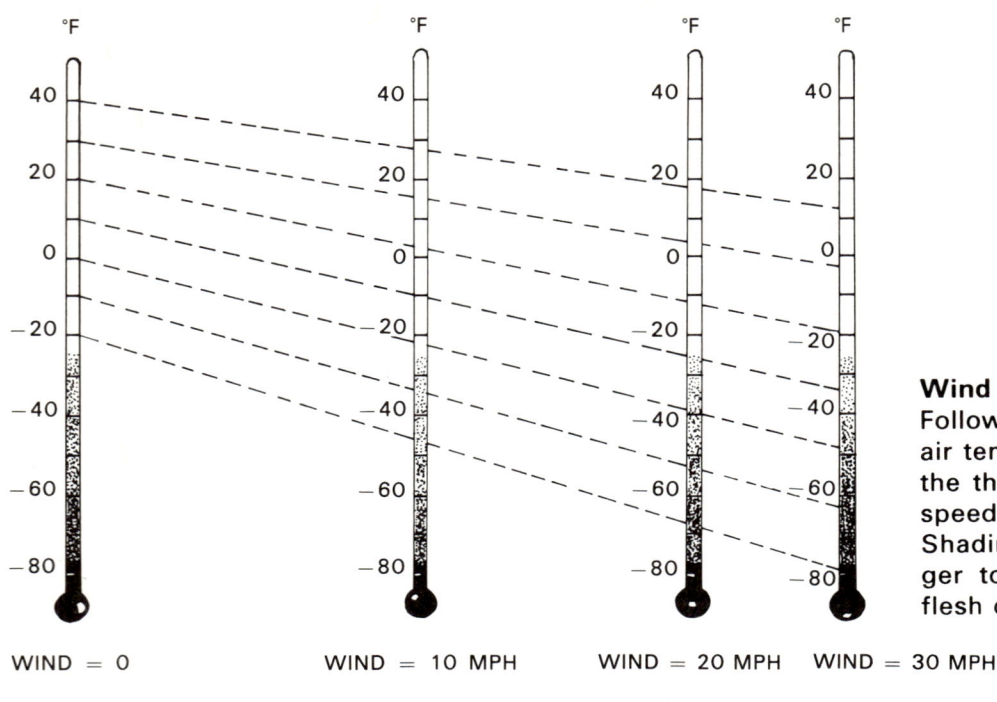

Wind chill chart
Follow the dotted line from the air temperature thermometer to the thermometer with the wind speed to read the chill factor. Shading indicates relative danger to exposed skin. At −25° flesh can freeze in one minute.

from the temperature. Thus, for a 10 m.p.h. wind subtract 20 degrees; for a 20 m.p.h. wind subtract 30 degrees, etc.

Humidity also changes the effective temperature, as water vapor whisks away heat faster than air. A damp or foggy day feels cold all the way to the bones. In cold clear weather, however, the air will frequently be very dry, moderating the effective cold. But this means your body loses water more rapidly through breathing. Couple this with extra exertion and it will be necessary for you to drink more fluids than normal to avoid dehydration. Dehydration makes you tire more easily and also feel the cold more. A secondary effect of dry air is that your skin may need additional moisture, which a face lotion can supply.

Loss of body heat affects your extremities first. Goosebumps and shivering may occur as your body tries to restore the heat balance. Surface blood vessels constrict to lower the blood flow, and hence the heat loss to arms and legs. Your fingers and toes will get cold and sting as your body conserves its heat in the vital organs. Your nose and cheeks may hurt from their exposure. In frigid weather have your companions look at you frequently, and you at them, to watch for frostbite. This is a mild freezing of the skin which appears as a white, numb patch. If you get it, immediately warm the frozen area back to body temperature. *Do not rub with snow or place in hot water!* For the nose and cheeks, warm the area with your bare palm. If your fingertips are affected, put your hands inside your clothing next to your body. Frostbite is not serious if treated right away, but once you have gotten it you will be more susceptible to freezing that area again.

Now let's fight back against the cold. The first rule is to conserve the heat you have. That means appropriate clothing and dressing for warmth rather than style. Warm clothes work by trapping air, which is an insulator. Dressing in layers creates air traps to save body warmth. An old adage says, "If your feet are cold put on an extra sweater." That's still true today, for conserving heat lost in one area saves it for another. Your bare head can lose over 50 percent of your body heat, so cover it with a hat. Avoid exposing skin, such as the neck or wrists. On bitter days, swallow your pride and save your skin with a face mask. Protective cold weather creams offer limited protection, like an invisible mask, if you don't mind a greasy feeling.

Since moisture carries away heat you must avoid dampness. Boots and gloves are giant sponges. They'll collect snowflakes and perspiration by the gallon, even though they may look innocently dry. Be sure to place them in a warm spot each evening. Better yet, dry them with a warm (not hot) hair dryer or remove the liners. If possible, dry them at lunchtime also, or change to dry socks and gloves. Perspiration is moisture, and it collects in clothes to draw heat from the body. Try to avoid sweating in cold weather. When warm, remove your hat and perhaps a layer of clothes. Open up collars and zippers to vent your steam, especially when inside for a break. One word on blue jeans: No. They're fine for après ski, but they collect every flake of snow for miles and then freeze permanently into a sitting position on the chair lift.

When your clothes can't conserve enough heat, you must generate more. Active skiing produces six times more body heat than just sitting. Before starting a run, jump around, stretch, and bend up and down to get the muscles limber. Your legs contain the largest muscles in the body, so use them to make a lot of small turns down the hill. Turn frequently where you normally would cruise. Windmill your arms to force blood into cold fingers. Stamp feet up and down to warm cold toes. If you're still chilly a sure warmerupper is to climb uphill on skis. Even while riding the chair wiggle your toes, clench and relax your grip on the poles, and hold your legs straight out from the chair to work the thighs.

Food is converted to muscular activity plus heat. In the cold you need a lot of calories to keep going, so don't try to diet and ski. Fats and protein supply needed day-long energy, but aren't instant warmers. Carbohydrates provide quick heat energy, giving you a great excuse for an extra Danish pastry at breakfast. During the day snack on candy bars, fruit juices, or other foods with sugar. Among the many negative things tobacco does is constrict the capillaries, allowing less blood to reach the extremities (colder toes). Alcohol dilates blood vessels, giving you a flush of temporary warmth, but this is at the expense of internal heat, and after a while you'll be colder than ever.

In short, cold will attack with temperature, wind, and moisture. You must respond with adequate clothes, activity and food. However, the battle is never-ending. Take a break now and then with a hot chocolate while you swap tales with friends about how much colder it was last year when you skied Mt. Frosty.

In planning a trip to a high altitude resort (one over 5,000 feet) there may be one detail you've overlooked. That is how the unaccustomed altitude will affect you.

Very simply, the higher you go the less air you'll find. You can figure on 10 percent less air pressure for every 3,000 feet of elevation you gain. This causes some unexpected phenomena, one of which is lowering the boiling temperature of water. You'd better get up five minutes earlier because your five minute egg at sea level must cook almost ten minutes in a mile high kitchen. At western resorts you'll finally get a chance to use those special directions for high altitude baking on the cake mix package.

What will concern you most is the lack of oxygen to breathe. The percentage of oxygen remains constant, but there's considerably less air than at sea level. This makes your heart and lungs work harder for the same physical output. How much the altitude affects you depends on what shape you are in at sea level and how hard you exert yourself. If you have a medical problem with your cardiovascular or respiratory system you should check with your doctor before taking the trip. The first day or two will be the hardest. If you make a major gain in elevation, for instance, suddenly rising 7,000 feet, you may feel lazy or even dizzy. You'll think your luggage and skis gained several pounds on their flight. You may find yourself breathing faster and your heartbeat may increase. As a rule of thumb, subtract 15 percent from your normal physical performance for each 3,000 feet you've come up. Thus, at 7,000 feet don't expect to exert more than two-thirds your normal sea level energy before tiring that first day.

Your body will acclimate quickly by readjusting such things as the proportion of oxygen-carrying red corpuscles in the blood. After a couple of days you probably won't notice much difference from sea level, but in the meantime make it easy on yourself. Avoid overexerting the first two days by stopping frequently to look around and breathe deeply. Diet will also help. Stick to easily digestible food with a high energy content. At breakfast pass up that second helping of sausage in favor of an extra doughnut or other "carbo." Be aware that smoking and alcohol will hit much harder those first days (talk about a Rocky Mountain high!).

Sunlight, always a hazard at any ski area, will be especially intense at high altitude. The air is thinner and cleaner and lets a larger percentage of ultraviolet rays through. At 7,000 feet this radiation can be three times as strong as it is at sea level and it's all trying to burn your eyes and skin. Never ski in sunshine without good quality sunglasses. Even overcast days will be much brighter than you expect and still hazardous. Anyone who's ever experienced sunburned retinas will never forget sunglasses again. Too much sun also reduces your night vision.

You'll tan several times faster than at home, so apply sun lotion (not baby oil) liberally. Lotions are labelled with protection factors from 2 to 15. A "4" label means you can stay out four times as long as without any protection. Many ski professionals use 6 to 10 factor labels and still end up with a great tan. To prevent further tanning, a colorless "block-out" will screen out all burning rays.

Lips come in handy now and then for talking, eating, or whatever so prevent them from cracking or swelling by using a stick-type sunscreen and moisturizer. Carry it in a parka pocket so it's always accessible.

Once you return home you'll look healthier and have some great stories to tell. Also, as an unexpected bonus, until your body readjusts to sea level pressure (which takes a couple days), you'll be full of extra energy.

7

SURMOUNTING ADVERSE WEATHER

Nasty weather skiing can be fun. Don't let a storm drive you inside for the day. Let's assume you're properly dressed for protection from wind, cold, and wetness, and take a trip onto the slopes.

Looks sort of gloomy out, doesn't it? Put on those yellow goggles! Immediately everything appears cheerier, but most importantly, your visibility improves. The yellow color increases contrast by filtering out light scattered by fog and snowflakes, thus highlighting features and intensifying shadows. This reduces the "flat" light so you can see interesting features, such as mogul fields. Keep the goggles over your eyes. Once they get pushed up over your wet hat they'll start fogging inside. To help prevent fogging, wipe the inside lens (eyeglasses too) with an anti-fog cloth. I prefer double lens goggles, as they are quite resistant to fogging.

Avoid skiing wide open areas. Sure, they may seem to have less to ski into, but you'll also get a touch of vertigo. You may lose your balance, not see bumps, and wonder which way is down. It happens to everyone in a *white-out,* that uncomfortable situation where your whole world turns into the inside of an icy cotton ball. Ski near trees, perhaps along a trail edge or in a glade. They'll provide an up and down reference point for balance. Also, they give you perspective, which means an idea of the relative size of things, allowing proper judgment of speed and terrain. Trees offer some contrast to the whiteness and provide a subtle shading to the snow, improving vision. If you run out of trees, try skiing near people, lift towers, or trail markers. Don't forget you're carrying a set of "curb feelers." Occasionally touching your ski pole baskets to the snow gives sensory information on which way is up.

Visibility may appear to be your major problem, but if you have been fortunate enough to watch a blind skier on the slopes, you'll realize skiers use more senses than just sight. Be loose and especially flexible in the knees to compensate for a bump or gully you may not see. Let your feet become sensitive to subtle changes in pitch and snow conditions. You must be aggressive without being reckless. Skiing slower is a good idea, but do it by staying over your feet, always ready, rather than shying away from going downhill and reverting to poor technique. Exploring is for sunny days. Stay on familiar trails so that you'll ski with confidence, always knowing what to expect.

Mountains intensify storm fronts. The higher you go the more severe the storm. If it is bad at the lodge it will be worse on top. The one exception will be a calm weather valley fog, with possible sunshine above. During storms, clouds will hang in around upper slopes causing fog, while the lower slopes may be clear. Ski the lower, sheltered runs where the wind and snow are more tolerable. Always check doubtful weather with the ski area information desk. They should be able to tell you temperature and wind velocities on the hill.

You won't need a degree in meteorology to figure out which way the wind is blowing. Head for trails that are protected, both for your

Slope exposures
In this photo the sunlight from the south helps to show which directions various slopes "face."

(Photo courtesy Sun Valley Ski Area.)

43

comfort and for better snow. The wind can whip away loose snow, exposing an icy base on unsheltered runs. This fluffy snow is then deposited on the lee side of hills or trees. If the wind hits you from the left as you face downhill, then ski next to trees on the left side of the trail or find runs nestled on the left side of a protecting ridge.

Recognizing slope exposure is useful, even under sunny skies. North-facing slopes, the most common ones at ski areas, have less exposure to direct sunshine and retain a better snow cover. But these slopes are colder and during icy conditions will be the last ones to soften. Learn to follow the sun around the mountain to your advantage. When you need its warmth or light, ski the east-facing slopes in the morning, and the west-facing in the afternoon. Avoid exposed slopes when looking for the lightest powder or the firmest snow in spring slush. If you need warmth on a chair lift, try riding around noon when the sun is highest and less likely to be blocked by terrain or trees.

Skiing on a nasty day can be an uplifting and almost mystical experience as you battle the elements. Often it's just you and the mountain, as most others don't know the joy of skiing harsh conditions. But remember to recognize your own limitations when you get tired and cold. Head in for a hot drink by a warm fire—that's where we frequently do our best skiing!

8
CHOOSING A SKI AREA

Deciding where to ski is part of the joy of skiing. About July, when ski fever strikes me again, I start mailing for area brochures. They're fun to read on the beach and give me an idea where to head for a change of pace when I'm not instructing.

In evaluating your local areas, you can talk to friends to find out about types of runs, crowds, and prices. You may want to join a local ski club. They frequently have cabins at areas where you can stay reasonably. Every club runs several trips a season, particularly on long holiday weekends. They hire charter buses and arrange group rates on lodging. It's a great way to meet people, and some ski club parties are legendary.

Area brochures, skiing magazines, and ski area directory guidebooks provide your best sources for discovering the facts about an area. When writing for a brochure, also request a trail map. The brochure will always have gorgeous color photos (not necessarily of their own area) and glowing descriptions of the skiing. They will give you an idea of what shops, restaurants, and nightspots are nearby, what additional diversions are available, such as skating, swimming or cross-country skiing, and what the costs are. Reading between the lines you may be able to decide if they meticulously groom slopes, if they leave bumps for those who like them, if they cater to families or singles and so on.

The trail map will provide a more accurate idea of what's actually on the mountain. However, be wary of the illustrations of the hill. Ski areas employ artists of inordinate talent who could make Mt. Everest look pale beside a drawing of the highest point in Florida.

The first statistic you should notice is the *vertical drop*. This is the elevation difference in height between the top and the bottom of the area. Some areas will liberally round this figure off to the next highest 100 feet, or also count the lower end of the parking lot in the vertical. Generally, the greater the vertical drop, the longer the runs and the more skiing terrain. An area with one chair over a 2,000-foot vertical will have three or four times the skiable terrain of an area with one chair but only a 1,000-foot vertical.

Many areas make up for a lack of vertical by spreading out sideways along a mountain or skiing several faces on a mountain. You should therefore consider the number of lifts and also the number of trails for your ability level. There is no standard for trail rating, so one area's intermediate may be another's advanced. Trail steepness is frequently measured in "percent slope," which divides the vertical drop by the horizontal distance covered. Generally trails marked "easiest" include runs up to 20 percent slope, dropping 20 feet for every 100 horizontal feet forward. "More difficult" trails cover 20 to 40 percent slopes, and "advanced" over 40 percent. The steepness of a chair lift will give you a clue as to how tough the runs really are. Consider a 1,000 foot vertical covered by a chair 5,000 feet long. The runs under that chair would be considerably easier than runs under a chair somewhere else with a 1,000 foot rise in only a 3,000 foot length.

One area may specialize in narrow trails, and another in wide cut slopes. Sometimes the resorts will quote a figure called *skiable area*,

(Photo courtesy Aspen Skiing Corporation.)

Vertical drop

11,100 FT.

VERTICAL DROP OF 3,100 FEET

8,000 FT.

which in theory is all their acreage with ski turning space. Unfortunately, these figures frequently include tree regions where you'd need a 14-inch chainsaw to hack your way through.

Ski reports provide you with a clue as to what to expect. Don't be too impressed by snow depth figures. They are always unpacked depths. Sometimes they are measured by a nearsighted owner with a broken yardstick. Some areas have their slopes groomed so well that you can ski on six inches. Others will need three feet just to cover the stumps and rocks. What's more important is the percentage of the area that is open on any given day. This may be stated in terms of the number of lifts running or by naming the trails that are skiable.

Ski areas in the same locality will have the same general conditions, allowing for small variations due to altitude, exposure, and grooming. One significant difference in general "skiability" of an area can be attributed to the presence of manmade snow. This artificially produced snow is manufactured by shooting sprays of water and compressed air from nozzles into the freezing atmosphere above the ski runs. As it falls it crystallizes into snow, somewhat dense, but very similar to "real" snow. Many areas use this snow to assist Mother Nature in building up a base. In slim snowfall years it can comprise the majority of the snow pack.

Although the Eskimos have dozens of words to describe snow conditions, we have only a few terms to classify the various types of snow. Unfortunately, some ski area owners seem to know only one phrase. They use the term "packed powder" to describe anything vaguely white on the ground. Take several grains of salt when listening to snow reports. The ideal condition is packed powder; then there are many others including soft pack, hard pack, corn, frozen granular or even the dreaded ice, not to mention "spring conditions," which can be anything including a few bare patches for good measure. Conditions change rapidly in winter, so be prepared for anything by the time you get to the slopes.

A general knowledge of weather patterns will help your trip. If it is chilly at your home, and you're heading north or up into the hills, it's going to be chillier. Even though the latest ski report said thirty degrees, if you're going to northern New England in January, be prepared for cold. If you're taking a spring ski trip to the Rockies, carry along a parka. Their heaviest snowstorms come in April.

When you're choosing a spot for a vacation, don't shy away from the major resorts. The well-known areas are justly famous because they have a lot to offer everyone. If you want to avoid crowds or stretch your dollar, you may be happier at a smaller area, or a combination of two or three areas in one trip. The choice is yours. That's what makes horse races, and also what makes reading the area brochures in July so much fun.

9

SHOPPING FOR A SKI SCHOOL

It's not always necessary to take lessons to learn something, skiing included. Perhaps you don't have the financial means to take them, or are simply headstrong enough to want to do it yourself. Many fine skiers have developed without organized lessons. But the trained eye of a professional instructor can quickly spot your problem areas and help you improve rapidly. If you should decide to take lessons, the sequence of exercises in this book is basically the same as you will find at many ski schools; the terminology is also common. Lessons can be fun as you share your problems, misfortunes, falls and successes with your fellow learners. They are also a great way to meet people.

Lessons are classified as group or private. The latter cost from four to eight times as much per hour of instruction, but you do receive concentrated attention. Sharing a private lesson with someone of your own ability can substantially reduce the cost per person. But don't forget that in a class you can learn from watching your classmates too, so the choice boils down to how you feel you learn best. Usually, beginners take group classes rather than private lessons. If you have a lot of skills to refine at any level of skiing, classes can be best. But if you have one specific thing you want to improve or are limited in time, a private lesson may be better.

How do you choose a ski school? Most large resorts will have a competent professional staff, as will many smaller areas. Here are some points to consider to aid you in your choice:

1. Find out what technique is taught. Ask if the ski school is affiliated with the Professional Ski Instructors of America. If so, they probably teach a unified method, one that is tried and proven. The American Teaching Method (ATM) is a standard, and you will fit into other ski schools around the country. Be wary of fantastic claims of instant parallel skiing, new international techniques, and

any ski school that starts you out on skis so short they look like toys.

2. Find out how many students are in each class. Ideally it should be four to six, but this is seldom economically practical for a school. Seven or eight is workable and during an extremely busy season expect as many as eleven. Forget about classes with more than a dozen students.

3. Ask how many of the instructors are professionally certified. Each region of the country has a Ski Instructors Association whose members take rigorous tests to become certified. A ski school with a good percentage of certified instructors shows that it cares about the quality of instruction.

4. Find out if you will need a lift ticket in addition to a lesson ticket. In higher-level classes you inevitably will, but this is desirable, as you'll want to ski before or after the lesson. But many areas will let you take a beginner's lesson without a lift ticket. As long as you are in class you get to ride free on the beginners' lifts.

5. For any level above beginners, a good ski school will put you into a class by skiing you down a test hill. Then you will fit right in with others of your same ability. If no test hill is available at the meeting place, be sure that you can easily transfer between classes to one of your exact ability during the first run.

6. If you're taking several days of lessons, see if you will stay with the same instructor. That way you can progress without repeating steps and the instructor will know exactly how you ski and what will work best for you as an individual.

7. Look for emphasis on long lesson periods. Generally a four-hour lesson, with the same students and instructor, will prove more beneficial than two separate two-hour lessons with different students and instructors, and it may be less expensive. One long lesson avoids wasted organization time and allows your instructor more time to find out what you as an individual need to learn. Some resorts offer four-hour lessons which are actually five-hour sessions, taking a lunch break with your group.

8. See if any extra services are offered in the ski school, such as actual classroom time to learn how to care for skis or watch films. This is still a rarity, unfortunately. But some areas may have a videotape for ski school, so you can actually see yourself ski.

9. Ask if there is emphasis on starting on shorter skis (a good idea), and if so, if there are special classes for people on Graduated Length Method (GLM). At the beginner level, having students on both four- and seven-foot skis in the same class can slow down everyone's progress.

10. See if classes can cut lift lines so you don't waste time standing around.

Once you are in a lesson, remember it's your time and money. Feel free to question anything you don't understand or ask for special things you'd like to learn. To learn fastest, when the instructor demonstrates a maneuver, imagine yourself in his place doing the same thing and actually feeling which way you should move.

Don't be prejudiced by an instructor's gender, appearance, accent (or lack of one), etc. Keep an open mind to the principles you are learning. If you think you want to parallel but the instructor shows you a wedge, he's doing it for a good reason. If you have a particularly good (or bad) lesson, let the ski school director know. Often this is the only feedback he has as to how well his staff is doing.

Finally, consider the instructor. He's only human, trying to be a teacher, psychologist, stand-up comedian, guide and first aid dispenser, among other jobs. He's probably instructing because he loves the sport and enjoys meeting people who are interested enough in skiing to try to improve. If you honestly enjoyed your lesson, let him know—he'll appreciate it. Most ski schools pay instructors a flat hourly wage, so he's receiving only a small percentage of what your class has paid. If he gives an exceptionally good lesson in content, showing extra preparation, attention, and time, then a tip, whether as a class or individually, is certainly in order.

Every ski school defines class levels differently. It really doesn't matter what your class is called, as long as everyone skis at about the same speed. However, since we like to classify ourselves, I'll list the general levels and what you can expect:

(A) *Absolute Beginner.* If you've never been on skis, you'll learn how to put them on, walk around, straight runs, wedges for stability, and turns. (Most schools have an A-2 section, for people who have been on skis about two hours or once before.)

(B) *Higher Beginner.* If you've been on skis one or two days, you'll learn traverses, improving turns using edges, and sideslips. You'll be skiing beginner runs and riding lifts.

(C) *Intermediate.* You'll learn stems to control speed and to initiate turns, skidding to finish a turn, and simultaneous knee actions to turn and stop. You'll be skiing some intermediate runs.

(D) *Advanced (High) Intermediate.* You'll learn the use of poles, definite weight transfer aided by unweighting, initiating parallel turns, and handling the bumps. You'll be skiing any intermediate runs.

(E) *Advanced.* You'll learn how to improve parallel turns by refining movements, carving, rebound unweighting, powder and ice. You'll be skiing most advanced runs.

(F) *Expert.* You'll learn racing techniques, avalement in the bumps, shortswing, and step turns. You'll ski any run with snow on it.

If you take lessons at an area and plan to return to the area, ask your instructor if you are ready for the next higher class. Several days of consecutive lessons at the same resort may automatically progress you through one or more stages.

Perhaps the above technical terms sound confusing at this point. As you take a lesson, concentrate on the basic skills of steering, edging, and pressure and remember, whatever the exercise is called, it's only a refinement of those skills.

Section II
FIRST MOTIONS ON SKIS

Your first days on skis will be a bewildering yet enthralling time. You'll discover things you didn't know your body could do, and experience the first thrills of delight and terror as your skis head downhill. This section is designed to help you safely enjoy those days. You'll find that some conditioning prior to skiing will aid your coordination and endurance. You'll learn how to carry and put on the equipment. Once on the snow you'll discover that many basic motions are similar to walking with very long feet. Straight runs will introduce you to sliding, while sidestepping will get you back up a slope and provide a feeling for edges. In a wedge position your balance will improve and your speed slow. You'll make your first turns with a natural steering action. Next you'll be riding lifts to beginner slopes where awareness of skier safety is important.

10

WILL I BE ABLE TO SKI?

Frequently beginners have serious doubts about their ability to learn to ski, whether due to physical condition, age, or lack of coordination. Let's try a simple test. Walk to the center of your living room. Stand there relaxed and move your knees left about six inches and then right six inches. Now bend straight down in the knees about half a foot and straighten up again. If you can walk, move your knees left, right, up and down, *then you can ski!* It's that simple.

Maybe you feel that you will never be an expert skier. I have seen individuals begin the sport in their sixties and become experts. I've enjoyed skiing with people with such "handicaps" as blindness, obesity, amputated limbs, artificial limbs and acrophobia. I guarantee that you have within yourself the capability to ski any part of any mountain. Ski purely for the fun of it, find the positive side of each learning experience, and you'll progress rapidly. Part of the challenge of skiing is that no one is ever as good as he or she would like to be. Anyone who claims he had a perfect run down the mountain may as well hang up his skis and look for a new sport. It's the seeking of perfection, the ability to master any slope in any condition that drives a skier to improve.

Statistics show that skiing is a safe sport. Anyone who avoids skiing by saying "I can't afford to incapacitate myself for work" may as well also avoid driving cars, using power tools, or stepping into bathtubs. With modern equipment and ski lessons the risk of serious skiing injury continues to decrease. Accidents generally happen to those whose bindings are misadjusted or to those who are skiing far beyond their ability technically or physically.

Being in shape leads to smoother body action and enhances your skiing fun. This doesn't mean you must be a Mister America to ski. Professional skiers have firm muscles, but aren't musclebound.

Some moderate exercise, done several times a week as a year-round program, (or at least a month prior to skiing) will strengthen, stretch, and elasticize the muscles, tendons, and ligaments. You will tire less, reduce the risk of injury, and improve faster.

Three physical conditioning factors will aid skiing:

1. Agility, the nimble ability to move and react quickly. Women often outclass men in this category. Sports demanding quick footwork and coordination are useful, such as tennis, racquetball, badminton, table tennis, volleyball, soccer and basketball. Yoga and dancing, which encourage limber muscles, are also good disciplines.

2. Endurance, the ability to keep continuously active for five minutes or more. Almost any activity which induces heartbeats of around 120 a minute for several minutes at a stretch develops endurance. This is known as aerobic exercise, increasing the air carrying capacity of the blood by heart and lung action. In addition to agility sports, recreation such as swimming, jumping rope, jogging, skating, and bicycle riding will help.

3. Strength, the muscular capacity to handle a task. In skiing, as in walking, the legs are used. Thus any activity which especially develops the leg muscles helps, such as hiking, climbing stairs, and most active sports. Exerting yourself beyond normal levels, as in weight lifting or isometrics, develops strength. When building up muscles, remember that they always work in pairs in opposite directions. Riding a ten-speed bike would only develop half the needed muscles, the "pushing" ones, unless you use toe clips on the pedals to exercise the "pulling" muscles as well. After any muscle developing exercise, it's important to stretch and relax those muscles.

To be effective, exercise has to be fun or it is quickly dropped. I find nothing more boring than jogging around a track, yet I love to jog random paths through the woods or different streets in town. When bicycle riding, I set a destination, a goal such as the beach or a store, and then push myself on the tougher stretches of hills. If you're really devoted and can stick with it you may set up a daily program of a few minutes of various exercises, but most people would rather get out with friends or an organized group several times a week for a physical activity. Find a sport you can enjoy doing in the backyard with the family; phone your local parks department or schools to see what evening sports are offered in the gyms; take a long walk several times a week. Whatever you do, any exercise is infinitely better than none.

Help yourself get into shape for skiing by eating a balanced diet and getting enough sleep. Through an exercise program you may even find some nice side effects, such as a more alert mental attitude, less stress in everyday living, and simply a healthy feeling. Pretty good, considering we haven't even gotten on the snow yet!

11
GETTING TO THE SLOPES

No matter how near the slopes you park, you'll always have to do a little walking in those awkward boots while simultaneously juggling your skis and poles. Here's where you have the choice of looking like a complete bunny, with heavy skis slung across the forearms and poles spearing people left and right, or looking cool and collected with skis under control. Let's choose the latter.

Before you take a step, unfasten all your upper boot buckles. This gives your ankles freedom to flex, making walking and climbing stairs easy.

Carrying skis
Note that the top buckles on the skier's boots are unfastened for ease of ankle bend when walking.

Place the skis bottom to bottom and clip them together with inexpensive rubber straps made for the purpose. Wrap one strap around the tips and one around the tails. You can also fasten skis together with safety straps or with some of the ski brake devices. (With practice you will be able to dispense with the fasteners.) Now rest the skis flat on one shoulder, tips in the air, so that your shoulder is between the heel and toe piece. This is the balance point of the skis; your hand near the tails will keep them in place. Remember, your skis will sweep a large arc wherever you walk, especially when changing direction. The more vertically you carry the skis, the less chance you have of hitting other objects and people. By carrying both poles in the other hand you now have additional support for icy walks. To avoid beheading people in a more confined area, remove the skis from your shoulder and carry them upright in front of you, grasping them with one hand below the toe pieces. Rest them on their tails in the snow when you stop.

If you're an equipment nut, you may buy useful devices to aid getting to the slopes, such as clip-on rubber walking soles, and plastic gizmos to hold your equipment together. I think they are great, except once I get to the hill I don't know what to do with them. Too bad they don't also convert into earmuffs.

Now to put on your skis. Find a level area and stick your poles straight into the snow. If you don't have ski brakes, turn one ski on its side so it has less tendency to run or be pushed away. If the snow is soft enough you may stick the ski upright, tail first into the snow.

Putting on skis

Removing snow from boot sole

Place the other ski flat on the snow and open your binding. Leaning on a pole for balance, check your boot sole for sticking snow, which would prevent the boot from fitting into the binding. Resting the lower leg against your other knee, knock any snow off the sole with the pole shaft. If there is caked ice on the sole, dislodge it with the point of the pole. Holding onto a pole on each side for support, step into the open binding, latch it closed, and fasten the safety strap if you have one. Repeat the procedure with the other ski.

Once you have progressed to a hill, you will usually attach your skis on a sloping area. To do this, stand at right angles to the slope and put your first ski—the downhill one—at right angles to the slope so it won't slide forward or backward down the hill. To be sure it doesn't slide sideways downhill, firmly press the ski into the snow until it is level. On icy terrain you may temporarily place a glove under the ski to help hold it in place. Once you are securely in the downhill ski, repeat the process with the uphill one.

Next put on your poles. If yours have straps, insert your hand upward through the loop, so that the strap rests in your palm as you grasp the grip. If you have a strapless type, just make sure the left and right poles are on the proper hands. Place a piece of tape or a dab of paint on one pole to enable you to see instantly which is which. With everything fastened, your boards are now ready to slide.

Putting on pole straps

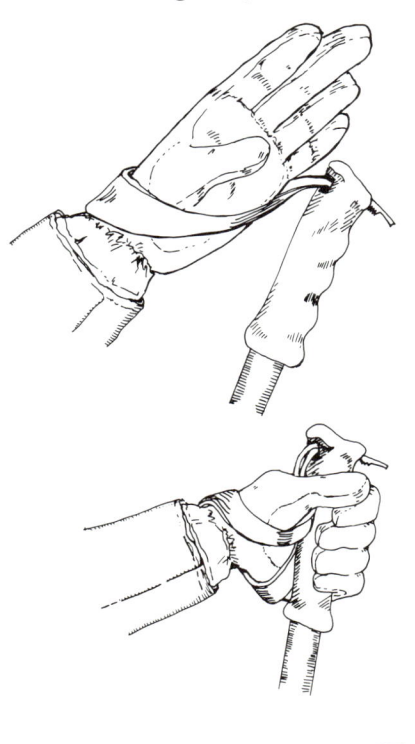

57

12

WHERE POINTETH THE FEET, SO GOETH THE SKIS

Now that you've put on the skis and have stood up on them, congratulations! You have won a good part of the battle, since standing on skis means you have found a balance point and have coordinated dozens of muscles already.

Skis are merely big feet, with a few improvements to adapt them to the snow, namely slippery bottoms and steel edges. Pick up one foot at a time and notice that any direction your foot twists, the ski also twists. Let's discover more about balancing on them.

Spread your skis comfortably apart, as in a walking stance. Your ankles will be bent forward by the boots, and your knees are bent to compensate. Keep your upper body flexible at the waist, with the trunk upright, as in walking. Center your hips over your feet. Hold your poles by lifting your hands slightly in front of you, with the baskets pointing back. Now, rock forward and backward at the ankle to press first the toes and then the heels down. Find a point at which your weight feels slightly forward on the balls of the feet —there should be no strain on your body. This will be your balanced stance.

FINDING A NATURAL ATHLETIC STANCE

I call this position an athletic one as it is basic to many sports and to walking. You are relaxed and balanced over the feet, but ready to respond in any direction. With the feet eight to twelve inches apart you have a wide, stable stance. You should feel your lower legs pressed against the front of the boots and no strain on the back or calf muscles. Your knees are flexed to compensate for the ankles being bent forward in the boots. Imagine a weight on a string hung from your midsection behind the belly button. This center of gravity line should pass through the balls of your feet. This means your skeletal structure (backbone, pelvis, leg bones) is supporting your

Relaxed athletic stance

weight, without any muscle strain. Your head is erect and looking forward; if you glance down, you should not see the front of your ankles as the knees are in the way, flexed over the feet. Hold your hands out as though riding a bicycle, with the elbows bent and slightly away from the body. Have a friend look at you to verify that your back is upright and that your fanny is not sticking out behind you. (As the Austrians say, "Den Hintern nicht hinausstecken!") If all this seems picky, remember that a balanced stance is fundamental and vital to every phase of skiing.

You'll find if you can stand balanced on skis without moving you can also stand balanced on them while moving. Let's try motion and maneuvering on a level area.

FIRST MOTIONS ON SKIS

On flat terrain, ski straight ahead by sliding first one ski ahead, then the other. Let the arms swing as in walking, and push on the poles slightly, with the baskets alternately touching the snow. Glide the skis across the snow, without lifting them.

Put both poles in the snow just behind your boots and push, so that both skis slide ahead. Repeat several times before you come to a stop; see if you can work up some speed.

To change direction while standing, lift one ski tip and move the toe outward so that the tip spreads apart from the other one. Put the first one down and lift the second foot to match the first ski. Repeat until you have stepped around in a circle. Try it in the other direction. Now combine sliding with the change of direction to make a big figure eight.

Walking   **Sliding**   **Stepping toes to change direction**

Again, to change direction, lift a ski tail and move the heel outward so that the tail spreads apart from the other one. Move the second foot to match the first ski. Step around in a circle in both directions.

Step sideways by lifting one foot, moving it straight sideways (tip and tail equal amounts) and putting it down. Match it by lifting and moving the other foot toward it. Use your poles for balance. Repeat for several yards to the left and right.

From your normal stance, move both knees left and then right. Notice how your skis get on an edge when you do this. Keep your pole baskets in the snow for balance and see how far you can move the knees laterally.

Hop up and down on the snow. (Omit this one if it should happen to be New Year's Day.)

Sidestepping

Stepping heels to change direction   **Hopping**

First motions on skis

All right, it's fine in the flats but you've noticed most people like to take advantage of gravity to slide downhill. Now you're ready, too. The first step is to get up a hill, so let's find out about ski edges (and also why ski lifts were invented). Obviously, walking straight up a hill on skis doesn't work; they slide backward just as well as forward. It is time to learn how creating resistance to the snow keeps us from sliding.

SIDESTEPPING

Approach a gentle hill and turn sideways to it. Step up the hill as if stepping sideways on a level surface, but walk on the edge of each foot which is closest to the hill (uphill). Keep your knees pointing uphill at all times to stay on the edge of your feet and skis. Move the tip and tail an equal amount as you step and keep the skis across the hill so they don't slide forward or backward. Take small steps,

3   4

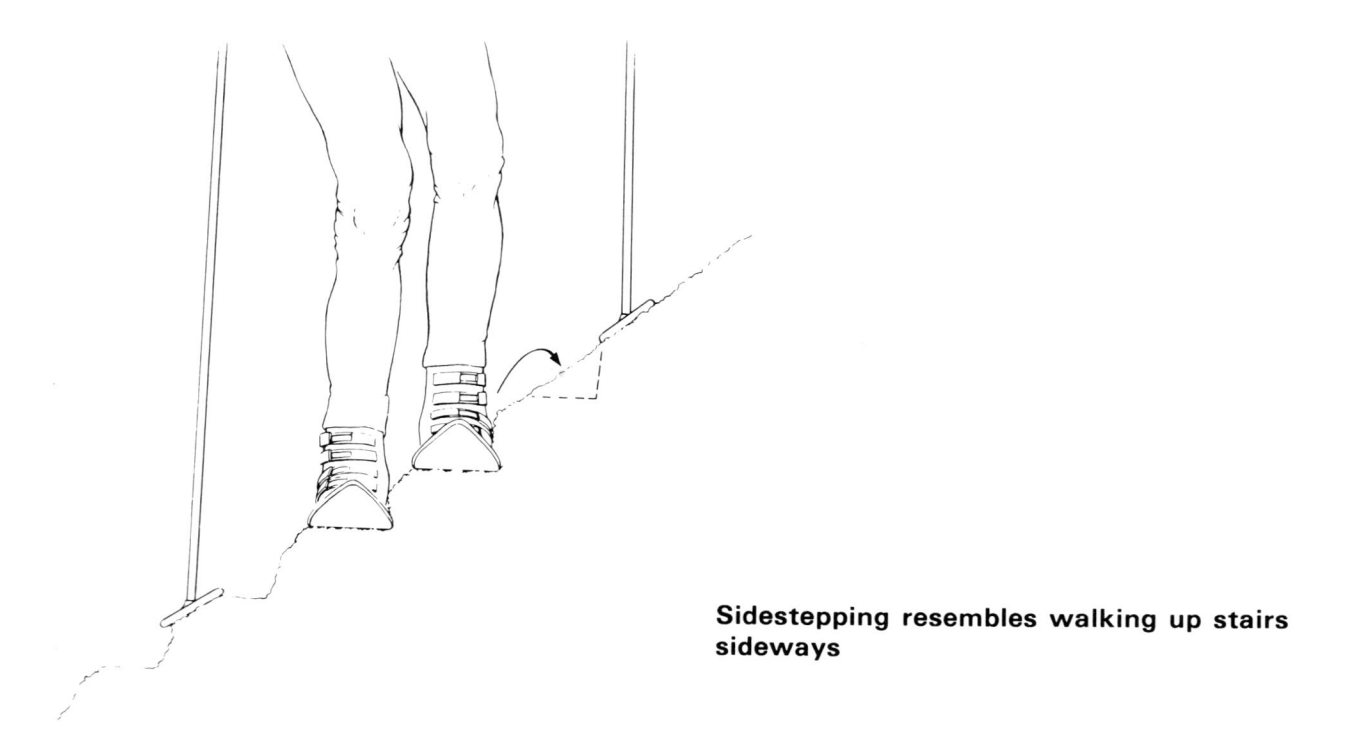

Sidestepping resembles walking up stairs sideways

balancing with the poles. Pretend you are walking sideways up a set of stairs.

You'll find that skis are slippery little devils. They want to slide downhill anytime they are flattened on a slope. The steeper the hill, the more you'll need to push your knees uphill in order to stand on an edge and keep the skis from sliding sideways. Keep this idea in mind, as we'll soon use edge resistance on the snow to slow down and turn.

It's now time to learn our first technical term. Instead of skiing "down the hill," let's ski the *fall line*. The connotation of this word

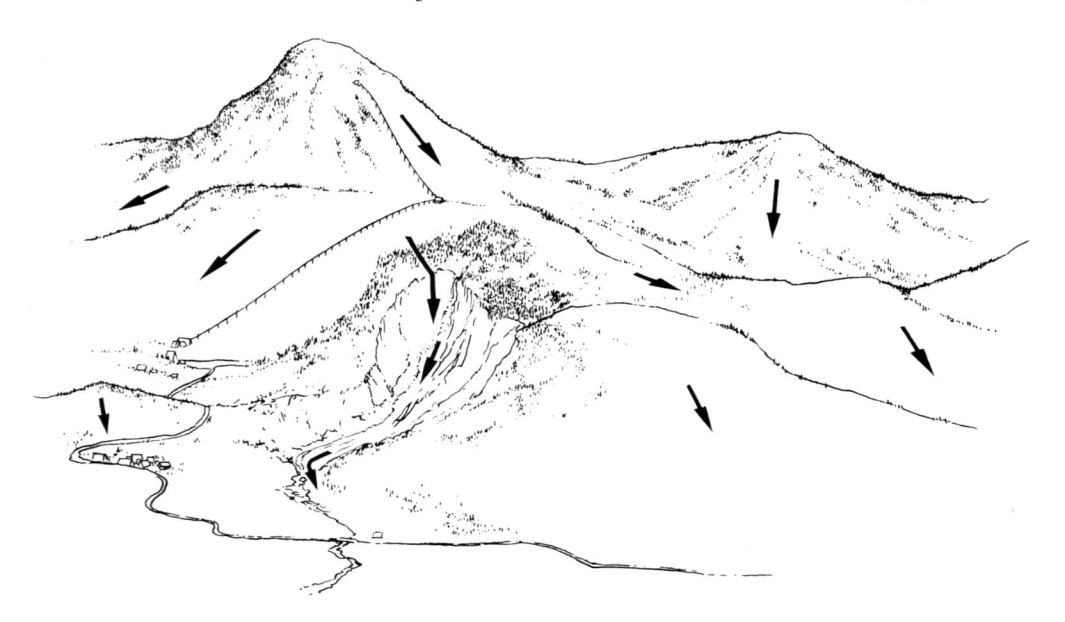

Fall lines

isn't too encouraging, but think of it simply as the path down which a snowball would roll if released from your feet. Frequently, it may not be the same direction your trail will be taking, and it can change direction depending upon variations in the slope contours. If a ski begins to slide forward it is no longer at right angles to the fall line. Learn to read the terrain and recognize what direction is truly downhill at any point.

From a sidestep position, let's turn around and face downhill.

STANDING CHANGE OF DIRECTION

While standing sideways to the fall line, place both pole baskets shoulder width apart in the snow, directly downhill from your boots as far as you can reach. With elbows straight and hands on top of the poles, lean on the poles to keep from sliding as you face downhill. Step each ski around, using small steps. You'll end up facing the desired direction.

An important point to remember is that the elbows should be locked straight with the hands cupped on top of the poles. This lessens the strain on the arms when leaning on the poles.

So, there you are, facing downhill, finally ready to ski. Make sure you have chosen a short gentle slope for the first run (about the same pitch as a Kansas driveway) with a long, level or slightly uphill finish to the slope, clear of trees, people, and other obstacles. Relax, uncramp those curled up toes, and take some deep breaths. Now feel the force of gravity and discover how to flow with it.

YOUR FIRST STRAIGHT RUNS

Standing in a balanced, upright position, with feet comfortably apart, pull the ski pole baskets from the snow and point them behind you. Stay loose and relaxed in your natural athletic stance and let your skis run down the hill to a stop on a level run-out. Keep your body over your feet as your skis accelerate down the fall line.

Standing change of direction (bullfighter turn)

Your first straight runs

Repeat this a number of times. On one run bend up and down in the knees while moving. On another, push with the poles to increase speed as you go downhill. On a third, briefly pick up one ski, put it down and pick up the other. Try stepping sideways while moving straight ahead to avoid imaginary (or real) obstacles in your path. Finally, flex down and extend up in the knees and ankles enough to actually hop the tails off the snow as you ski downhill.

Have you felt the wind in your face and decided maybe skiing can be fun? Good! You're hooked for life with no cure. The first runs are the hardest—from now on things will get easier. To keep it fun, be sure you have sunglasses and sun cream on bright days. Take a break when you get tired and come back after a rest.

Perhaps you don't have a hill with a level run-out long enough to stop. Let's examine one way to change the path of travel, so that you may direct your skis to avoid obstacles, or even direct them uphill, letting you gradually slow to a stop. Everything we have done standing in place can be done just as easily while moving, so let's relate a direction change on the level to one on the hill.

STEPPED CHANGE OF DIRECTION

While in a straight run, change direction by picking up the tip of one ski and moving it outward, then matching the other ski to it. See if you can step to either left or right by moving one ski tip at a time. Try to step around in a half circle while moving so that your skis face back uphill and you come to a stop. Repeat by lifting the tail of one ski at a time to step change your direction.

Of course, in all these actions you've been skiing the way you walk, moving the feet and knees. The upper body stays balanced over the feet. This is a ready athletic stance, one used by a tennis player perhaps, awaiting a serve. The hands are in sight, but keep

Stepping skis to change direction

the pole baskets slightly back of the boots, out of the way. *Poles are never used to stop,* as the body has too much momentum. Attempting to stop with a pole may cause the handle to jab into the body, which hurts even more than it sounds like it would.

Just on the off chance you are tripped by a "snow snake" (creatures that hide under the snow and reach out to snatch at your ankle as you ski by), a few words on getting up may be in order. If you feel yourself falling, and are unable to recover your balance, don't fight it. We're all endowed with plenty of natural padding. Simply crouch and let the fanny contact the ground first, to the side of the skis. This will skid you to a stop. Don't be discouraged. If you don't fall you're not trying. Into each life a little snow must fall, and after all, what's life without a little adversity? Actually, falling is a learning experience, and part of the fun of skiing. The snow is relatively soft, and when you touch down to the side of your skis it can be harmless and refreshing.

So, there you are on the hill—literally. After you've finished in-

TAKING A SPILL

specting the snowflakes, untangle yourself with both skis pointing the same way *across* the fall line. That way, when you stand up they won't slide forward or backward. Place your feet downhill so gravity will help you stand up. Now, pull the feet close to your body. Put the uphill hand next to the fanny. Place your poles vertically, basket down, in the snow next to your uphill hand, and place your downhill hand on top of the poles. Now give a good sharp shove off the snow by pushing yourself up with the uphill hand (on the snow) and pulling yourself up with the downhill (on the poles). This throws your weight onto the downhill foot. At the same time, move the uphill ski farther uphill, getting it underneath your body. Stand up using the leg muscles. It should be one smooth continuous motion. The secret is to get your "nose over your toes" as you rise. This puts your weight directly over the feet and you stand up by using the strongest muscles in the body, the thighs.

Don't be psyched out by this, as it's really no different from standing up in your living room (a good place to try it with skis on). If you push straight upward and outward, get the fanny over the feet, and use the leg muscles it should be no problem at all. Your problems, if any, will come from pushing your feet out ahead of your body. If you do have difficulty, try getting up in two stages, by first rising onto the uphill knee, with the fanny clear of the snow, and then pushing straight up, moving the uphill foot under your body to stand up. If a ski has come off, it's usually easier to first stand up, knock the snow off the bottom of the boot with a ski pole and then put the other ski back on.

Getting up

Getting up by first rising on the uphill knee

You'd probably rather not fall, which is understandable. So, three words of advice when you get in trouble: keep your cool! All the arm flapping in the world won't regain your balance, but standing comfortably over your skis will. Keep the feet apart in a wide track stance and move your whole body back into balance over them. The mind is willing but the flesh is weak, so allow for a spill now and then, until your subconscious learns to control everything. Use your head to keep your balance.

LOOKING AHEAD FOR BALANCE

Ski while looking at your ski tips, then simply raise your head to look down the slope where you are skiing. Your balance will improve when your head is up. No one will take your skis while you're wearing them, so you don't have to watch them continually. Watch where you are skiing instead.

The body is used to walking while seeing a horizon, as that establishes a reference line for balance. (If you don't believe it, try jogging sometime while watching your feet. Your neighbors will swear you are drunk.) Ski with your eyes ahead and chin up. Seeing the ski tips with peripheral vision is adequate and frees your eyes to look at more interesting things, such as people, scenery, and approaching trees.

Look ahead for improved balance

67

13

THE WEDGE

Perhaps you've heard about the "snowplow." We're going to discover its modern counterpart, the *wedge*. From a wide track stance simply pivot each foot in slightly (toes facing each other) and push the heels out so the tails are farther apart, in a piece of pie shape. This "V" position is called a wedge. (If you prefer to think of it from the reverse, it's an "A" position, or egdew.) You'll find the wedge useful both to introduce you to the feeling of turning your skis and for the added stability it allows. For a while this will be your most stable stance; pyramids rarely topple and you now have a wide base tapering to a narrower top. If you get in trouble, don't panic; "rethink the wedge" and regain your balance. It's your basic athletic stance, with a broader base. Let's see how a wedge helps control speed.

EDGE CONTROL IN A WEDGE

While standing still in a wedge, move your knees (and ankles) outward until you are on flat skis. Now, move the knees toward each other and notice how the skis get on their inside edges. Distribute your weight equally on each ski. On a gentle slope with a good run-out, try a *gliding wedge:* a straight run in a wedge with flat (or very slightly edged) skis. Midway through the run, move your knees toward each other and feel the resistance against the snow in both feet. Your speed will diminish in this *braking wedge*. Try several runs moving from flat to edged skis and back again. Feel yourself speed up and slow down at will.

You now have a means to control your speed, simply by knee movements (or ankle movements, which translate to knee movements in stiff boots). On flat skis you have a gliding wedge with minimal edging; on edged skis, a braking wedge. Keep a small wedge and learn to vary the amount of edging by moving your knees in and out.

Edge control in a wedge
Both skiers started simultaneously from the same place. The braking wedge slows speed.

Look at your tracks in the snow. Was there equal brushing of both skis against the snow? Did you feel equal pressure on each foot while skiing straight down the hill? It's very important that each ski be across your direction of travel by equal amounts, with hips and upper body centered between the feet; this should be evident from your tracks. If one ski is pointing straight down the fall line, there is no braking action from it against your direction of travel. In other words, the tails of both skis should be displaced equal amounts from the fall line in a straight downhill braking wedge. (Memorize these words and you'll be the life of the party in the après ski gatherings.)

Perhaps you found that your skis have a tendency to cross at the tips when you are in a braking wedge—marvelous! You've discovered a turning technique we'll soon be using effectively. For the time being, hold your horses, make the skis flatter on the snow, and perhaps push your toes apart slightly. If you do get one ski across the other, you can simply lift up the top ski and move the tip back where you want it.

Now is a good time to realize that skiing is not a static sport. It is continual motion. Although we've been talking about certain static positions, your body must always remain flexible and loose. Here's a great way to test your balance while in motion.

As you climb up the slope, mark each side of your intended downward path with gloves or snowballs. While skiing down in a wedge, pick up each of these objects by flexing deeply in the waist, knees, and ankles and then straightening to a normal upright position.

BODY FLEXIBILITY

If you have any problems, think back and decide if your weight was equal on both feet. How about your wedge? Were your feet apart, with your hips centered between them?

As a prelude to discovering the way our skis turn, let's find out how to change from a wide track to a wedge.

Body flexibility
Stay flexible and balanced over your feet.

Start straight down a gentle hill with your feet comfortably apart. While skiing, pivot both feet by pointing the toes in and pushing the heels out so you are in a gliding wedge. Let your feet slide apart slightly for a wider base as you pivot them. (A hopping motion may help you to push the heels out.) Go back to a straight run from a wedge by pointing both toes straight ahead and letting the feet come comfortably closer under the body. Alternate back and forth between a wedge and a straight run as you ski down the slope.

WEDGE FROM A STRAIGHT RUN

Did you feel that you could change from a straight run to a wedge and back again just by pivoting your feet? This pivot is a basic maneuver we'll soon use to turn. It's simply a rotational movement of the leg, as though you were squashing a cigarette butt under your foot.

Since we will be learning a new technique, let's first learn some new terminology. You already know that when standing across the hill, or across the fall line, everything below a line drawn through your center is *downhill* and everything above is (surprise!) *uphill*. This applies to each ski and also to each foot, leg, hip, and hand. Each ski has an uphill and a downhill edge, one on the uphill side, and one on the downhill side of the ski. (Thus in sidestepping, we dig in with our uphill edges.) When you change direction in relation to the fall line, as in a turn, your uphill and downhill sides interchange. This can get confusing. To simplify which ski we are talking about in a turn, the *outside ski* is defined as the one which takes the longer radius, or outside path, during a turn. The *inside ski* is

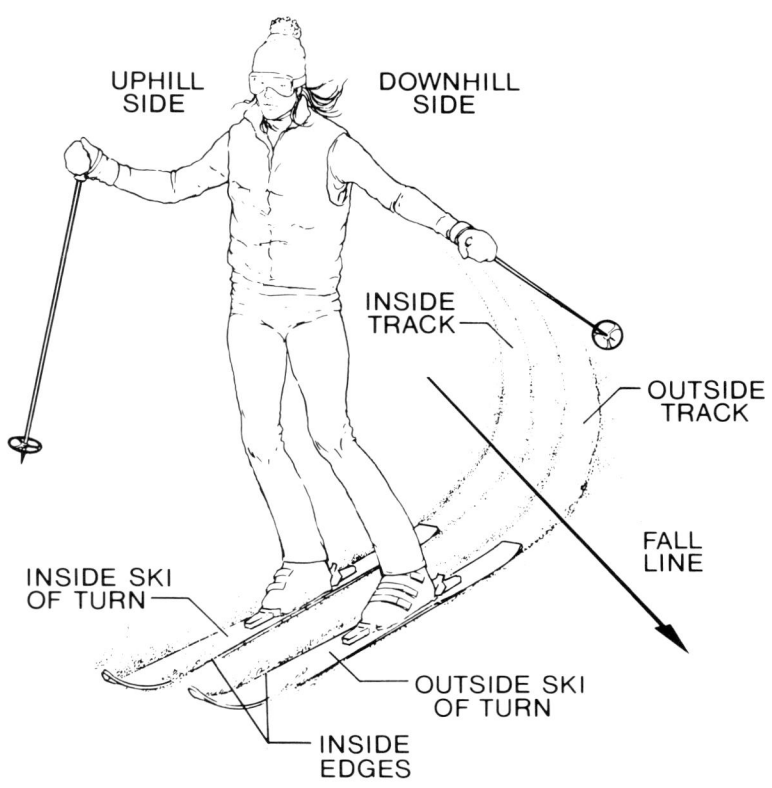

Turn terminology

Straight run to a wedge
Pivot the feet for a wedge or a straight run.

closest to the center of the turn, as is the inside foot, leg, etc. To avoid confusion in defining edges, we may refer to the two ski edges closest to each other as the *inside edges,* and the other two as the *outside edges.* (Thus in a braking wedge you dig the inside edges into the snow.)

Now that you know the wedge, you may want to try a reversed wedge, or herringbone, to climb up a moderate hill.

THE HERRINGBONE

Facing uphill, put your tails together and spread the tips so your skis form a "V." Push the knees inward so you are standing on the inside edges. Now lift one ski at a time uphill, staying on the inside edges so you do not skid back downhill. As you duckwalk uphill, balance with the pole baskets in the snow downhill of your skis and thrust with the palms on top of the grips for support. Move the pole baskets when lifting the opposite ski (right pole with left ski).

From the track your inside ski edges leave in the snow, you can see why this step is called a herringbone. It's not a particularly graceful maneuver but it is a fast way up a gentle slope. Since the skis are pointed backward relative to the fall line, the pole support is necessary to keep you from sliding downhill. As in a standing change of direction, placing your palms on top of the poles gives better support. On a steeper slope this calls for extreme force on the arms; it is easier to sidestep on these slopes, keeping your skis across the fall line. Now that you know how to climb uphill, it'll be all downhill from here!

The herringbone

14
STEERING TURNS

We walk and change direction simply by turning our feet where we want to go. The foot is twisted by rotating the lower leg about the axis of the bones connecting the knee and ankle. The same effect works in skiing, but since skiers do everything the easiest way, we don't even have to lift our feet to turn. Simply pivoting our feet in the direction we want to go is a means of directing our skis known as *steering.* It's easy to demonstrate this twisting force right at home.

Stand in a gliding wedge on a throw rug over a smooth floor (or in socks on a slick floor). Feel your feet pivot as you twist both of them left and then both of them right. Move your balance point back to the heels and forward to the toes to verify that your feet steer easiest with your weight just forward of the arch. Change to a narrow, feet-together stance to see how difficult steering is from this position.

With some experimenting you'll find that steering can be done with either foot separately if you want. You can stop steering and then resume the pivoting action in a noncontinuous fashion at any time you wish.

If you feel ambitious, try the above exercise with ski boots on. You'll readily observe that from a braking wedge stance (lots of edge to slow down) steering is more difficult. A pure steered turn will work best on a flat ski, as in a gliding wedge. This rotating force is basic to every turn you will make, so let's try a few steered turns on the snow.

On gentle terrain, ski in a gliding wedge with flat skis. Turn both your feet in one direction, then in the other. Feel your toes press

STEERING ACTION

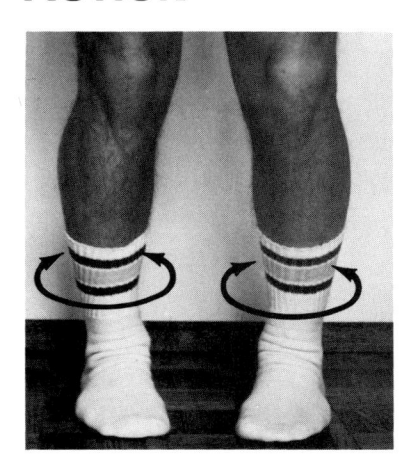

Twisting the feet in a steering action

BASIC FOOT STEERED TURNS

Foot steered turns

against the inside of the boots in the direction you want to go, and your heels on the opposite side. Make many small turns left and right from the fall line. Now, from a slightly braking wedge go through the same motions with your feet.

Do you feel that turning your feet turns the skis? If so, good, as this rotation can be used in any turn at any level of skiing. Steering is an apt term to describe this means of directing the skis. It's difficult to turn the steering wheel of a parked car, but easy to turn the wheel of a moving vehicle. Similarly, you can't turn your skis while standing still, but once you're moving it's easy. To demonstrate the tremendous power available to steer your skis, here's an exercise you can try with a friend.

Sit on a bench with your feet pointing straight ahead and flat on the floor. Have someone hold one of your boots in that position. Now try to steer, or pivot that foot, pushing your toes one way and your heel the other. Feel the power you possess to turn the foot as the other person struggles to hold it. Now turn your knee the same direction as your toes. Ask the person holding your boot how much stronger the steering force was when you turned your knee also.

DISCOVERING FORCES INVOLVED IN STEERING

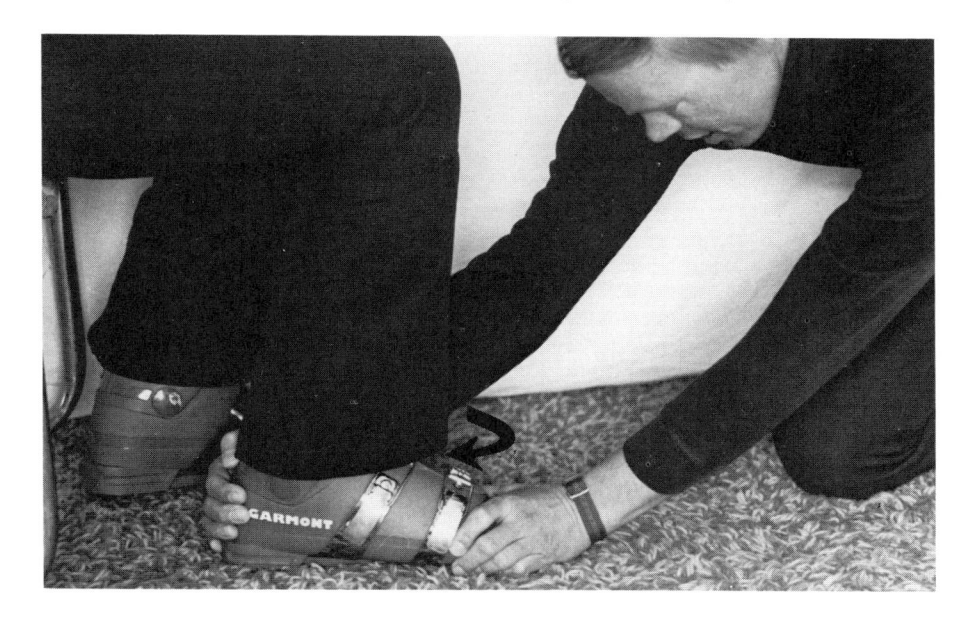

Feeling a steering force
Twisting the foot and knee exerts a large force.

Note that your hips, shoulders, and hands do not have to move to create a turning force. In fact, they won't help a bit in the above exercise. We should ski just as we walk, from the knees, ankles and feet and nothing else. (We certainly don't need our heads, or we wouldn't be out driving long distances in blizzards just to fall down in the snow.) We may balance occasionally with the arms, and angle our upper body to compensate for certain knee movements, but all the action will come from the knees and feet. By turning the knee, you rotate the upper leg about the axis of the femur from the pelvis to the knee, which greatly increases the torque (a fancy term for rotational force). Let's try some turns using the knees.

On gentle terrain, ski in a gliding wedge. Turn by steering the feet and knees, rotating (or pushing) the toes in the direction you want to go. Make many turns right and left down the hill. Do the same turns from a slightly braking wedge.

STEERED FOOT AND KNEE TURNS

Turn the feet and knees in the direction you want to go. What could be simpler? We'll soon find how to take advantage of ski design to help our turns; otherwise, we might just as well ski on waxed two-by-fours.

Now is a good time to explore the advantages of bent knees and a balanced stance. It's important that the knees be flexed slightly

Foot and knee steered turns
Twist feet and knees in the direction you want to go.

in your natural stance. Let's relate this to steering and see one reason why.

Stand on a floor or the snow with your legs straight at the knees. Distribute your weight equally on each foot, and keep the feet comfortably apart under the hips. Rotate the right foot inward (toes left, heel right) as far as it will go. Now flex your knees and see how much more the foot can rotate inward when the knee rotates also. Repeat by rotating the foot outward, going from unflexed to flexed knees.

KNEE FLEX AFFECTING STEERING FORCE

Thus bent knees increase the amount of steering and consequently the force which can be applied to turn skis.

It is also important to keep your hips centered over your feet. A similar exercise will help show why.

Hold onto a ski pole or chair back for balance. Stand with your knees slightly flexed and your feet comfortably apart under the hips. Now move each foot about twelve inches to the right, without moving your hips, so you feel as though you are standing on the left side of the left foot. Rotate the right foot inward as far as it will go. Now move your hips back over the feet, keeping the same knee flex, and see how much more the foot can rotate. Have someone hold your foot to feel the difference in the force you can apply in both positions.

HIP POSITION AFFECTING STEERING FORCE

76

So, unless you're practicing the hula, let your feet function most effectively by keeping your hips centered over them.

If you're good at charades you may especially enjoy the following exercise.

Crouch as low as possible, with a deep knee flex and feet apart. Keep your weight balanced on the balls of both feet. Start down a gentle slope and pivot your feet rapidly left and right, making many small turns.

Normally we don't ski in this position but it's a good one to demonstrate the steering force.

After only a short time on skis you now know how to remain upright, control your speed, and turn. You've learned the fundamentals; now you can go on to improve your technique.

Body position affects steering
The greatest foot rotation (and easiest turning) occurs with the hips centered over the feet and the knees flexed.

GORILLA TURNS

Gorilla turns

77

15
LIFTS

By now you're tired of walking up the hill, and maybe you have already sneaked a few rides on a lift. If not, you are more than ready to be skiing on a beginners' hill and riding the tows.

Almost all areas will require you to purchase a lift ticket to ride a beginners' lift. (A very few areas have a free one.) However, check the rates, as sometimes the charge is less for a "beginners' lift only" ticket. If you're getting a late start, most areas have a reduced half day rate, which generally starts between noon and 1 P.M. Read the directions on how to attach the sticky side of the ticket so it stays on. Area operators frown on placing tickets on gloves, hats, or other apparel easily traded from person to person. However, do attach the ticket to something you'll wear all day, and not to a parka you may want to discard in the warm afternoon sun.

You should study the area trail map or ask the patrol to verify you'll be riding a lift to a trail or slope within your ability. I remember my second day on skis, standing in one of two side-by-side lift lines. Only after the lift whizzed me past the beginners' slope and up to the top of the mountain did I realize it was the wrong line. Incidentally, you may enjoy the name of your particular beginners' slope. My favorites are at Snowmass, Colorado. The original beginners' trails were on Fanny Hill. When a new section opened, its beginners' area became Assay Hill.

Before you board a lift, check to make sure all loose clothing is secure. Items like long scarves, parkas tied around waists, unworn gloves dangling from zippers, and pigtails all have a nasty habit of winding around lift parts and holding like super glue when your turn comes to get off. If you're not familiar with how to ride a particular lift, ask the operator ahead of time, and watch other people as they board the lift. Basically, these are the types of lifts you may encounter.

ROPE TOW

Step over to the rope tow with your skis pointing straight ahead up the track. Grasp the rope gently so it slides through your hands. Gradually increase hand pressure until you find yourself traveling as fast as the rope. Poles may remain attached to your wrists by their straps or carried in one hand. Experienced riders put their outside hand behind their back and grasp the rope with it to relieve the strain on the arms. They also wear old thick leather mittens. To get off, just let go of the rope and step away.

MITEY MITE

The Mitey Mite is a slow moving rope tow with handles. Approach it as you would a rope tow. As a handle comes by you, grasp it with both hands and you will be pulled along. Let go at the top and ski away.

T-BAR

Observe others riding the T-bar tow. It is not intended to be sat upon, but rather to pull you along by the bar, which is shaped like an upside-down (you guessed it!) "T." This rests behind your fanny. After the skiers ahead of you have loaded, move right in. Stand next to your partner with poles held midway in the outside hand (the hand away from your partner). Point your skis straight up the hill. Look over your inside shoulder to grasp the bar as the attendant hands it to you. Place the "T" under your bottom and it will pull you along. There may be a lurch as you start out but your flexed knees will absorb the shock and any others you may encounter along the track. While gliding along decide if you or your partner will unload first. Whoever has the honor skis out of the way at the top and the remaining rider pulls the "T" out from under him, releases it gently and skis away. If you should take a spill while riding, just let go of the bar and move quickly out of the track. Reassemble yourself and ski back to the loading ramp for another try.

Riding a surface lift
Stand upright and let the Poma or T-bar pull you uphill.

POMA LIFT (PLATTER PULL)

Similar to the T-bar, the Poma lift is made for one person. Again, move in to the loading area with skis pointed up the tow line and poles in the hand away from the attendant. When he hands you the poma, pull the bar down slightly to place the platter between your legs and against your fanny. Just rest against the seat-shaped disc with your legs supporting your body, and the platter will pull you along. To unload, pull down on the bar to release pressure from your rear, bring the disc between your legs, let go of it gently and ski away.

GONDOLAS AND TRAMS

Gondolas and trams don't require explanation, although after a winter at Jackson Hole I could write a book on riding trams, including how to get a window spot, using elbows to create breathing room, and avoiding the garlic eaters. In some resorts these lifts will actually transport you to the beginners' area, which may be located high up the mountain. At other resorts, check your lift ticket privileges. You may be able to ride them without skis to enjoy a marvelous view and perhaps lunch on top.

CHAIR LIFTS

Chair lifts were reputedly invented by the company which builds hooks on conveyor belts to unload banana boats. However, chairs are actually the easiest and most enjoyable lifts to ride. They generally hold two people cozily although triple and quadruple lifts are increasingly popular. As you move into line find a partner to ride with. Remove your pole straps from your wrist. After the chair has swung past to load the skiers ahead of you, move in quickly and stand next to your partner on the indicated spot (usually a recessed board that has been cleared of snow). Point your skis straight ahead the way you want to go. The poles are used to move in, but once in position hold them by the middle and out of the way in the hand away from the support bar. Some chairs have one support bar rising from the middle of the sitting area, in which case look for it over your inside shoulder (toward your partner). If the chair has two support bars, one rising from each side of the seat, look for it over your outside shoulder. As the chair comes, pretend someone is handing you a kitchen chair. Grasp the support bar with your free hand and sit down when the chair touches the back of your legs. Let the skis run straight ahead on the ramp and you are soon airborne. Pull down the foot rest if your chair has one, relax and enjoy the ride. Push the foot rest back up before you get off. When you reach the unloading ramp stand straight up from the knees so that you are no longer in the chair. Poles are held out of the way in one hand and the other hand may be kept on the edge of the chair until you ski away from it. As you ski down the ramp *lean forward* to stay balanced over the skis. Once you are clear of the ramp and away from your partner, use a braking wedge for control.

The last section on the chair lifts applies to all skiing. If suddenly your skis are going from a level position to one heading downhill, you must stay up with them by leaning forward, keeping your body centered over the skis. If you don't believe it, watch people falling as they unload from a chair—back on the fanny every time. To

Getting on the chair lift

Getting off the chair lift

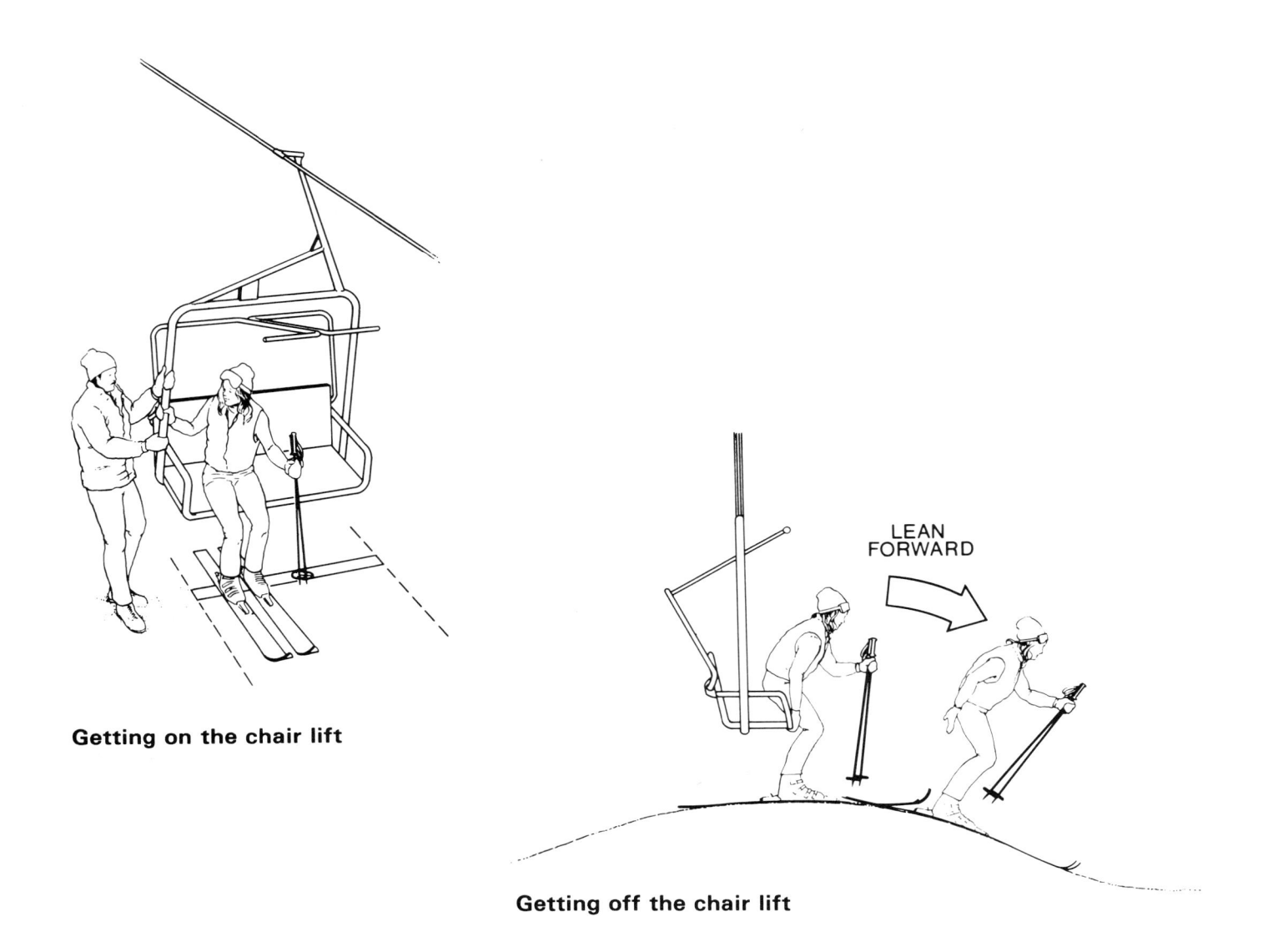

unload, stand erect and lean forward from the ankles. To avoid congestion, when you unload move well away from the immediate area so that others have adequate room.

Once off the lift, you should limber up before skiing, particularly if your muscles became chilled from the cold. Stretch your legs out, one in front and one in back; stretch legs to the side; touch your toes; swing your upper torso around; lift up each leg as high as you can. Once you feel loose, go ahead and ski.

All lifts will stop occasionally, so when you're on one that does, have patience as it will soon start again. Operators control the lifts and stop them the instant anyone has difficulty loading or unloading. A safety device also automatically stops the lift in case someone forgets to get off at the top. In the rare instance of a lift breakdown, a backup motor will be started to get it going again. The ski patrol will also ski under a lift in case of breakdown to tell you what is happening.

Don't be so enamored of skiing down that you miss the pleasures of riding uphill. Lift rides are great times to talk to your partner. Look around you to see the whole length of a trail you'll soon be skiing down. Observe other skiers below you and their technique to see why it's good or bad. Watch the clouds drift by, identify trees, see the snow sparkle, find animal tracks in the snow, or lift your eyes to the magnificence of the hills around you. It's a time to relax your muscles, catch your breath, and refresh your soul.

16

SKIER SAFETY AND COURTESY

Safety and courtesy go hand in hand, since one leads to the other. They are both pretty much a matter of common sense and respect for the rights of others. Someday perhaps the areas will require an individual to have a skier's license, showing he knows the rules. (Unfortunately, I suppose that would lead to the ski patrol hiding behind firs to look for violators, a sophisticated electronic "fuzz buster" to spot the patrol, and on and on.) Anyway, now that you're venturing out onto the mountain, knowledge of the major rules of the road could save your own neck as well as someone else's.

We share the slopes with others, so have control of your skis, whether they are on or off your feet. Always ski slopes within your ability and be able to stop at any time. Use safety straps or ski brakes to prevent injury to someone else.

Before starting out on a trail look uphill and make sure you won't be suddenly cutting someone off. When on the trail, look behind you before making unpredictable moves. Learn to sense when other skiers are near by the sounds of their skis and by your peripheral vision. Be especially alert at trail junctions and catwalks crossing slopes.

The skier farthest downhill always has the right of way when he is overtaken. Generally, the faster skier passes the slower to the left when skiing straight downhill, on the uphill side in a traverse situation, or on the more dangerous side on a narrow catwalk.

When you want to stop for a breather, go to the edge of the trail to allow room for others to ski by.

Know the trail marker designations denoting difficulty of slopes. The general standard is a green circle for easiest, blue square for more difficult, and black diamond for most difficult. Plan your route ahead by referring to trail maps so you don't suddenly end up on a trail beyond your ability.

Trail markers
Green circle—easiest;
blue square—more difficult;
black diamond—most difficult.

In the event of an accident, place crossed skis in the shape of an "X" in the snow above the injured skier. Do not move him. Keep him warm with extra clothing and comfort him. Notify the patrol immediately by skiing to the nearest patrol phone (as shown on your trail map) or to the nearest lift station. Make sure you know the exact trail name and location to report so the injured skier can be found promptly.

Leave the slopes as you would like to find them by putting your litter in your pocket or in a trash barrel. If you fall in soft snow, you may leave a "sitzmark," or large hole in the snow. This should be stamped in with your skis so someone else doesn't catch a ski tip in it.

Stay off closed trails or other posted closed areas. Besides risking your own safety on them, you could have your lift ticket revoked or you might even be liable for the expense of search and rescue should you get lost.

These are pretty simple guidelines, and they won't restrict your freedom. Make them good habits.

section III
KNEE MOVEMENTS LEFT AND RIGHT

At this point you've been on skis for a few days. You're ready for longer slopes, and you want to be able to control your speed and your turns. In this section you'll discover that a ski will turn more easily if you edge it, using a sideways knee movement. Along with the edging, you'll find the ski must also have weight applied to it. This leads to an easy stem turn. You'll learn to use gravity to vary your speed in skiing across slopes and in round turns. As the slope steepness increases, you'll also skid on the edges to brake your speed. You'll use this same skidding to finish a turn in a comfortable stance, known as parallel. The emphasis will be on efficient, relaxed skiing, using your feet and legs.

17

WEIGHT TRANSFER AND EDGING

If you have felt your turn improve by steering with the knee as well as the foot, you have already discovered something about *edging*. An edged ski is designed to turn, not to run straight. It is narrower in the middle than it is at the tip or tail. Thus, when it is put on its edge in the snow and weight is applied, it tends to run in an arc. Resistance from the snow to an edged ski will cause it to turn. You've already discovered this when your skis tried to cross in a braking wedge. Besides steering (turning) the feet and knees in a rotating mode, you will now also be able to turn a ski by edging it and applying weight to it. Let's ignore all those technical words, and see if you can feel a ski turning all by itself.

BASIC CARVED ARC

On a gentle beginners' slope, stand in a wider than normal stance, with your feet about eighteen inches apart. Keep both skis straight ahead. Edge the right ski by pushing the right knee inward, to the left, while keeping the left ski flat on the snow. Keep your weight equally distributed on the balls of both feet. Push off down the slope and feel your right ski carve a gradual smooth turn to the left. Repeat, edging the left knee inward (to the right) while the right ski stays flat on the snow. Experiment with the amount of knee angle and the amount of pressure you put on the edged ski by standing more heavily on it.

Look at your tracks to see how the ski edge carved a long gentle turn in the snow. These gradual turns should convince you that a ski will turn for you if you move the lower leg to place the ski on its inside edge and also keep weight on that ski. The greater the edge, or the more weight on the ski, the sharper the arc of the turn. Of course, to help these turns, you would add the twisting force of steering.

Basic carved arc

Another way to aid a turn is to start with your skis in a wedge position, so that the skis are already pointing at an angle to the fall line. Let's examine how to apply turning forces in the basic wedge.

Stand on a flat area in a gliding wedge position. Leave your poles aside and put your hands on your knees. Note that each ski points in a slightly different direction. To edge the right ski, push your right knee simultaneously inward (left) and forward. You'll feel extra weight pressing down near the big toe of the right foot. Notice how the right foot and ski get on an inside edge as you do this. You can vary the amount of edging by varying how far inward the knee is pushed. Now let the knee go back to its normal position and resume a gliding wedge (essentially no edge). Push the left knee inward (right) and forward. Observe the edge angle of the left ski and feel the weight on the inside left forefoot increase. Alternate edging your skis by pushing on one, then on the other knee.

EDGING A SKI FROM A WEDGE

Obviously, you don't go anywhere on a flat grade, so you've already figured out the next exercise.

On a gentle slope, leave your poles aside, and keep your hands on your knees. From a gliding wedge, turn by edging a ski and weighting it. Push one knee at a time inward and forward, bring it

GLIDING WEDGE TURN WITH EDGING

88

Edging a ski
A simple knee movement puts a ski onto an edge.

Wedge turn with edging
Weight and edge a ski to turn.

back to the normal position of a flat ski, and then push the other knee inward and forward. Vary the amount of edging. Use a more weighted edge for a sharper turn and a less weighted edge for a more gradual turn. Make many turns left and right of the fall line.

Keep working on this one with your hands on your knees until you really feel through your feet how the skis turn. Once again, as with steering, the actions are in the lower body, in this case, the lower leg. As you bend a knee inward and forward, more weight is automatically put upon that foot from the upper body. Try even exaggerating it by moving your upper body over that knee as if you were stepping to that foot. This principle of *weight transfer* is basic to walking. Once you get the feel of this it will be basic to skiing also, as it comes from natural motions. That's one reason for practicing with your hands on your knees: you won't get into the habit of moving your whole body. When standing in street shoes, putting weight from one foot to the other isn't a complicated maneuver, and the same is true in skiing. Pushing the knee forward also puts additional pressure on the ski tip to help the turn. Now try an exercise from a braking wedge.

BRAKING WEDGE TURN WITH EDGING

Repeat the gliding wedge turn exercise from a braking wedge. Feel first one, then the other ski "bite" into the snow as you increase your edge and weight on it. Observe your tracks in the snow to see how the ski edge digs into the snow to turn you.

Do you feel that the whole ski edge carves into the snow to turn you? Really push the knees forward and inward. Let them bend! Now you know one reason why boots are so stiff. When you move the knees left or right, the ski must respond without free play. Bending forward or backward at the ankle doesn't change the edge angle and movement in this direction is much easier. You have seen that the boots are angled forward to keep your knees bent. Straight knees do not move left or right. Try it. You can't walk with straight knees and you surely can't ski that way.

You have probably observed one important principle: as the right ski was put on the inside edge and weighted, it began to turn to the left. This always confused me, thinking right ski for left turn and left ski for right turn. I had generally skied smack into the base lodge by the time I got that straight. An easier way to think of it is that in a wedge, the ski pointing where you want to go is the one to edge and weight. That ski will then take a longer path for that turn, like the outer horse on a race track, so it's called the outside ski. Gradually, you'll realize that your weight is always transferred *to the outside ski of the turn.* Weighting the inside ski would only fight the turn.

Now just a slight modification takes advantage of two knees. Imagine you're in a braking wedge down the fall line. You move the right knee forward and inward. Edge and weight on the right ski start it turning to the left. Your left ski is still braking, trying somewhat to turn to the right. If you move the left knee the way you want to go (left), you flatten that ski into a gliding one. It no longer offers resistance and you'll turn more easily. So let's try moving both knees.

Ski with your hands on your knees in a braking wedge. To turn left, move both knees slightly left, thus increasing inside edge and weight on the right ski, and flattening the left ski. To turn right, move both knees to the right, increasing inside edge and weight on the left ski and flattening the right ski.

WEDGE TURN WITH KNEE EDGING

Knee edging in a turn
Pointing both knees in the direction you wish to go aids your turn.

If you're really keen on technique, you'll see we're heading into the concept of edge changes and weight transfers, which facilitate parallel turns. But let's not get ahead of ourselves. For the time being get the feeling of a ski edge biting or carving into the snow when you edge it and put weight on it. Once you have that, remember the motion and the result.

By now your back is probably tired from bending over, so let's stand upright again. Grab your poles, but pretend you have imaginary hands pushing on your knees for this one.

From an upright athletic stance, make turns from a slightly braking wedge by driving your knees in the direction you want to go. Feel the outside ski bite into the snow and turn as you edge it and apply weight. Aid your turns by steering your feet and knees in the direction you wish to go. Vary the radius from long to short turns. Stop by continuing your turn until you have skied back up the hill to a standstill. Make a slalom course out of snowballs or gloves and ski in and out of the objects.

WEDGE TURN: UPRIGHT

Standing upright certainly beats bending over with hands on the knees. But remember the feeling—keep your weight forward and press those knees into the turn. You've returned to a natural upright position with your back pretty much perpendicular to the skis. Ask someone to observe your stance to make sure your pelvis isn't tipped forward. In other words, don't let your fanny stick out. Your hips belong centered over your feet.

You've now discovered one nice effect of turning: it slows you down. Rather than fight a hill with a braking wedge in the fall line, you can use one turn after another to flow with the hill. This will come in especially handy on long *catwalks* (skier's trails also used by maintenance equipment or "snow cats" to get up the mountain). Rather than plowing straight down the center of a catwalk, turn continually from side to side. As in all skiing, smooth fluid movements are necessary.

SINGING IN THE SNOW

Sing, whistle, or hum your favorite tune while skiing. Synchronize your turns to the beat of the music.

EQUALLY WEIGHTED SKIS IN A WEDGE TRAVERSE

Now, let's make the start of our turns easier. You've probably found that instead of skiing straight down the hill, it is often convenient to ski across the hill; this is a form of the *traverse*. You can ski across a hill from the finish of a turn by keeping a little extra weight on the downhill ski. Let's see how we start the next turn.

Ski straight across the hill in a slightly braking wedge, with more weight on the downhill ski, as though a turn has just been made. Now, transfer some of your weight to the uphill ski, so that both skis are weighted equally. Allow the skis to gradually turn into the fall line by themselves. Finish the turn by letting more weight go to the outside ski and increasing the edge angle.

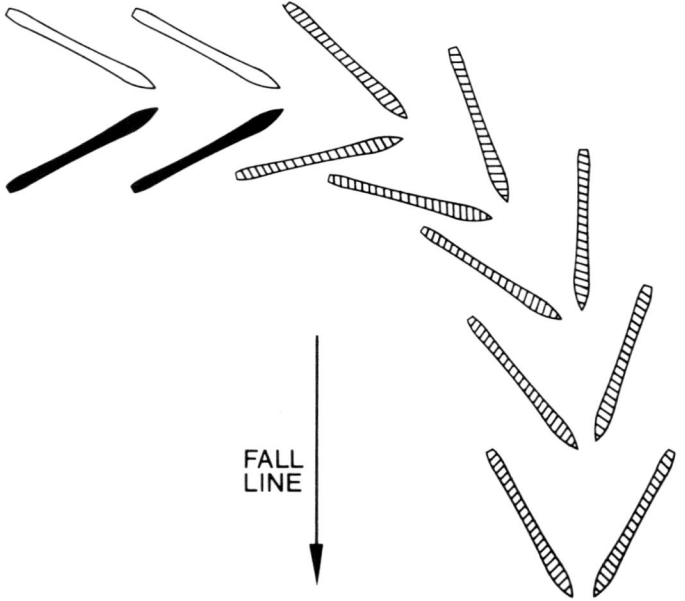

Equally weighted skis drift into the fall line

Even though you did not increase the edging of the uphill ski, or produce steering actions, equally weighted skis (provided they are edged equally) will turn by themselves into the fall line. This is the way they are designed. If you have trouble experiencing this, start from a gliding wedge to avoid worrying about equal edge angles. Instead of working to turn the skis, you can now just stand on them, and they will slowly turn into the fall line by themselves. Of course, you need steering, edging, or both to finish the turn, and applying those techniques at the start of a turn will speed up the whole process. But letting the skis work for you is an important concept, one that I'll expand upon in the next chapters.

Now that you know how to turn and to control your speed, you are moving into the intermediate category and can handle any beginner slope with ease. Think back upon what you have accomplished. You now know how to stand balanced over your skis, use a wedge to slow your speed and change direction, turn your skis by steering the feet, and also turn by edging and weighting skis. None of this was especially hard to learn, and you've gotten a lot of fun and satisfaction out of it. Things get even better from here on!

18
THE TRAVERSE

Skiing across a hill without turning is called a *traverse.* It is just like your first straight run down the slope, except you ski across the fall line on your uphill edges. Your position is similar to sidestepping but now you'll also be moving forward. The traverse is easily accomplished by just standing balanced on your uphill edges and letting the skis run. (I'll later refer to this balanced position as *angulation.*) You'll find the lower body edges the skis and the upper body angles over the edged skis for balance. Here's a snap exercise.

Stand across the hill with your feet parallel and pointed slightly downhill, using the poles to keep from sliding forward. Make sure your uphill ski is ahead by several inches. With your feet comfortably apart and more weight on the downhill ski, remove the poles and let your skis slide. Enjoy the wind in your face. When you reach the end of the slope or get going too fast, come to a stop with a braking wedge. Turn around (poles downhill while you step around) and traverse across the slope in the opposite direction. See if you can lift up the uphill ski briefly and remain balanced over the downhill one.

Not too hard, was it? You've now traversed left and right, the only two ways you can do it.

Just as in sidestepping, you must stand on two uphill edges to resist sliding sideways down the hill. The steeper the hill, the greater the angle between skis and slope. Control this edge angle by pointing the knees uphill and balance by angling the upper body out over the skis. This may take some sideways bend at the waist in addition to the knees. Feel your body weight transmitted through the uphill edges of your feet to the snow. At first your instincts may tell you not to lean toward the valley with your upper

TRAVERSE

The traverse

body, but you'll also soon find "hugging the hill" will get you into trouble. The steeper the slope, the more body weight you must place on the downhill ski. Your uphill ski, foot, knee and hip must be kept slightly advanced. This allows your upper body to comfortably face slightly downhill, ready for a turn or a stop.

Perhaps you found that your traverse became a shallow arc or turn, rather than a straight run across the hill. This is perfectly natural, as a ski on its edge tends to turn. Let's see how controlling edge angle can help.

While traversing, roll the knees uphill to increase the edge angle. Feel your skis start to turn gradually uphill. Now, roll the knees downhill to decrease the edge angle until you reach a point where the traverse becomes more of a straight line.

VARYING EDGE ANGLE IN A TRAVERSE

Varying edge angle in a traverse

That was pretty easy. Let's try another variation on the traverse. It is an actual sidestep while moving.

While moving in a traverse, pick up the uphill ski and step it uphill parallel to the lower ski. Then pick up the downhill ski to match the upper. Repeat stepping uphill as you move forward. Now try stepping downhill, lower ski first. Repeat for several yards downhill.

CHANGING A TRAVERSE BY STEPPING

That may have been a little trickier, as you alternated lifting skis completely off the snow. However, it's good for balance and an excellent way to change your traverse to avoid obstacles (skiers or other nuisances) in your path.

Speed increases in a steeper traverse. Thus, you can vary your speed simply by varying your traverse angle to the fall line. This is part of learning to read the terrain and using it to your advantage. Let's do a moving exercise based on a stationary one you already know. Notice that the law of skiing relativity comes into play: things that can be done standing still can be done as easily while moving. So, onward to the step turn.

From a traverse, bring your skis to a stop by stepping uphill, moving first the uphill ski tip outward, then matching it with the downhill ski. You are now in a shallower traverse. Keep repeating until you have skied uphill to a stop. Now from a traverse, step the tip of the lower ski downhill and match it with the upper ski. You are now in a steeper traverse. Vary between steep and shallow traverses. On a gentle hill, keep stepping across the fall line until you have changed your traverse direction entirely and are going back uphill in the opposite direction.

Perhaps you found crossing the fall line on a gentle slope somewhat difficult. In this exercise your knees had to move up and down to step. But, if you crossed the fall line entirely, they also moved *laterally*, or left to right. Changing from a traverse in one direction, say to your left, to the other direction, your right, requires that your knees move from left to right also. Therefore, all a turn will require is a change of edges, controlled by lateral knee actions. (Cogitate on these words for five minutes a day and one day a light will dawn.)

Stepping in a traverse
Step to raise or lower the traverse line.

STEP TURN

Here's one more traverse exercise combining the elements of balancing on the edges and steering with the feet, but eliminating all that tiring work involved in picking up the skis.

VARYING A TRAVERSE BY STEERING UPHILL

Ski to a stop by changing your traverse to one that's going uphill. To do this, simply steer your feet uphill. Try driving your knees uphill slightly also. Repeat this from steeper traverses, arcing your skis back uphill. Look at your tracks to verify they are round and smooth.

Once you've mastered the preceding exercise, you deserve congratulations, because you have completed the finish of a parallel turn. Parallel skiing is a part of every skier's goal. This does not mean that the feet are locked close together but rather, they simply both point the same way. Here's a more advanced exercise to give you a feeling of starting a parallel turn.

Step turn

Steering uphill in a traverse

97

VARYING A TRAVERSE BY STEERING DOWNHILL

From a traverse, roll the knees downhill slightly and steer your feet downhill. When you feel the tips move downhill in a steeper traverse, push your knees back uphill and steer the skis back to their original traverse. Do a series of these across the hill, moving knees left and right.

If you had any problems with these traverse exercises, go back to your original sidestep position. Check to see that the uphill ski is ahead, that your knees are pointing uphill, and that the upper body is balanced over the skis.

Now let's see how to combine your familiar wedge turn with a traverse.

WEDGE TO A TRAVERSE

Ski in a wedge position across the hill. Pivot both your feet to point straight ahead in a traverse, with your feet comfortably apart under the hips. Both knees are now pointing uphill. To resume a wedge, pivot the toes toward each other, spreading your feet apart slightly. The uphill knee now points downhill. Ski across the hill in a traverse, pivot to a small wedge, turn, and then twist your feet back to a traverse.

You've already done a wedge to a parallel position while skiing straight down the hill. The only refinement here is that now you are going across the fall line, traversing on your uphill edges. If you had any problems pivoting the uphill ski into a wedge, think of first making that uphill ski flat on the snow. Once it is flat you can push out the tail to a "V" by twisting your foot. You have just "changed an edge." Don't worry technically about this yet. For the time being, enjoy your newly found skill of a parallel traverse across the hill, combined with a wedge turn.

Traverse to a wedge

98

19
ABOUT FACE

Skiing frequently consists of short bursts of activity punctuated by long breathing periods. Upon stopping, the hill ahead may suddenly seem a lot steeper, and you'd like to be able to turn around to traverse back the other way. Or, at the edge of a trail, trees may prevent you from continuing forward. Both instances necessitate a sharp 180 degree change of direction. You already know the stationary "bullfighter" turn, where you place your poles downhill with arms straight and step around one ski at a time. However, on a steeper slope this will be cumbersome and hard on the arms.

A better way to change direction is with a turn. Even from a nonmoving position you can step out the uphill ski into a wedge to make a short turn.

TURN TO CHANGE DIRECTION

Standing across a hill, step out your uphill ski into a wide wedge. Put that uphill ski onto its inside edge. Now push forward with your poles, and immediately transfer most of your weight to the uphill ski. You'll feel your ski edge bite into the snow to turn you sharply 180 degrees. Aid the turn with strong steering from your knees and feet. You'll end up facing the opposite direction a few feet below your starting point.

The big trick is to point that uphill ski down the fall line and put all your weight on it. Any weight on the original downhill ski will delay your rapid turn. Try placing your downhill pole basket in the snow and leaning on it for balance as your ski turns.

Sometimes the space is too confined or the slope too steep to turn, even using the above way. Then it's a good idea to know the kick turn, which will enable you to about face without any forward movement. Try it on a flat or very gentle slope the first time.

Changing direction by turning
From a standstill you can change direction in a short distance by a turn using extra edging and weighting.

KICK TURN

Face your upper body downhill, but keep your skis directly across the fall line. Place your pole baskets on each side of you in the snow above your uphill ski. Using the poles for balance, transfer all your weight to the edged uphill ski. Kick out the downhill ski so that the tip is straight up in the air, with the tail resting on the snow where the tip formerly was. Swing the elevated tip around to touch the snow where the tail used to be. Immediately put your weight onto this edged ski and in one smooth motion lift the uphill ski and corresponding pole, swinging them around 180 degrees. This uphill ski now becomes the new downhill ski as it is placed beside the other ski.

Action speaks louder than words in this one, so visualize this exercise first and then try it. Remember, the key points are to face downhill and to kick the *downhill* ski straight out and swing it around a full 180 degrees, followed in the same fluid motion by the uphill ski. This uphill ski need be lifted only high enough to clear both the snow and the other ski. Bringing your uphill pole around with the uphill ski will help your balance. Of course, your uphill edges prevent you from sliding sideways downhill, just as they do in sidestepping or traversing. Long skis will be a little more difficult to kick turn than short ones but the principle is the same. Practice this and then spring it on your friends. It really looks classy. With a little more practice, you may find it easier to balance by keeping the original downhill pole in front of you until the downhill ski is kicked almost all the way around.

If you ski at an area where some trail is named "KT," it may be interesting to find out whether it was named after the Himalayan mountain or the kick turn. KT Gully at Snowmass, Colorado, for example, was supposedly named by a ski patrolman who ventured into a very steep gully, encountered wind pack conditions and ended up by traversing and kick turning the entire run.

Kick turn

101

20
THE SIDESLIP

Perhaps this chapter should be entitled "How to Ski Down Any Hill in the World," because you're going to perfect a skill which will let you do just that. Let's imagine you've suddenly skied up to a steep pitch, one beyond your present ability. Of course, you could always take off the skis and walk down, but that's no fun. It's too much work and, on a hard packed slope, quite dangerous. The braking wedge won't slow you down on a steep hill. Traversing and kick turning are tedious. How about sidestepping? You already know how to sidestep up or down a hill. With your skis crosswise to the fall line you use their whole edge to dig in and hold you in place while you step sideways downhill. Through lateral knee actions you can get enough edge angle to hold you on any hill. Although sidestepping down is easier than up, it's still a lot of work, and very slow.

Thanks to your slippery skis and hard edges, you can actually ski while still using the advantages of the sidestep position. In sidestepping the knees are angled up the hill to get on an edge. If the knees, and nothing else, are moved toward downhill, that edge angle will decrease. A point will be reached where gravity overcomes the hold of the edges. You will then slide sideways downhill in a controlled skid or *sideslip*. Since your knees control edging, moving them back uphill will increase the edge bite, thus slowing you down and stopping you. All of a sudden you have the ability to sideslip, or in other words, to ski in control down a hill previously much too steep. Let's get the feel of sliding sideways.

Find a moderately steep but short pitch of firmly packed snow. Assume a basic sidestep position with your skis across the fall line on their uphill edges. The upper ski is ahead and your upper body is facing downhill. Place your upper pole basket in the snow close

FIRST BASIC SIDESLIP

EDGE   SIDESLIP   EDGE TO STOP

Release edge to sideslip

to your uphill ski, about a foot or so ahead of your boots. Place the lower pole basket as far downhill as you can comfortably reach and directly below your heels. Now, with your weight more on the downhill ski and back slightly onto the heels, flatten your skis by moving your knees downhill slowly until your skis sideslip. Move your knees back uphill to stop before you reach the downhill pole. Move the ski poles and repeat until you feel confident enough to sideslip without poles in the snow. Feel the snow sliding by underneath your edges!

Here are two alternate exercises which are particularly useful if the snow is soft or if the hill is gentle.

BASIC SIDESLIP A

From a sidestep position, hand the baskets of your ski poles to a friend standing directly downhill from you. Weight your heels and have your friend pull you directly toward him until your skis start sideslipping. Then drive your knees (*not* body) uphill to stop. Repeat with a gentler pull, helping by rolling your knees toward your friend. Finally, try with no pull at all, just by moving your knees.

BASIC SIDESLIP B

From a basic sidestep position, place both ski pole baskets just uphill of your skis, shoulder width apart, one by your uphill toe, the other by your uphill heel. Push on the poles to start your skis sideslipping. Stop the skid by pointing your knees back into the hill to increase edging. Repeat but push less by flattening your skis first. Continue until no push is needed to start the sideslip.

In your first attempts you may find the tips of the skis starting downhill. This is quite normal and is actually the start of a turn. Since you want to slide straight down the fall line for the present, put your weight back as if trying to press your heels down. This

103

Sideslipping with the help of a friend

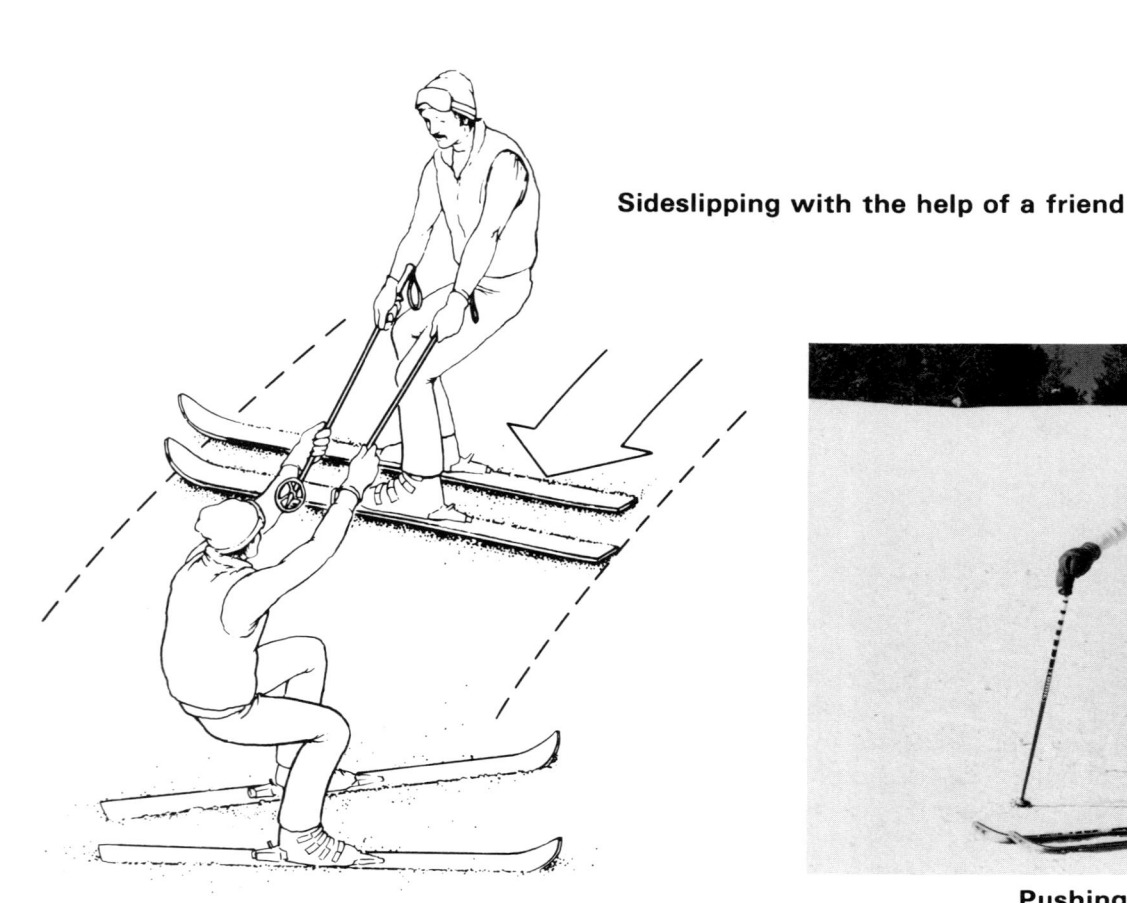

Pushing with poles to sideslip

weight distribution is done by rocking backwards from the ankle while keeping the body upright. You may find that a little steering of the feet up the hill will enable your skis to stay across the slope. Don't forget that you must angle your upper body out over the downhill foot. Failure to face downhill with the upper body or to keep the weight centered over the lower ski will cause loss of control over your edges. This means your fanny must be square over the skis, not sticking out. If you want to experience "catching an edge," try sideslipping and facing back uphill with your upper body. You'll only want to do that once. If you find a downhill edge does catch, make sure the snow is not so soft as to pile up against your skis.

To sideslip successfully, all you have to do is move your knees left and right. Have someone watch you to make sure you are moving the knees and not throwing your hips out.

A sideslip straight down the hill is only one specific instance of the basic concept of skidding. Among sports, this sideways movement is unique to skiing. It probably will feel strange the first time you do it. Keep working on it! To improve edge control in this sideways motion let's practice knee motions back and forth.

Start a sideslip at the top of a steep, firmly packed longer slope (at least thirty yards long). Move the knees left and right while sideslipping straight down the fall line, until you are confident you can start and stop a sideslip just by lateral knee movement.

KNEE ACTIONS IN SIDESLIP

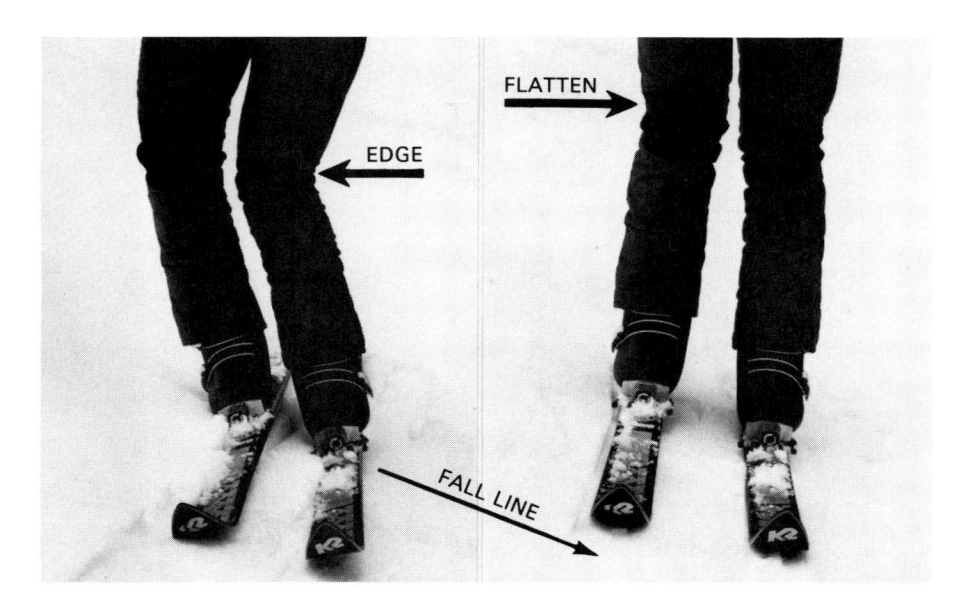

Knee actions control sideslips

A long sideslip with speed is a great maneuver. It's really straight skiing down a slope, with the upper body facing the direction of travel and the skis across this direction of travel to curb your speed. Try this one.

Start a sideslip at the top of a long, steep, firmly packed slope. Release the edges and sideslip straight down, gaining as much speed as you can. Stop just before the bottom by gradually pointing your knees uphill to increase edge and slow down. Make sure your final body position is the same as your starting body position.

LONG SIDESLIP

Long sideslip

You've probably already discovered why it's important to keep your weight back somewhat on the heels. Due to ski and boot design and binding placement, if your weight is forward and the edges are released, the tips turn downhill. The distribution of weight forward or backward on the foot is known as *leverage*. We can use this concept to help control the direction of a sideslip.

While sideslipping straight downhill, bend forward at the ankles to place your weight primarily on the toes. Your sideslip will now go forward while still going downhill. Then bend backward at the ankles to place your weight primarily on the heels. Your sideslip will now go backward while still going downhill. Vary this leverage fore and aft as you sideslip to help control your direction of skid.

The falling leaf is a maneuver very few skiers are even aware of, yet it's one that will come in extremely handy, especially during mogul skiing. For now you can utilize leverage to sideslip down slopes without following the fall line. Play with this leverage while

THE FALLING LEAF

The falling leaf
Shifting weight to tips or tails changes the direction of a sideslip.

sideslipping until you really feel comfortable at it. Since skiing is symmetrical, don't forget to do all these exercises in both directions (if we were intended to sideslip in only one direction, we would have been made with one leg shorter than the other).

Now that you've learned to enjoy skidding on the edges, let's take the sideslip out of the specialized category and use it in more general skiing, where you travel forward and sideways at the same time.

Start across a moderate hill in a parallel traverse on your uphill edges. While moving forward, release the edges by pointing your knees downhill just until you feel yourself skidding downward at the same time you are moving forward. Move your knees uphill until the edges grab and you resume a straight traverse. Make many long traverses, moving your knees left and right to vary the edge angle (alternately skidding and tracking). Look at your tracks to see how a sideslipping ski can get you down a hill at the same time you are skiing across it.

SIDESLIP FROM A TRAVERSE

Sideslip from a traverse
Release edge hold to lose elevation while continuing to ski forward.

Once you've mastered sideslipping while traversing, try the following fun exercise.

Standing on a slope, pick out an object (a tree, person, ski poles, etc.) across the hill and lower than you are. Aim your skis directly toward it in a traverse. While approaching the object, flatten your skis so you are also sideslipping. Without having changed your traverse angle you thus end up below the target object. Repeat by starting a traverse which is aimed above a chosen object. See if you can sideslip just enough in your traverse to lose elevation and end up right at the target object.

SIDESLIP "GRADUATION" EXERCISE

That last exercise was a great "sink or swim" one, and it shows if you really understand releasing edges.

Decreasing edge angle is not the only way to start your skis sideslipping. If you lower the resistance with which edges "bite" into the snow, gravity may then start you skidding. A good way to do this is by momentarily lessening your weight on the edges by either sinking down suddenly, or springing up and sinking down. Both methods will work.

SIDESLIP BY UNWEIGHTING

On a moderately steep hill stand with just enough edge to keep you from sideslipping. From a deeply flexed knee position, spring upright and sink down to your original stance to initiate a sideslip. Repeat from an upright stance by suddenly sinking down at the knees to start a sideslip. Also try this while moving in a traverse.

In the next section we'll discover more about up and down motions. For the time being, let your body feel that this type of vertical motion will release your edge hold just as will a lateral movement of the knees.

With mastery of sideslipping, the time has arrived to put a feather in your fedora. No matter how steep the hill, you can always sideslip as long as the snow is firm enough to support the skis. Perhaps you won't yet have an advanced flashy turning style, but you will be *skiing* it.

Sideslip by unweighting
Unweighting can reduce edge hold to cause a skid.

21

UPHILL STEM TURNS

Skiers find ways to make everything easier, and the stem turn is a step in this direction. It's a turn half as difficult as a wedge, yet just as effective. It contains elements essential to every advanced turn. Going from a traverse to a wedge requires pushing out the tails of both uphill and downhill skis. The uphill stem turn possesses the subtle difference of pushing out only one ski. Let's try the necessary motions.

Assume a stationary traverse position, with your skis across the fall line. Put your weight on the downhill ski by angling your upper body over it. The uphill ski should feel almost weightless. Now

UPHILL STEM POSITION

Pivoting to an uphill stem

simply flatten the uphill ski and pivot out its tail. Let the edge and base glide flat over the snow, until you are in a small wedge stance. Glide the ski back to a parallel position.

Notice I said "glide" on the snow. It isn't necessary to lift the ski. In a traverse, moving the upper knee from pointing uphill to pointing downhill is simply a few inches of movement. However, it takes you off of the outside edge and onto a flat upper ski. Pushing out the heel of that ski puts you on an inside edge. (And you thought edge changes were difficult.) This position, with one ski tail displaced, is called a *stem*. To resume a parallel position, point your upper knee back uphill. This puts you on a flat ski. Then pivot the same foot straight ahead. If your upper body is facing slightly downhill, and the uphill ski is ahead, this action is effortless.

Since the goal of ski instructors is to make your life more complicated, let's now incorporate a little forward motion in this same position.

Traverse across the hill, with your weight almost entirely on the downhill ski. Push out the uphill tail, letting the ski glide on the snow. Resume a traverse position by gliding the ski back to a normal parallel traverse. Check your tracks; the downhill ski should not have moved from its traverse track. Only the uphill ski should have been displaced from the track. Repeat several times in both traverse directions.

In a stem your position resembles a wedge. The uphill ski is starting to point downhill in the direction you would like to turn. All you have to do now is put some weight on that uphill ski, roll your knees downhill slightly and steer your feet. Pushing the knees downhill flattens the lower ski so that it will stop tracking across the hill; the upper ski can resist the snow and start turning. Let's get the feeling of starting a turn by making stem garlands. A garland is simply a term for a series of repeated exercises done without crossing the fall line. The word comes from the garland-like tracks you will leave.

UPHILL STEM FROM A TRAVERSE

Uphill stem from a traverse
Pivot the uphill foot to a stem.

Stem garlands

STEM GARLANDS

Ski across the hill in a traverse, with the uphill ski ahead and your weight on the downhill ski. Glide out the tail of the uphill ski. Now point that knee downhill to edge the uphill ski and press on the toes to weight the ski. When your skis move toward the fall line, release edge and pressure on the uphill ski. You will feel your skis start back uphill. Return the uphill ski back to a traverse by pointing the knee back uphill and gliding in the tail. Repeat several times, traversing in both directions.

As you will notice, this really isn't much different from the start of a wedge turn, except there is more emphasis on edging and weight transfer. These skills are essential to skiing, so give your body time to learn them. An additional step allows you to use the inner knee in a turn.

Ski down the fall line in a small braking wedge. Increase the pressure and edging on your left ski by driving that knee inward and forward. As your skis turn right of the fall line, point your right knee uphill and let that foot pivot in to a wide track parallel. Repeat from the fall line with a left turn.

FINISHING A TURN BY PIVOTING THE UPHILL SKI

Finish of a turn
Pivot the uphill foot in to complete a turn.

FALL LINE

This is essentially resuming a parallel traverse from a stemmed position. You have all the elements for a complete turn now, so let's put them together.

From a traverse, push out the tail of your uphill ski and then apply weight to that ski. Drive the knees slightly downhill, and help your turn by steering with the feet. You will feel the uphill ski "bite" and turn for you as soon as weight and edge angle are applied to it. After crossing the fall line, let the new uphill ski pivot in parallel to the downhill ski to resume a traverse. Do a series of stem turns down the mountain with traverses between each turn.

STEM TURN

Stem turn
It's as easy as it looks!

You should end up with your weight primarily on your new downhill ski, and both skis in a parallel traverse.

You may finish a turn with the uphill ski caught in a stem, unable to smoothly resume a traverse. Imagine a friend taking a photo of you in this position. Without seeing your tracks in this photo, there would be no way to tell if you had completed a turn or were merely traversing and had stemmed out that uphill ski. The position for the start of a stem turn and for the finish are exactly the same, only the left and right skis have changed places. Therefore, all you have to do to resume a parallel traverse is point the inner knee uphill and pivot in the tail of that uphill ski.

If you're still having problems, go back to skiing with your hands on your knees to verify that you are really skiing only from the lower body and not hindering your turns with excessive upper body movements. Make sure you're edging from the ankle-knee combination and not from the hip. The hip is a long way from the ski and won't help turn it. Don't contort or twist any part of your upper body to force a turn. If you're still "catching edges," you may also want to check that your bone structure is matched properly to your boots, as discussed in the equipment chapters. This is vital to allow proper edging.

While you are perfecting the stem turn, let's try one method to improve it.

DECREASING THE SIZE OF STEMS

As you gain confidence in making stem turns, decrease the size of the stem needed to start your turn. Try to feel the turn as being caused by edging skis and transferring weight rather than by a wide stem. Choose gentle smooth slopes to make wide round turns at moderate speed. Bring your skis parallel sooner by pivoting the inner ski parallel as soon as you cross the fall line.

Once again, you can see we're aiming at the pure parallel turn. If you skid at the finish of your turns, great! Keep doing it.

As you gain speed you'll find turns are easier. Centrifugal force will help you press weight to the outside foot to make the ski turn. This same force will also help your inside stemmed ski to return to a more natural parallel position.

RELAXING MUSCLES TO FINISH TURNS

Stand in a stem position and lift the uphill stemmed ski off the snow. Feel the extreme muscular effort required to hold it there. Keeping the ski in the air, relax only those leg muscles which pivot out the ski. Your foot will swing in parallel under your hips where it feels comfortable, even though it is still held in the air.

It's work to hold a stem longer than necessary. Apply this leg relaxation principle to the finish of your turns so that the unweighted stemmed ski slides back across the snow surface to a normal parallel position.

One advantage of a wide track position is that from this stance

STRAINED RELAXED

Relaxing leg muscles to finish turns

it is not necessary to make a large stem, or even any stem. Simply pushing the uphill knee in the new turn direction puts you on a new edge. Transfer weight to the uphill ski and you are turning. During this weight transfer you will feel a slight "up" motion, similar to a stepping action. Let your body become conscious of it.

Without exaggerating any actions, feel your weight flow from one ski to the other during a turn. Start a turn as though you were pushing off from the downhill ski. Then let your body flow with the motion, rising up to put weight onto the edged uphill ski and sinking down to a normal flexed position as you turn across the fall line. As weight settles onto the outside ski of your turn, the inside ski slides in parallel.

We'll be working on this active motion soon enough. At this stage you will feel a slight up-down motion, especially during smooth flowing turns. If you're already starting to ski somewhat parallel, terrific. If not, relax; we have a few more steps to go through to achieve a pure parallel turn.

"UP" MOTION IN STARTING A STEM TURN

22

SLOWING DOWN

Too many skiers of all abilities seem to follow Admiral Dewey's famous advice, "Damn the torpedoes—full speed ahead." Anyone can ski fast; slowing down requires some commonsense techniques. Only when you have learned to control your speed are you then ready to ski fast when you please.

First of all, let's use that common sense. Skis pointed down the hill accelerate. The more directly they point down the fall line, the faster they will go. Resisting gravity will slow you down, so let your skis run uphill to lose speed.

Choose a smooth hill, but one with a steepness near the limit of your ability. Point yourself straight downhill, bracing yourself against your poles. Keep a narrow wedge, or a parallel position if you feel confident. Now take a deep breath, and let yourself go. When you have reached a comfortable but not quite toe clenching speed, steer your skis back uphill, say to your left for the first time. Let your skis run in a long arc, like the bottom half of the letter "S," and see how far back uphill you can go before coasting to a stop.

SPEED CONTROL BY SKIING UPHILL

Now look at your track. Was it honestly an arc, and not an abrupt turn, traverse, and panic stop? Keep practicing it to both sides, as skiing is a symmetrical sport. Then practice some refinements.

Experiment with varying the radius of your uphill stops, steering a more abrupt arc uphill to slow down sooner, or a more gradual one when you have more room. Pick out a target (a person, tree, two ski poles, etc.) across the slope and downhill from you. See if you can turn your skis in one round arc and come to a stop right at that object, merely by losing momentum traveling back uphill.

SPEED CONTROL IN VARIOUS ARCS

Have you now felt acceleration and deceleration in your whole body during these arcs? (Unfortunately, you'll never go quite as far uphill as you started, or we'd have a perpetual motion machine and would put the ski lift industry out of business.) Differences in slope pitch and snow conditions will affect your stopping distance. The size of your turn will be affected by the amount of edging and the amount of steering with the knees and feet. If you can honestly say you have conquered speed, you have now put gravity to work for you. A round smooth turn back up the hill is the best way to slow down at any level of skiing.

Notice I said "slow down." This does not have to be completed to a stop but can be used throughout a continuous ski run.

Instead of a complete stop, merely slow down to a moderate speed by skiing back uphill and make a turn in the other direction. Link one turn after the other, making a series of arcs down the slope. You should be slowing down almost entirely by losing momentum. Keep doing these on slopes of varying steepness.

Rounded turns apply to any means of turning, whether steered or edged, and to any style, wedge through parallel. Perhaps you had been making short little turns on the proverbial dime. Concentrate on rounding the turns—don't rush them. They should make an "S" in the snow, not a "Z." You'll gain speed going into the fall line, but will lose it again as you continue to ski uphill. The speed will be invigorating but not frightening, since you'll be in control.

Unfortunately, you can't always count on having enough space to simply ski back uphill to slow down. Slopes are frequently narrow and crowded. Although the "S" turn approach can certainly be used to ski down the fall line in confined areas, let's explore a way to skid to slow down (or to use frictional edge resistance against the snow to dissipate kinetic energy, if you're technically inclined). The braking wedge controls speed, providing the slopes are gentle. But let's imagine you're skiing across a challenging slope in a parallel traverse, and want to slow down. Perhaps you can't turn uphill due to a tree, people or assorted other objects in the way. A full braking type wedge would work, but because you're traversing across the slope, most of your weight is on the downhill ski. Half a wedge would work as well. This is called a *downhill stem*, or *downstem* for short. All it requires is pivoting out the downhill ski tail so that the ski is now across your direction of travel.

You must keep your weight on the skidding downhill ski to slow down effectively. This requires additional flex in the downhill knee, and angling more from the waist. The upper body follows the lower ski as it is stemmed downhill. Just as in a braking wedge, a greater edge angle to the snow will slow you down faster. This edge is controlled by the downhill knee. Let's try one.

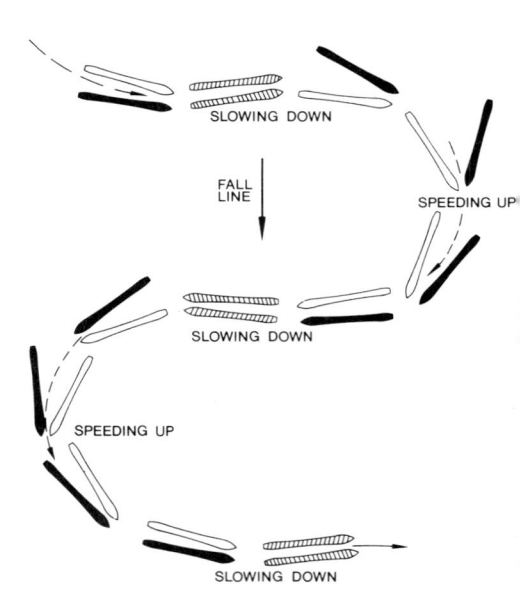

SLOWING DOWN BY ROUND TURNS

Slowing down by round turns

SLOWING DOWN BY A BRAKING STEM

From a moderate traverse, reach a comfortable speed. Flex the downhill knee and simultaneously pivot that ski out so the tail is below its original track. Your upper body must bend more at the waist, facing slightly downhill. Play with the amount of downhill knee angle. You should be able to drive the lower knee outward (downhill) so there is almost no braking action, and then inward (uphill) so that with an increasing edge you will slow down faster. If the ski tends to turn, put your weight back slightly onto your downhill heel. Slow down this way to a complete stop. Try it to both sides, at all speeds, at all angles of traverse. Look at your track to verify that the uphill ski maintains its straight course and only the downhill ski is displaced.

Mastery of this exercise will enable you to ski steep slopes. You should feel the resistance from your whole ski edge through your foot. You may find that a lot of inward knee angle will cause you to turn uphill. This is natural; skis tend to turn when they are edged. Learn to skid the ski by applying edge gradually, and put more weight back toward your heel, as weight forward (pressing the toes down) initiates a turn.

Perhaps you've already discovered the pressure generated in this maneuver. It's almost as though the snow underneath your lower foot is trying to push you upward. Let's exaggerate this feeling during a more rapid stop.

Downstem to brake speed

DYNAMIC DOWNSTEM

Perform the downstem action more dynamically. Push the lower ski tail out more rapidly, flex the downhill knee more, and abruptly apply an edge to the snow to stop. Make sure the snow flies up from the edge of your downhill ski and that you feel a momentary pressure push up on the bottom of your foot.

As long as the uphill ski has little weight on it, you can slide it parallel to the downhill ski during a stop. This is a more advanced exercise, but I have confidence in you.

PARALLEL SLOWING EXERCISE

From a traverse, perform the downstem in a gradual slowing action. The weight is on your downhill ski. Since the uphill ski has little weight on it, match it parallel to the downhill one by rotating the upper knee and pivoting in the uphill tail. The uphill knee must flex the same amount as the downhill one. You now have two skis skidding across the hill. Move the knees uphill simultaneously to increase edge angle and come to a stop. Now do this maneuver more rapidly and make the snow fly up from your edges. Feel the pressure on both feet pushing you up as you apply the edges to stop. Work on reducing the time between stemming the downhill ski and pivoting the uphill ski to match. See if you can pivot both skis simultaneously across your direction of travel.

Pivoting both skis is similar to the completion of an uphill stem, where the twisted muscles of your upper leg are relaxed to a parallel position. We'll be exploring this more in the chapter called "The Hockey Stop." But first, it's time to learn about skidded turns.

Slowing down by skidding on uphill edges of both skis

23

A BASIC SKIDDED TURN

You are skidding anytime you angle a ski across your direction of travel, causing the ski edge to slide sideways over the snow. You've already done this in speed control situations, namely the braking wedge and the sideslip. A downstem is also a skidding position, and pivoting in the uphill ski during the downstem maneuver results in a parallel skid. Similarly, in a turn, pivoting the inner ski after you cross the fall line also results in a parallel skid.

You've probably already done a basic skidded turn without even realizing it. Indeed, if you've been turning with any speed at all, centrifugal force around the turn has probably overcome your edge holding power and started a skid.

Whenever you finish a turn across the fall line in a parallel position, skidding on the uphill edges, you've made a basic *christie*. This is an old term named after the Norwegian town of Christiania, now known as Oslo, where the technique originated. Now is the time to play with edging to learn how much and when to skid.

BASIC CHRISTIE

From a moderate traverse, steer the skis back uphill in a sweeping arc. Roll your knees and ankles enough downhill during this turn to flatten the skis so that you are skidding as you continue to steer uphill. Repeat from steeper traverses until you are starting from the fall line. Starting from an upright stance, try to initiate the skidding action by rapidly sinking down in the knees. This releases your edges as you continue to steer the skis uphill.

Actually, a christie may be considered as a sideslip with steering. It is simply an extension of sideslips from a traverse, but you are now applying it to the finish of a turn. You should have felt skidding previously when you pivoted in the uphill ski while finishing a stem turn (technically that would be a stem christie).

SKID

Basic christie
Finish a turn by skidding.

Since you already know how to start a turn, the following will make you aware of completing a turn with a skid.

As you turn across the fall line, keep your skis flat enough so the edges slide sideways on the snow. Experiment with the angle of your knees while crossing the fall line so that you can vary from no skid at all to a skid which results in an almost straight sideslip down the hill. If necessary, exaggerate the steering as you cross the fall line to help the skis skid. Start your uphill ski into a small stem for the next turn.

SKIDDING TO FINISH A TURN

The above exercise is one you will have to try many times. The amount of skid will depend on your knee angle, of course, but also upon the radius of the turn, your speed, and the steepness of the hill. The faster and sharper the turn, the easier it is to skid. When sideslipping straight down the hill, your weight goes back to your heels slightly. This will also help finish your turn with a skid. Vertical knee action up and down (up to start a turn, down to finish with a skid) will also help your skid.

Why do you want to skid? First of all, it's a way to control your speed. Any time a ski is skidding it has braking resistance against the snow, and this slows you down. In addition, pivoting in the uphill ski to a parallel christie position is less tiring on your legs than a wedge. It also gives you two edges on which to skid. A major reason to skid is simply to get down the slope with fewer turns.

Pick a long moderate slope and ski it at one constant speed, at first without skidding. Traverse, turn, and traverse all the way down, counting the number of turns required. Now ski the same slope at the same speed, but skidding as much as you can after each turn, so that you are sideslipping downhill while still going forward. See if you can decrease the number of turns required by half.

SKIDDING TO AID IN COVERING DISTANCE

TURN - TRAVERSE - TURN   **TURN - SKID - TURN**

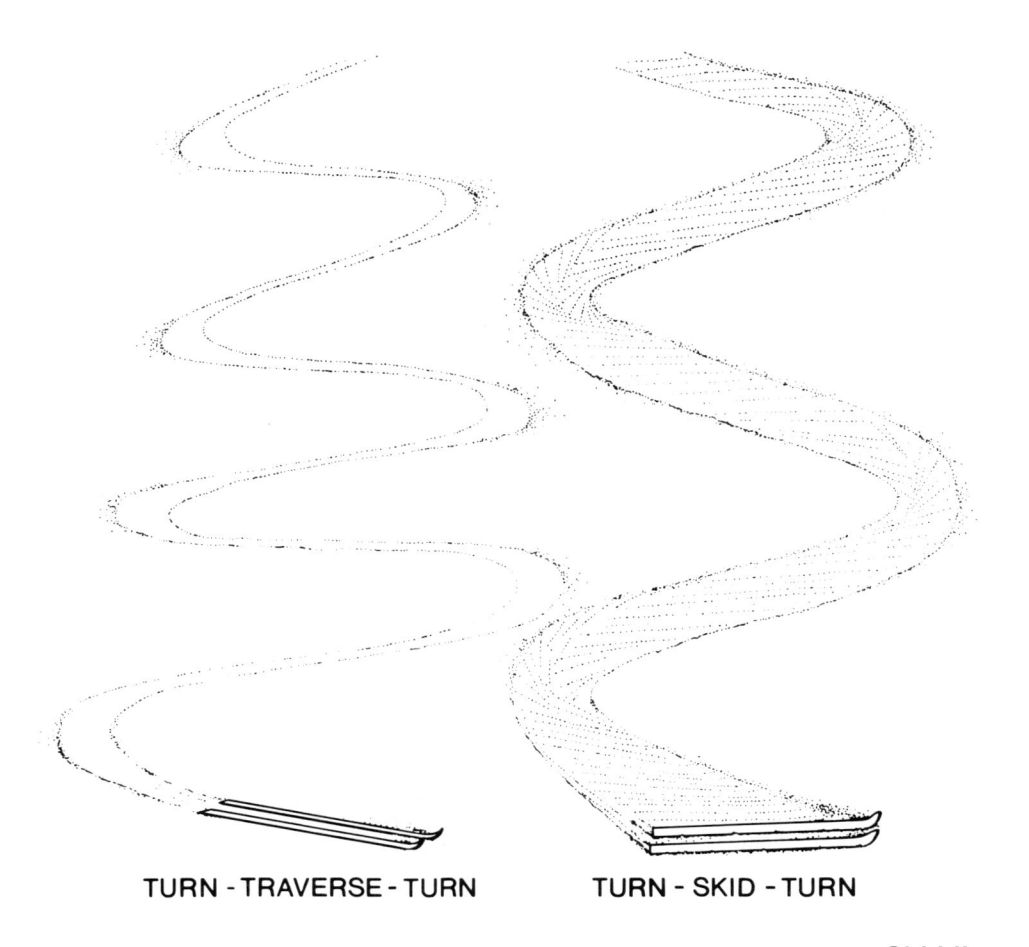

Skidding to cover vertical distance

Frequently skiers come around a turn with a stiff, straight outside leg. This means the inside ski will have too much edge while the outside ski will be too flat and not weighted. The result is the splits, ending in a noseplow. Try it in your living room, to verify that only a flexed outer leg will edge properly. On the slopes, make sure your uphill ski is ahead and your upper body is angled outward over the downhill ski. Try this exercise to see just what your knee is doing.

As you finish your turn, see for yourself if your downhill knee is really bent or not. While crossing the fall line to finish a turn, bend over sideways from the waist and feel the back of the downhill knee with your lower hand. If it is bent, fine. If not, then bend it by pushing in the back of your knee. Straighten up after feeling the knee, and immediately start another turn. Sink down while crossing the fall line to feel the back of the new downhill knee. Straighten for the next turn and continue this sequence down the hill.

BEND ZEE KNEES, FIVE DOLLARS PLEEZE

Verifying downhill knee flex

Once you have a bent outside knee, you can control both edges to skid whenever you desire.

Knowing what a skid is and how to control it will enable you to decide when to use it. You won't always want to skid. Don't forget that the best way to control speed is still to ski rounded turns back up the hill. Racers in particular will want to avoid skidding and losing speed. On ice you may find it especially difficult to maintain your balance in a skid. But for most of your skiing, skidding sideways on the edges can be very useful for speed control. More than that, skidding can be fun, and that's what skiing's all about.

24

UPPER BODY POSITION

"Feet bones connected to de ankle bones," states an old song. The hip, back, and head bones are a long way up the chain. Too frequently skiers contort their upper bodies, trying to force a turn. This interferes with the natural lower body motion which could manage an effortless turn. Your feet are smarter than you think. They're connected to the skis, and along with your lower legs and knees they should be allowed to make your turns efficiently.

Watch a racer or expert skier execute a series of short radius turns through gates, bumps, or powder. Put your hand out in front of you to block your vision of him from the hips down. It's almost impossible to tell which direction he's turning. Every accomplished skier will ski from his knees and feet, maintaining a quiet upper body.

The following exercise is great for skiers at any level. If you're at the wedge turn stage, it will aid you to parallel. At more advanced levels, it will help you to ski bumps and steep slopes.

SERVING A TRAY

Stand across a gentle slope and imagine you are an attendant on an airplane. Hold your poles aligned straight with the forearms, baskets in back out of the way. Pretend you're holding a serving tray. Swinging your upper body from the hips, you'll notice that this "tray" points wherever your torso points. Imagine serving a passenger sitting directly downhill from you. You must bend slightly at the ankles, knees, and waist, and angle your upper body out (downhill) toward him. Watch out for your hips; the aisles are narrow so you can't push your fanny uphill into the next passenger. Keep your hips centered over your feet. Now simply ski down the hill, always serving this tray directly down the fall line. Have a friend stand far below you in the fall line to watch. Serve this tray to him as you ski down, making numerous turns in a narrow path. To make this more fun for your friend down the hill, let him make a few snowballs.

Every time you spill the drinks he gets to throw a snowball at you.

The "tray" merely serves as an indicator of what your upper body is doing. Keep working at this exercise until you have it! Don't worry about what your feet are doing or how they are turning. If your torso is quiet your feet and knees will find the easiest, most efficient way to turn, without your conscious mind having to worry about the hundreds of actions needed to get you safely down the hill.

If you're having problems, check to be sure your hips are really quiet too, facing downhill and still centered over your skis. Don't cheat by only facing your arms down the hill and not your whole upper body. For this exercise, think of your hips, stomach, chest, arms, and head as being locked in one position, with your knees and feet absolutely free to twist beneath you.

You'll find that all of a sudden it's easier to ski, because now your upper body isn't putting weight where it doesn't belong. Ever cross your ski tips? Here's a sure way to do it.

TIP CROSSER

Make a slow wedge turn. As you cross the fall line to finish the turn, point your "tray" back up the hill. Immediately the uphill ski lags behind the lower one and tries to cross over. Do the same wedge turn with the "tray" pointed downhill all the way through the turn. Automatically, the uphill ski comes out ahead, and your weight ends up on the edged downhill ski.

Anytime you face uphill in a wedge or stem, you force the upper ski onto its inside edge and also weight it. Instead of becoming parallel, the upper ski has no choice but to cross.

Obviously you don't see good skiers in this extreme tray-carrying position all the time. I've exaggerated to give you a feeling for turning just the feet. Let's find out to what degree you really need to face downhill.

VARIOUS SIZE TURNS WITH A QUIET UPPER BODY

Stand at the top of a smooth moderate slope. Imagine a large narrow upside down "V" with the point where you are standing. It culminates at the bottom of the slope, where it is perhaps ten yards wide. Serve a tray and ski down the slope, just touching the outside boundaries of the "V" in your turns. As your turns get wider and the tray begins to feel awkward point your upper body more in the direction your skis point.

The amount your upper body will actually face downhill will depend primarily on how short the radius of the turn you are making is. We have been exaggerating by always pointing the tray straight down the hill. But exaggeration is a good teacher. Play around with this concept until you find the correct amount for every skiing condition. Even when holding your poles normally pretend you have a tray; always keep your hands in sight. Or, if you

Serving a tray
Face your upper body downhill and let your feet turn underneath you.

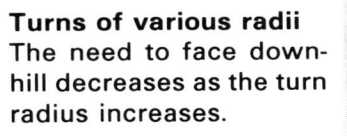

Turns of various radii
The need to face downhill decreases as the turn radius increases.

Tip crosser
Instead of continuing to face downhill, face uphill. Your tips will immediately cross.

like, pretend your bellybutton has an arrow coming straight out of it and pointing downhill. This is a variation on serving the tray that will make you very aware of your midsection.

Edges are used in every skiing situation. Skis must be at an angle to the slope to be on an edge. The only efficient, balanced way to do this is to push the knees uphill and to angle the upper body slightly downhill to compensate. Standing comfortably on the uphill edges in this balanced body stance is known as *angulation*. The uphill foot, knee and hip must be ahead to stand like this, which means the upper body is naturally facing somewhat downhill. The uphill ski is higher than the downhill one; similarly, the upper shoulder, arm and hip are higher than the downhill ones. Let's see why this is a stable position.

Find a steep, wide patch of hard packed snow. Traverse across it in an angulated stance. See if you can leave two sharp tracks in the snow by riding on the uphill edges of the skis. "Serve a tray" to verify that this feels balanced and enables you to ride the ski edges without slipping. Now experiment with these various body positions, one at a time, while traversing: point the tray back uphill; point just the hips back uphill; advance the downhill shoulder and hand ahead of the body; rapidly move the downhill hand from its normal position as far forward as you can reach, while also moving the uphill hand backward; raise the downhill hand and lower the uphill hand as far as you can reach. In each instance note how unbalanced you feel as you face uphill and possibly how your skis suddenly lose edge control and skid out. They no longer leave two sharp tracks in the snow.

Psychologically, facing downhill and even leaning out over the downhill ski are formidable barriers to overcome. Your instinct is to hug the hill for safety, but when you do, you lose edge control in the lower legs. For proper balance, your center of gravity must be between the skis, not above the upper ski. Just imagine if you were on glare ice, became a little apprehensive and "reached for the hill." You'd slide all the way to the bottom on your bottom. Even something as simple as driving your downhill hand forward (as in an exaggerated pole plant motion) causes loss of edge control. There is nothing wrong with a controlled skid, but that means one you initiate from the knees when you want to. All this leads to a great exercise, since the only effort required is to open your eyes.

uphill ski, foot, knee, hip, hand and shoulder are ahead

FALL LINE

Upper body ahead in angulation

ANGULATION IN A TRAVERSE

Angulation
Stand comfortably on your uphill edges with your weight mainly on the downhill ski. Your shoulders and body should be at the same angle as the slope.

OBSERVING UPPER BODY POSITION

It's fun to be a critic. Try it. While riding the chair, take advantage of the time to observe skiers on the slopes. Watch those in trouble—you'll see excess upper body movement, and as soon as they "grab for the hill" by turning their upper bodies back uphill drastically, get ready to see a spill. Contrast them with the smooth, controlled skiers with quiet upper bodies.

Though it's not necessary to always ski imagining a tray held in front of you, do be conscious of your upper body. It does not have to be static, as skiing requires fluid motions throughout the whole body. But keep it always facing somewhat downhill, so that your knees and feet can take charge and ski for you.

25
DOWNSTEM TURNS

So far you've downstemmed to control your speed. However, the action can also dynamically initiate turns, particularly at higher speeds.

The downstem resembles a wedge position, just as does the uphill stem. Once in a downstem you don't have to retract the downhill ski and then stem out the uphill ski. The latter has already been flattened automatically on the snow as you downstemmed. To turn, all you have to do is edge the uphill ski and put weight on its inside edge.

TURN FROM A DOWNSTEM

From a traverse, push out the downhill ski tail to slow down, bending more in the downhill knee and keeping the upper body angled over that ski. Now put the uphill ski on its inside edge by pointing the upper knee downhill. Rise off the downhill ski to put weight onto the uphill ski, and aid the turn by steering. Turn across the fall line, pivoting the inner ski parallel at the finish of the turn. Downstem the lower ski and repeat. Do a series of downstem turns, varying the radius from large to small.

Here you're skidding a ski to slow down and then turning. This rapid slowing is called a *check*, because the downstem "checks" or retards your speed as it sets you up for a turn. Here's a repeat of a feeling awareness exercise you did for an uphill stem.

"UP" MOTION IN TURNING FROM A DOWNSTEM

From a traverse, downstem sharply to slow speed. Feel your body weight push off the downstemmed ski to flow upward and settle back down onto the edged uphill ski. Let the weight sink onto this outside ski as you turn across the fall line, sliding the inner ski in parallel.

Downstem turn
The downstem controls your speed and also aids the edge change for a turn.

As the downstem becomes more vigorous, you should easily feel your weight flow from foot to foot.

The time is ripe to experiment with your poles. Since you paid good money for them, you should get some use out of them besides spearing candy wrappers. I'll talk more (lots more) about the use of poles later on, but for now we'll get an idea of their function in balance and timing.

Traverse across a hill at moderate speed. Vigorously pivot out the lower ski in a downstem. As the edge engages, touch the snow below the lower boot with your lower pole. Immediately push up and off the lower leg and transfer your weight to the uphill ski. Swing your lower leg in parallel to the upper ski. Resume the traverse before your skis cross the fall line, and again repeat the downstem maneuver.

The pole plant is accomplished by a forearm and wrist movement. Always use the right pole when downstemming the right foot and starting a turn to the right, and vice versa, of course. You can lean on the pole slightly to help balance and to help push off the lower foot to the upper. If the poles still confuse you at this point, wait and try them in the future.

After a garland with a pole plant, the next logical step would be

DOWNSTEM GARLAND WITH A POLE PLANT

"Up" motion in downstem turns

Downstem garland with a pole plant
The downstem edge set and the pole plant occur simultaneously. From the third position, with skis in the fall line, you could complete the right turn if you desired, although in this sequence the skier resumes the traverse and practices the downstem again.

FALL LINE

a complete turn. You can try that for yourself. To keep you on your toes, let's do a really fun one.

Stand on a gentle slope in a braking wedge. Without moving forward, establish a rhythm by shifting your weight entirely onto one ski and then the other. Continue back and forth at a comfortable rhythm, switching perhaps once a second. When you have a rhythm going, push off down the fall line. Feel yourself turn from side to side. Let the unweighted ski relax each time to flow with the turn.

DOWNSTEM WEDEL

Downstem wedel
Turn continually, stepping from foot to foot.

Wonder of wonders, you may suddenly make some parallel turns. This wedel (pronounced with a "V") is simply one turn after another without traversing. Each turn is preceded by a downstem motion. As you relax the inner leg of the turn, it automatically swings parallel. If you think you have it, try a gentle pole plant with each downstem edge set. Remember, right pole with right edge set, left with left.

With your heightened control and turning ability you're probably venturing onto intermediate slopes now and then. Here you've hit (figuratively only, I hope) some *moguls*, rounded bumps in the snow. Contrary to rumor, they are formed by skiers turning in the same spots, and not by a secret crew of sadistic mogul makers who work at night. When you find some gentle moguls, use the downstem to help turn on them.

While traversing at slow speed, approach a small mogul at an angle. Downstem, so that your lower ski pushes against the uphill side of the mogul. Immediately transfer your weight to the uphill ski and turn around the mogul by edging and steering that ski. After a bit of practice, touch your downhill pole to the mogul crest just as you push off from the downstemmed ski to start turning.

You can use the same technique on any rounded terrain, such as on a long, convex ridge. The big secret is to push against the uphill side of the mogul, rather than skiing over its summit or trying to downstem below its summit. In this way the shape of the terrain is such that you will be drawn right around the mogul. It's an easy spot to turn.

DOWNSTEM IN MOGULS

Downstem in moguls
Downstem against the mogul crest (here partially hidden by flying snow), turn around it, and look for another mogul on which to downstem.

section IV

KNEE MOVEMENTS UP AND DOWN

By now you are enjoying some intermediate runs, and you want to make quicker turns and handle bumpy terrain. In this section you'll find that vertical knee movement helps control the pressure on your skis. You'll learn to use a downward knee movement to make a parallel stop, and will apply that action to control speed on steeper slopes. Then you'll eliminate stems and perform an elegant parallel turn. These turns will be useful in the moguls, where you'll take advantage of the terrain to turn easily. Next, you'll learn to use vertical knee motion in an unweighting fashion, to reduce ski pressure for faster turn initiation. By that time you'll be increasing your speed and will discover how to compensate for it.

26
THE HOCKEY STOP

The hockey stop is named after the way ice skaters make a sudden stop. I think it is easier than a skating stop, thanks to the skis' long edges and the soft snow. This stop is simply a parallel skid. As in any skid, sliding the ski edges across your direction of travel provides a resistance or slowing effect. You've performed many skids, including the braking wedge, downhill stem, sideslip, and christie. For the hockey stop you'll need a down motion in the knees to release the edges, combined with a steering action to turn your skis more radically across your direction of travel. Let's try one.

Traverse across a smooth hill at moderate speed, with your feet comfortably apart. From a high stance, sink in the knees and simultaneously pivot your skis under you to point them up the hill. Put your weight back slightly on the heels to maintain a skid in your original direction of travel. Increase edge by pointing your knees uphill to come to a stop. Keep your upper body facing downhill while pivoting your feet beneath you. Feel your weight primarily on the downhill foot, both in the traverse and the stop.

HOCKEY STOP FROM A TRAVERSE

The hockey stop is simply an improved, two-legged version of the downstem. If you find yourself falling over, make sure your weight is still over the downhill ski. Leaning backward during a hockey stop could result in your skis sliding out from under you. You must continue to face your direction of travel with your upper body. A narrow stance makes your balance very precarious; keep the feet apart for stability and for stronger steering action.

Let's analyze the basic concepts of the hockey stop.

1. The feet pivot uphill beneath you. You are already familiar with this steering action. Stay on the same uphill edges on which

Hockey stop
This is an efficient, quick stop.

you are traversing and merely rotate your feet radically uphill to put the skis across your direction of travel.

2. The knees flex downward. Lowering your body in this manner momentarily lessens the weight pressing on the ski edges, much like the start of a descent in an elevator. The faster you flex downward, the less pressure on the edges and the easier it is to pivot the skis. Experiment with how fast you can sink and turn the skis beneath you. This concept is called *down unweighting,* and as we progress we'll see how it can be applied to help finish one turn, or to help start a new one.

3. Your body weight goes back slightly onto the heels. In a straight sideslip down the hill, weight on the heels prevents a turn. Similarly, in a hockey stop a subtle weight shift toward the heels allows you to continue a skid in your original direction of travel.

4. The upper body remains facing somewhat downhill. As you well know by now, this is very basic and *very* important. It is the only means you have of standing balanced on your edges, and controlling them.

5. The edge angle is increased to bring the skis to a stop. There's nothing new here, as this is the old lateral knee action. All we've done is add a little downward knee action to facilitate an easier turn into a skid.

To stress the importance of this maneuver here's a refinement exercise.

Vary the steepness of your traverse and your speed before performing a hockey stop. With careful knee action, try to skid on a flat ski for a long distance before increasing edge to stop. Then practice increasing the edge more abruptly to stop quickly. See if you can "hit" the edges hard enough to make snow spray from them onto a stationary object below you. With your downhill pole, touch the snow below your boots as you make the final edge set action.

The pole plant is simply a touching of the basket to the snow, which will be a good habit to develop for future turns. As your body sinks, your downhill hand comes closer to the ground, and that pole touches during the final inward thrust of the knees to stop completely. Planting the pole assures that you are still angulated out over the downhill ski.

A final abrupt edge set is a great way to spray snow on friends below you. (Make sure you can ski faster than they in case there are any objections to being soaked.) It's the classic stop with style and flair.

HOCKEY STOP FROM VARYING TRAVERSES

The classic parallel stop

The hockey stop is often done from the extreme case, which is a straight run in the fall line. Here you go from a flat ski with weight equal on both skis to an edged ski with weight on the downhill.

With your skis running straight down a hill, perform hockey stops to both left and right. Imagine you are on a ten-foot-wide trail and maintain a straight descent while stopping, so that your skid is also straight down the hill within the trail boundaries. From weight equal on both skis in the fall line, feel your weight go to the downhill foot as you pivot and skid.

So far we've been talking about pure stops, but there's no reason

HOCKEY STOP FROM A STRAIGHT RUN

why this skidding action cannot also be used to control or slow your speed.

While skiing in the fall line, sink in the knees and pivot the skis uphill to parallel skid (hockey stop action) and decrease speed. Rise in the knees to start a turn and again sink and pivot to skid, losing speed gained in the fall line. Continue down the hill in this manner without traversing between turns, staying in a narrow track down the fall line. Feel your weight first on one downhill foot, then the other, as though you are pushing off from one downhill ski at the finish of a skid to the new downhill ski in your next skid. Your lower pole should touch the snow at each final edge set to help you push from ski to ski.

I sneaked in the words "rise in the knees." You cannot constantly keep sinking lower and lower; at some point you have to rise to the natural athletic stance position. The time to rise is at the end of your skidding action, as you start into a turn. You will feel the skis trying to push you up as you slow abruptly. Flow with this motion to rise. The pole plant means an edge change, from one set of edges to the other, and it occurs the instant you finish a skid and start to rise into a new turn.

FALL LINE SKIDDING

Fall line skidding
Keep skis mainly across the fall line to control speed on steep narrow slopes.

In the event you had problems with the preceding exercise, let's go back to one we did for the downstem.

Stand in a small wedge in the fall line on a moderate hill. With your poles in front to prevent sliding forward, sink down first in one knee, then rise up and sink in the other knee. Get a rhythm going, changing weight from foot to foot about every second. Press down on the right pole when pushing the right foot and vice versa. Now remove the pole baskets from the snow and ski down the fall line with this rhythm. Skid first on one ski and then push off to rise, sink, and skid on the other. When you feel confident in this, and have your weight entirely on one ski or the other, relax the unweighted leg (the one from which you pushed off) and let that ski swing around to join the new weighted, skidding ski. Soon you will be skidding on one ski or the other and swinging both of them across the fall line. Stay within a ten-foot-wide path all the way down.

When you have this rhythm going you are making a series of skidded turns without traverses (a wedel). The skis turn underneath a quiet upper body. Find a comfortable rhythm and keep the knees moving with it. Don't be static at any point. Sing a song to keep the rhythm all the way down the hill. If you can do this you may want voice lessons, but you certainly won't need additional hockey stop lessons.

HOCKEY STOP WEDEL

Hockey stop wedel

27

VERTICAL KNEE ACTION

Moving the knees up and down is such an ordinary experience in walking we don't even think about it. Yet, amazingly, in skiing it's easy to forget this movement and to become so tense that the knees lock up rigidly. We ski with the knees slightly bent for two reasons. We already learned in the last section that bent knees permit movement laterally, or left and right, to edge. The other reason is so that they are loose to contract or extend as necessary. Imagine you're skiing along with straight legs, knees locked. Every bump you come to will first throw you in the air, then drop you in a gully. Having your head bounce up and down all day is no fun. Let's become aware of the bump absorbing capacity of the knees.

Ski at slow to moderate speed across a series of small bumps, or moguls. Imagine your head traveling in a straight line and your feet moving up and down with every variation in terrain. Allow your knees to flex up and extend down like shock absorbers to join your feet and head.

THE KNEES AS SHOCK ABSORBERS

You may even feel you are aiding the knees to move up and down, smoothing the ride, particularly as you ski faster. Of course, each knee works independently, just as each wheel of a car has its own shock absorber. Thus, if you hit a bump with the right ski, that knee contracts to absorb it, while the left knee remains in its normal flexed position. Your body stays in perfect balance. This should be the case regardless of how close together you keep your feet. It's the important principle of *independent leg action*.

Reverse the absorption process and try your knees as compressed springs.

While going up a bump, actively sink in the knees. Then, just

JUMPING

The knees as shock absorbers

Independent knee action

Jumping

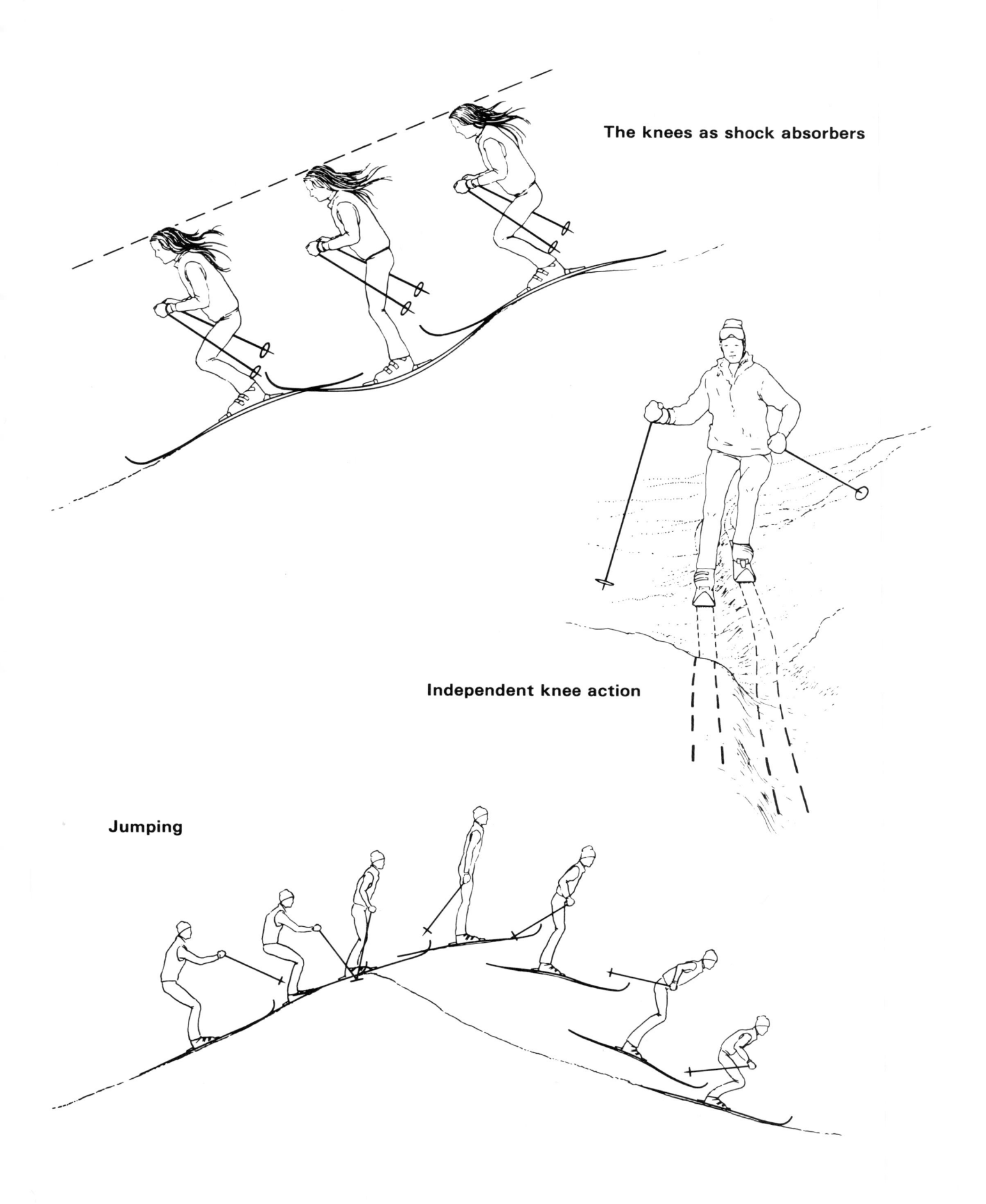

prior to the top, push up by rising as rapidly as possible in the knees to get airborne. Both poles may be planted ahead of you on the crest of the bump and a push given with the arms. When landing, let your knees flex to absorb the shock.

Jumping can also be done without a bump, but it requires more effort. One way to get higher ("More air!" is the term) is through speed. Ski fast enough over a bump so that the crest pushes you into the air, as in a ski jump. To be fair, I should mention that on your takeoff your skis are pointing uphill and at the landing they will point downhill. That means that while airborne, you must angle your skis downward and get your body forward, so you don't land only on the tails and fall over backwards. Pushing forward onto the toes at takeoff will help. To firmly convince you of the knees' ability to absorb shocks, just make one landing without flexing the knees to soak it up—you'll feel three inches shorter for days.

Knees bend vertically in every walking step to push you up and forward. If you're an ice skater, you've probably already done the following exercise while skiing across a flat area, using knee thrust.

On a flat area assume a herringbone position, standing on your inside edges with tips outward. Sink down and inward in the left

SKATING

Skating across flat terrain

knee. Then extend rapidly to push off from the inside edge of that ski, skating onto the inside edge of the right ski. As your speed slows, sink in the right knee and then spring up, pushing off to the left ski. Skate in a constant rhythm from one foot to the other. Use the poles for additional thrust, pushing with the left pole when pushing off the left ski, and the right pole when pushing from the right foot.

Here you are essentially using a "jumping" motion to push off forward from an edged ski. You're taking advantage of edges and resistance to the snow, combined with a vertical thrust from the legs. With fluid motion and forceful leg thrusts, a respectable speed can be reached across a flat area or even up a small incline. By now you know how to coordinate lateral and vertical movements, and you certainly have the best educated knees in town.

28

PARALLEL WEIGHT TRANSFER TURN

Don't get hung up on whether or not you ski parallel. A stem is sometimes superior to a parallel turn. However, now that you are learning to move your knees up and down, you may find that a parallel turn is actually easier than a stem. In fact, you may already be making this basic parallel turn. If you have a good feeling for edge control and weight transfer it should come naturally.

This is a good time to remember that parallel doesn't mean the feet are locked together. Rather, it means both feet point the same way. Go up to a friend who is standing with his feet close together. Try to push him over by shoving him on the shoulder. (Better tell him first.) Immediately, he will automatically spread his feet apart for balance. For lazy skiing you might find your feet coming together, but when the going gets tough, several inches of space between your boots will help keep you upright.

You'll recall that stem and parallel turns are closely related. In a stem you displace the tail of one ski and then change the edge of the uphill ski before changing edges on the downhill one. In a parallel turn it is not necessary to stem out a ski and therefore both ski edges are changed before the fall line. As you have increased speed, you've found that smaller and smaller stem positions work fine for turning. A parallel turn is simply the limit of a stem turn —a stem so small it isn't even there.

Let's go back and emphasize the feeling of weight transfer from the downhill to uphill ski to initiate the turn.

As you make a round turn and cross the fall line, actually pick up your inside ski so that your weight is pressed entirely against the outside ski. Drive forward with the outer knee, balancing on the edge of that ski. Put the inner ski down parallel to the outer one. Turn the inner ski onto its inside edge and weight it to turn. Im-

PICKING UP THE INSIDE SKI IN A TURN

Picking up the inside ski
Transfer weight to the outside ski at the start of each turn.

mediately lift the other ski in the air. Continue down the hill always skiing only on an outside ski, changing weighted skis at the start of each turn. If your inside ski tail drags on the snow at the start of your turn, bend your ankles to put more weight forward on the toes.

Lifting the inside ski in a turn exaggerates the weight transfer, as with one ski in the air you must have all your weight on the other. Putting down the lifted ski, it now becomes the uphill ski temporarily. Most importantly, it becomes the outside ski for the next turn. Edging that ski and putting your weight onto it starts it into a turn; steering then aids the turn.

The tip of the ski is designed to initiate a turn for you, but you must drive the knee forward to weight the ski's forebody. Your skis are accelerating since they are starting to head downhill; therefore your body must be forward to keep up with them. Lifting the inner ski as you start a turn also shows you if your weight is forward. If the ski tail remains on the snow, you are too far back! Get your weight forward until the tail lifts off, with the tip still on the snow.

For some fun, here's a trick to impress your friends.

While you are practicing picking up the inside ski throughout a turn, you may as well do something with that ski. Just for fun, cross it in the air over the outside ski to form an "X." Uncross the inside ski, put it on the snow parallel to your downhill ski and immediately start another turn, picking up the downhill ski and crossing it above

JAVELIN TURN

DIFFICULT TURN

EASY TURN

Weight distribution to start turns
Keep your weight forward to initiate a turn.

Javelin turn

the new outside ski as you turn. This is the old Javelin, or Iron Cross turn.

Whether or not you do the Javelin turn, keep practicing until you can ski on one or the other ski all the way down the hill, making repeated turns. You'll feel your outside ski edge carve a round arc in the snow.

Let's try a different approach to get the same result. If you have

146

ice skated this should appeal to you. You've already worked at skating across the flats. That exercise can be expanded to include the same active motions while going downhill.

On a very gentle slope, start to skate directly down the hill, pushing from one ski to the other in a slow rhythm. As you gain a little speed, also turn the ski on which you are standing by rotating that knee inward and pressing it forward. Once the ski has turned across the fall line skate to the other ski. Drive this knee inward and forward until the ski crosses the fall line. The unweighted inner ski swings around with the turning ski. Continue skating down the hill from one ski to the other, using the same rhythm you would use to skate across the flats.

Did you feel yourself push from one ski to the other? From skating in a herringbone position you have added forward weight and steering with the knee to achieve a turn, so that all of a sudden you are skating parallel. This is the same position as picking up the inside ski in a turn except that now you are being even more dynamic, actively moving your knees up and down to help "push" from one ski to the other.

Poles are helpful in transferring weight during a parallel turn. Frequently skiers get confused with the timing of the poles. The pole plant should be considered an integral part of weight transfer, and not a separate maneuver. We've already discussed poles in the chapters on downstems and hockey stops. The pole plant occurs

SKATING DOWN THE HILL

Skating down the hill
Push off one ski and skate to the other.

with an edge change, to start a turn toward the fall line. Now let's look at the pole as an aid to balance when your center of gravity moves, transferring weight from one ski to the other.

Standing across a steep hill in a sidestep position, take the ski pole baskets out of the snow and angulate so your weight is over the downhill ski. Now shift your body stance to transfer your weight to the uphill ski, lifting the downhill. Do you feel awkward and in danger of falling? Now stand just on the downhill ski again, but this time place the lower pole basket below your boot. Leaning on the pole, transfer your weight to the uphill ski, lifting the downhill one. Feel the balance and support from the pole!

Plant a pole the instant you are transferring weight to the uphill ski. This is when you need additional support for balance. Always use the downhill pole, placing the basket in the fall line, about a foot below the boot. This keeps your torso facing downhill, retaining edge control. Avoid planting a pole out at the ski tip. That destroys body position, takes time, and means you must ski all the way around it. Skating with poles can improve your feel for timing.

Find a spot where you can start off on flat terrain prior to a gentle slope. Skate across this level area using your poles for balance; right

POLES FOR BALANCE

POLE PLANT TIMING

Pole plants aid balance during weight transfer

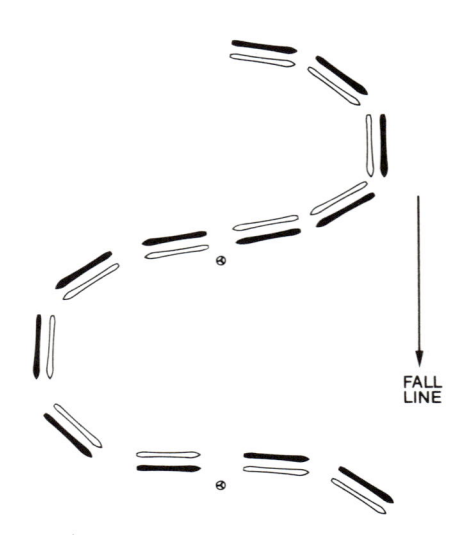

Weight transfer in a parallel turn
Change weight with the pole plant when starting a new turn, before reaching the fall line.

WITH A POLE PLANT

WITHOUT A POLE PLANT

pole as you push off the right foot, left pole as you push off the left foot. Gain speed skating down the hill, turning each weighted ski by a knee drive. Continue to balance by placing a pole downhill from your weighted foot just as you push off from that foot to the other.

If you can skate and pole plant on the flat, you should have no problem with pole plants during turns. Keep the elbows slightly away from the body and the hands aligned with the forearm. The hands should always be in sight. A slight push on the pole may help you to transfer weight from one ski to the other. If you've got it, super! If not, keep on trying. We'll be using poles more from now on and will try them in other ways. The beauty of the weight transfer turn is that it can be done with or without poles.

Let's take this turn beyond the mere exercise of lifting a ski and refine it into its most elegant form—an easy parallel turn.

From a traverse, transfer your weight from the downhill to the uphill ski, simultaneously edging the skis and driving your knees forward into the turn. Keep the inside ski on the snow and steer it parallel to the turning outside ski. Continue down the hill, stepping from one ski to the other, starting a new turn by transferring weight to the outside ski, and driving the knees. Work at making smooth rounded turns. Touch your downhill pole to the snow about a foot below your boot at the time of weight transfer. Aid your knee drive by tipping your body into your turn.

Everything you've worked on before still applies, including facing the upper body slightly downhill, steering with feet and knees, and not rushing the turn. This relaxed parallel turn is great for

Reach for the pole plant

PARALLEL WEIGHT TRANSFER TURN

Parallel weight transfer turn
A super easy turn done by changing edges and stepping weight to the new outside ski.

149

larger radius turns on open slopes. It's a good way to learn carving, which is useful in racing and in skiing on ice. Once again, you're simply eliminating stemming out a ski. Instead of a discontinuous, abrupt change of direction, you are now making a very smooth continuous, rounded turn. Your weight should flow from foot to foot. Some weight will remain on the uphill foot, but most of it should be pressed against your outside ski.

I could expound forever on this one Cadillac of turns but words can't do it justice. How do you know when you have this turn? It will feel wonderful, an almost effortless action with no wasted motions. Once you master the parallel turn, instead of calling yourself an "intermediate" skier, use some class with the Italian phrase *sciatore medio*. You've earned it.

29
MOGUL MASTERY

The time has come to get to know your best friends on the mountain, the moguls. Who said "With friends like these who needs enemies?" Give them a fair chance. Moguls are formed by many skiers turning in the same spot in soft snow and piling the snow into bumps. Once you learn to master them you'll prefer moguls to smooth slopes. They should be considered friends because they do so many nice things to help your technique. For one thing, they actually make turning easier, as you'll soon see.

You've already encountered moguls and wondered how to make all those turns needed to get through them, especially when you get zipping along practically leaving a sonic boom behind you. The secrets are to control your speed and to make short radius turns. For a moment let's go back to basics and see how short a turn you can make.

STEERED TURN WITH POLE PLANT

Stand sideways on a moderately steep hill, free of bumps. Place the downhill pole in the snow directly below and about eighteen inches from your lower boot. Lean on the pole. Now put your weight forward onto the toes and flatten your skis by pointing your knees downhill. Pivot your skis so that they immediately head into the fall line. Let the pole come out of the snow as your body passes it. To finish the turn, sink in the knees and drive them uphill, skidding to a stop on your edges.

In this steered turn you have changed direction within the length of your skis. Without a pole plant this turn is harder to do because the pole supplies an additional deflecting force to the skis. The pole helps to "block" the motion of the upper body, giving a solid point of contact outside the body system through which the steering force can be increased. This is somewhat like standing on a scatter

Steered turn with pole plant

rug on a very slippery floor. As you quickly swivel your feet to the right, the upper body twists to the left (action-reaction). But, if you hold onto a table (or plant a pole) to keep your torso from swiveling left, the feet will swivel right more forcefully.

The less friction between the skis and the snow, the easier it will be to pivot the feet. Here's an exercise to give you a valuable clue as to how moguls aid turns.

FINDING WHERE TO TURN ON MOGULS

In a gentle field of moguls, stand in the trough between two bumps and note the difficulty in trying to swivel your feet here. Now, stand on the crest of the mogul, balanced by the downhill pole, and twist your feet easily from side to side. Observe that the snow in troughs between bumps is more hard packed than the softer snow on the bumps themselves.

Now try a turn from an easy spot.

TURN FROM A MOGUL CREST

Make some turns from a stopped position by standing on the ridge of the mogul, upper body facing downhill. Plant the downhill pole with wrist motion so the basket ends up about eighteen inches

Finding where to turn on the moguls

DIFFICULT

EASY

Turn from a mogul crest

downhill of your feet. Leaning on the pole, weight the toes, pivot your feet, and push your knees toward the inside of the turn, letting your skis follow the curvature of the bump. Sink and skid to a stop on the back side of the bump.

You have discovered that the uphill ridge of a mogul offers an easy place to swivel your feet for a turn. Skiing across the troughs, the tips and tails are on the snow and the feet are sometimes off, which makes turning difficult. But on a mogul ridge or crest the tips and tails are free of resistance. This essentially transforms the ski into a super short one and the feet steer easily. In fact, a parallel turn in the moguls is easier to do than a stem! Generally, snow is better on the bumps than between them, as people tend to ski the troughs, hard packing the snow. Skiing up a bump to reach the crest also helps slow you down, which is very convenient. In addition, the angle of the bumps may actually flatten your skis for you, helping to change the edges for a turn. Now try some turns with forward motion.

TURNING ON THE BUMPS

In a gentle field of moguls, ski up the front (uphill) side of a mogul. Plant the downhill pole on the crest at the same time you pivot your feet on the ridge. Steer into the new turn. Skid down the back side of the mogul to control speed while sliding to the next bump. Turn on every one.

Three familiar concepts are essential for this turn. First, the upper body faces down the hill. In the moguls especially, there isn't time to rotate the whole mass of the torso back and forth. Only the feet and knees must turn. Although there are secondary miniature fall lines on each mogul, you must consider the fall line of the entire hill. The idea is to get to the bottom and that's where the upper body should face. Second, the pole plant is made down the main fall line below the boots; this downhill pole is planted with a slight hand movement (right pole for right turn). Leaning on it a bit gives an added impetus to steer around it. Third, skid on the back side (downhill side) of the mogul. By turning on the front the whole back side is available for a skid. This skid, a hockey stop motion, slows you down.

Turning on the bumps
Choose a path to make easy turns and remain in control.

Managing the moguls
Face downhill, plant the pole, skid to slow speed, and turn on the next bump.

Skids can also control your direction to the next mogul. This is an example of using leverage fore and aft, which you first learned about in Chapter 20, "The Sideslip." It is important enough to deserve a review.

Stand just past the crest on the back side of a mogul and sideslip down it. Move your weight forward and backward from the ankle to produce a forward or backward motion in the sideslip. Aim for where you want to turn on the next mogul and skid right to that spot. Keep skiing moguls, using leverage in your skid to help control your direction and turning on each bump in a narrow path down the hill.

LEVERAGE TO CONTROL SKIDS IN MOGULS

154

Leverage to control skids in moguls

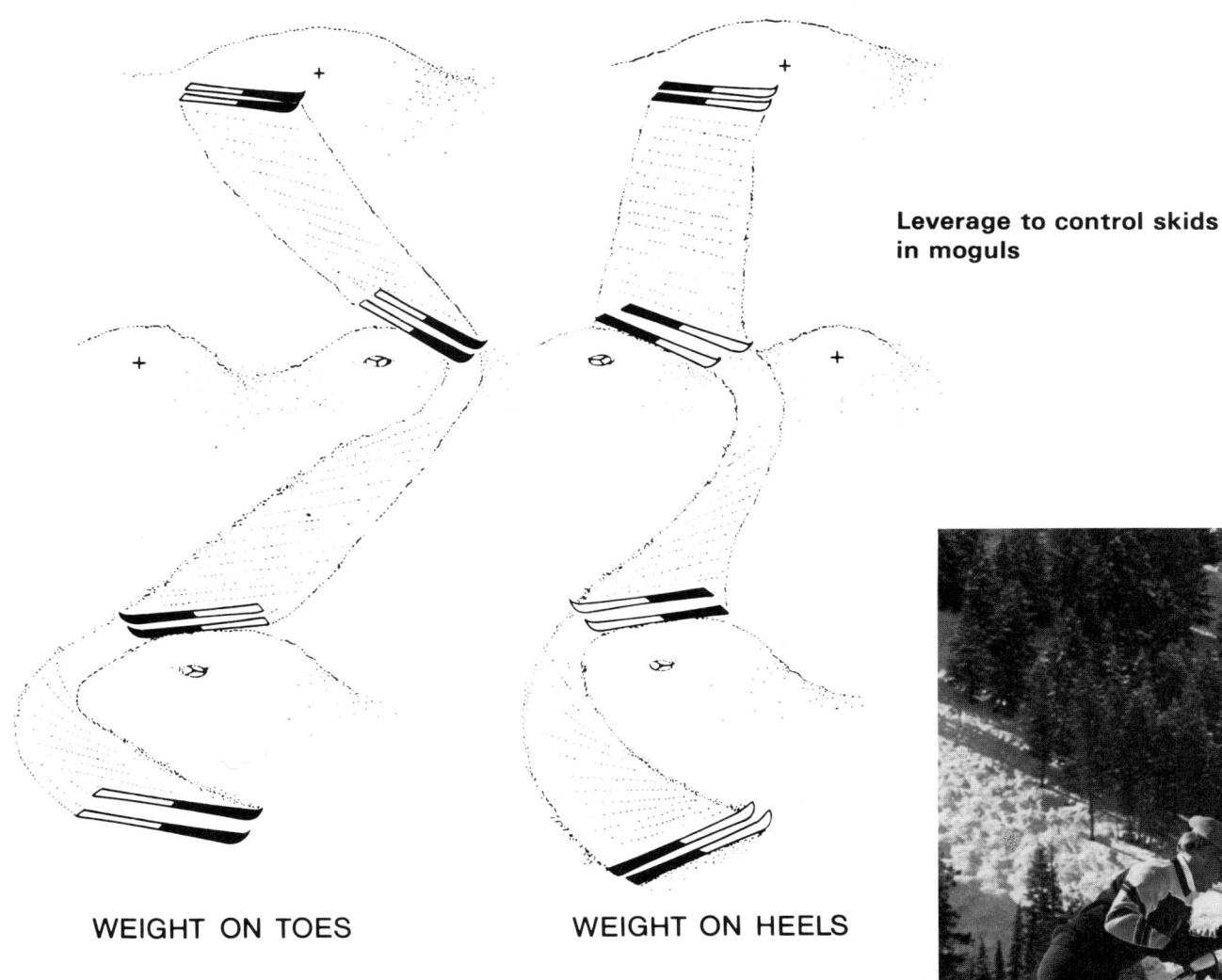

WEIGHT ON TOES   WEIGHT ON HEELS

In the chapter on the hockey stop, you learned to skid from side to side down the hill within a ten-foot-wide path. Use the same actions in the moguls with the addition of turning in an advantageous spot. Go through the bumps, turning on each one and staying within a narrow path. The person who traverses across a whole field of moguls looking for the perfect bump before turning doesn't have fun skiing them.

Once you acquire some confidence in the bumps, you'll start skiing them faster. With speed you will find that they have a tendency to throw you into the air as you reach the crest. You previously found how to ride across a field of moguls letting your knees absorb the bumps. Now let's absorb them while turning on them.

Start from a high body position heading for a bump. Relax your knees and let them fold under you as you approach the crest. Plant your pole and pivot your skis at the crest. Allow your legs to extend on the downhill side to stay in contact with the snow. At the bottom of the mogul you are in a high body position, ready for the next one.

Absorbing a mogul with knee flex

MOGUL TURNS WITH ABSORPTION

Of course, this is merely combining knee flexion and extension with a turn in an advantageous spot. As the bumps get bigger you will find that turning on the ridge portion prior to the summit of the bump is better to avoid being thrown in the air. You will essentially be skiing across a trough, part way up a mogul, skidding down its backside, across a trough, and part way up the next one. This is not the only way to ski moguls, but it's an easy, fun way.

Go back and try serving the tray through the moguls. Then try skiing the bumps, lifting up the inside foot for a turn, changing the weighted ski right at the mogul crest. Don't forget, you must lean forward and drive the knees to start the turn. The mogul field especially is no place to be so timid that you're off balance way back on the tails of your skis. Fear comes from worrying about what might happen. Instead, enjoy what you are doing well. Take a deep breath as you approach a bump and exhale as you turn on it. Be aggressive, shout at them if you like, and show them who's boss. Let your knees move up, down, left and right and swivel your feet in a convex spot. Stay loose. Get a rhythm, turning on every bump, and remember the old expression: "Gopher it!"

Shout at the moguls

30
ACTIVE UNWEIGHTING

By now you've skied enough moguls to feel that it's easier to turn on the convex area of a bump than on a smooth slope. How great it would be if you could place a single mogul anywhere you needed it to make turning easier! Well, you can. It will be an imaginary one, but one that works as well as a real one. To do this, let's first examine another reason why moguls make turns easier.

You remember that skiing up the front crest of a bump gives you a spot to turn free of resistance on the tips and tails. Just as importantly, the bump also pushes you into the air. Every mogul can be considered a miniature ski jump. Since you already know how to jump from a bump, make it more fun with a turn also.

Ski off a bump with enough speed to become airborne. While in the air twist your skis slightly, so that as soon as you land you start off in a new direction.

AIRPLANE TURN

When you reach the crest of a mogul, your momentum is such that your skis want to keep going upward; however, the mogul drops away. The pressure is taken off your skis' edges, or in other words, your skis are *unweighted* with respect to the snow. Whenever the edge pressure is lessened, the skis are easier to turn. An extreme example occurs while riding the chair lift, where the skis are completely unweighted and can be twisted with no effort at all. So, a bump provides a natural method to unweight, which technically is known as *terrain unweighting*. The trick will be to simulate a mogul action to unweight your skis and thus make it easier to change edges to start a turn.

One everyday example of unweighting can be seen on a bathroom scale. Just standing on it, the dial reads one constant weight. As you sink rapidly in the knees, the weight registered decreases.

Airplane turn
While in the air skis twist to land in another direction.

This is *down unweighting*, as in the hockey stop. When you cease the down motion and start rising in the knees, the weight becomes greater than your normal static weight. From the full knee extension, as you sink back down to a normal slightly flexed position, the weight goes toward zero. This sequence of rising up is *up unweighting*.

The longer the unweighting period, the more efficiently you can use it to initiate turns. Imagine you are holding a huge snowball. In dropping it from waist height, the ball is down unweighted and requires a certain time to hit the ground. If you heave the snowball

DOWN UNWEIGHTING   **UP UNWEIGHTING**

Unweighting motions

158

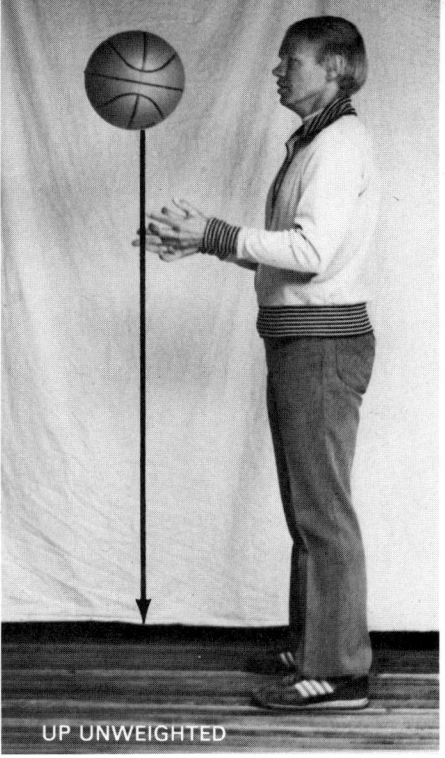

Duration of unweighting
Both basketballs are photographed at the beginning of their weightless period. The arrows indicate the unweighted path. Up unweighting provides a considerably longer period of weightlessness than does down unweighting.

into the air, it takes a longer time to hit the ground. The weightless period in this up unweighting is longer, as the snowball is pushed upward first. Let's see how this works on skis.

Skiing in a traverse, sink down in the knees, then rise sharply enough to push off the snow so that at least the ski tails become airborne. Upon landing, sink down in the knees and resume a traverse. Perform a series of these across the slope, assuming a normal relaxed stance between hops. As you sink down, let your downhill pole touch the snow to trigger the rapid up motion of the hop.

That's the basic motion: sinking down, rising up sharply, and sinking down to finish (down, *up*, down). You've already done these motions more gently while unweighting a single ski in stem maneuvers. In skating down a hill and in lifting the inside ski you more actively sink down, rise up, and sink down again. Let's try the same two-legged bunny hop motion in the fall line, combined now with the skis' rotational displacement (a fancy term for a turn).

THE BUNNY HOP

The bunny hop
The pole is planted to start the upward hop.

Hopping down the fall line

HOPPING IN THE FALL LINE

On a very gentle slope, ski in the fall line. Sink deeply in the knees, touch the right pole to the snow and rise sharply, hopping the ski tails into the air and also twisting the skis to point right. Continue to sink as the tails touch the ground and with a left pole plant rise sharply, twisting the skis across the fall line to point left. Continue hopping in a rhythm down the fall line, making small airborne turns.

You generally don't see people hopping down the hill. We've exaggerated, actually using enough motion to become airborne, in order to learn the basic knee action. The skis could be turned while in the air, but to make it easier on your heart and legs, keep the skis on the snow. Try to keep contact with the snow for better control. Note that the unweighting period comes after rising. While going up you are pushing with extra pressure on the snow, or *weighting* the skis. A stopping of this action, and a sinking down motion, causes the unweighted period. It is during the unweighted period that you initiate your turn. Continuing downward by flexing the knees as you start into the turn extends the unweighting period, allows a greater lateral knee angle and prepares you for the next up motion. That's a lot of words for something you've already done by other means, so on to a smooth turn.

PARALLEL UNWEIGHTED TURN

Skiing across the hill, sink down in the knees. Let your downhill pole touch the snow below your boots and rise up abruptly. While sinking down to a normal stance steer your knees into a turn, transferring weight to the toes of the outside foot. Experiment with varying amounts of unweighting at all speeds and arcs of turns. Less unweighting is needed for high speed, wide radius turns. Increase the unweighting motion to make rapid changes of direction during short radius turns.

Unweighted turn
Unweighting reduces pressure to make the turn initiation easier.

Compare the similarity of this turn to a weight transfer parallel turn. It is really the same process but here you're more dynamic. Rising up, besides reducing friction, has a tendency to flatten the skis, making turn initiation easier. Sinking down, the unweighting period lasts just long enough to change edges for the new arc. You are still driving your knees into the turn and transferring weight to a new (outside) ski, exactly as you have done in all previous turns. Now you are definitely working both knees at the same time. The unweighting gives you time to start rotational movement in a new direction (a turn initiation). You now have the ability to make an extremely short radius turn.

Now repeat an exercise from the hockey stop chapter, with the emphasis on unweighting.

WEDEL THROUGH UNWEIGHTING

Pick a moderate, smooth slope and imagine you are skiing down a ten-foot-wide section of it. Before starting out, begin a down-up-down motion in your knees with about one second between each down. Then push off maintaining this rhythm, making one turn after the other down the fall line. Make continuous turns without traverses between the turns. Once you have the rhythm, repeat on a steeper slope.

You should feel almost as though you are bouncing from foot to foot. Maybe you can relate it to skating on skis down the hill, as it's really the same thing. The downhill pole touches the ground at the end of each "down" as you are about to go "up." To remind yourself, modify the rhythm to say "Down, pole plant up, down, pole plant up. . . ."

The pole is an aid to timing and balance. You can also push on it to increase the upward thrust and to help deflect the skis. As in

Unweighted wedel

all turns, it's right pole for right turn, left pole for left turn; in other words, the downhill pole. If you are facing downhill, a very slight motion of the wrist and hand as you sink down for the hop will touch the pole to the snow just out from the boots. The pole remains in only long enough to start to ski around it, which is enough time to transfer weight to the outside ski.

When you have a good feeling for up unweighting you will find how much is needed in each turn and you can become more subtle in your motions. A gentle slow unweighting is all that's required to start a large round turn, whereas a dynamic rapid motion may be needed for a quick turn. Refine your movements so they are smooth, not jerky. Apply what you know about skidding to the finish of the turns, feeling the difference between a skidded and a rounded carved turn. Relate this unweighting movement to all the previous exercises which called for knee movements up and down.

In summary, when you can find a bump, turn on it. If there is no bump where you want it, simulate the bump's action by actively unweighting to start a turn.

Now that you realize how small bumps can help unweight you, it's time to observe macro (large) terrain changes and see how they also unweight you to aid a turn.

Find a hill with a gully or depression between two rounded convex slopes. Ski down one slope and turn in the gully. Repeat by skiing down the slope, crossing the gully, and turn while skiing up the slope on the other side. Note how much easier it is to turn high on the slope. You'll feel compressed against the skis while crossing the gully and feel light on your feet as you ski up the convex slope.

So you don't need a small bump to turn on. A large terrain change will also unweight you. Skiing from wall to wall in a gully is an exhilarating experience where you'll feel suspended in air, thanks to centrifugal force. Look for runs at a ski area followed by the name "Gulch." Some "Bowl" runs will also have gullies in them. Any convex terrain will make your turns easier. The sharper it is, and the faster you're traveling, the less active unweighting you'll need from knee actions. Any change in the slope to a steeper pitch (a *transition*) also offers a convenient convex surface on which to turn.

Have you noticed in this section that parallel turns are really

Pole plant
An efficient pole plant has no wasted motions.

USING TERRAIN TO ADVANTAGE

easier than you thought? You've found previously that lateral knee movements control the edge angles. Now vertical knee actions help control your effective weight, to easily change edges for turning. Your knees now know all the ins and outs of ups and downs.

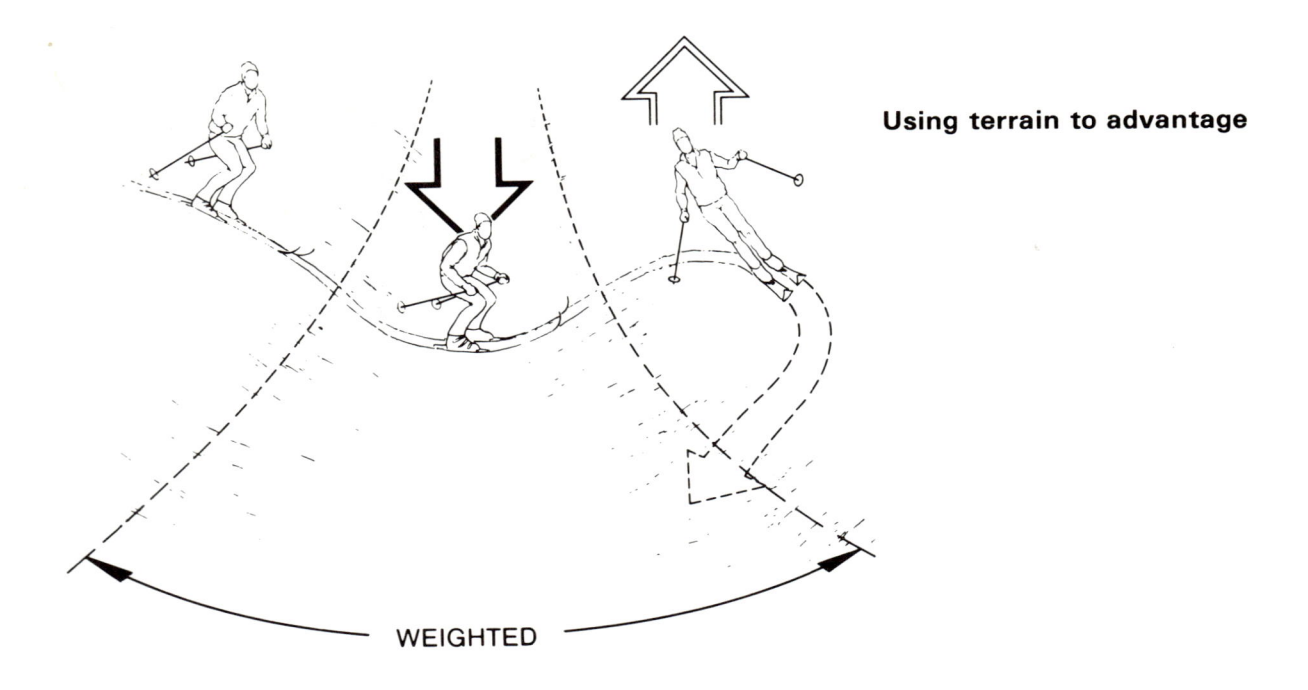

Using terrain to advantage

WEIGHTED

31

SPEEDY SKIING

By this time you can enjoy skiing fast when conditions permit. With your ability to control edges and to slow down at will, speed is adding a new dimension to your enjoyment. An expert makes speedy skiing look easy, and indeed it is. Turns require less steering and unweighting as the skis perform more of the work. However, at high speed you will encounter new forces that were overshadowed by gravity at slower speeds; you will have to learn to adjust to them.

The most obvious effect of speed is that you cover a lot of ground in a short period of time. Traveling at just 20 m.p.h., almost slalom racing speed, you travel thirty feet every second. Watching the ground at your feet only shows where you've been by the time your brain responds. You must look far enough ahead to plan your next two or three turns. Reaction time has to be fine tuned. That means practicing proper technique and body position until your subconscious can act instinctively. You don't have time to consciously "think aloud" all the complex motions needed for everyday walking, let alone fast skiing.

Confidence in your ability is the name of the game. A positive mental attitude frees your mind to concentrate on skiing. Fear only paralyzes the body. The trick is to reach a speed that is invigorating but not mind numbing. Too frequently we think about making turns a certain distance apart, and then get on a steeper slope and find the speed overwhelming. One solution is to change the turn rhythm.

VARYING TURN RHYTHM

Ski a slope that varies in pitch, starting out on a gentle section at a comfortable speed. Concentrate on maintaining a constant speed. As the pitch increases, increase your turn rhythm. You'll be making turns closer together to keep the same velocity.

The best way to keep your speed in control is to use gravity. As the pitch steepens, *finish your turns more*. This means rounding the end of the turn, so that you are skiing in an arc back up the hill. Start your new turn only after gravity has slowed you down.

At high speed all good skiers share a common characteristic. They ski efficiently from the feet and knees, because there simply isn't enough time to move the upper body around uselessly. If you're skiing fast in the fall line, you may want to review the chapter "Upper Body Position." Something as simple as a hand drawn back out of position may require an extra fifth of a second to move for a pole plant. At 20 m.p.h. that's an additional six feet, half the distance from one mogul to the next.

You're certainly familiar with gravity pulling you down the hill. This creates a certain inertia in your body, or as Newton put it, bodies in motion will continue in motion until acted upon by other forces. Speed doesn't hurt; suddenly stopping against a tree does. Whenever you change direction you resist inertia. Imagine you are skiing down a hill and rapidly ski up a bump. Your body had been traveling downward, but suddenly your feet are pushing you upward. This physical reluctance of your body to immediately move upward causes a downward weighting onto the skis. In other words, when skiing up a bump you become heavier. The faster you ski up a bump, or the sharper the bump rises, the more centrifugal force tries to squash you into the hill. Gravity is easily overcome by centrifugal force, which is why we can scare ourselves silly hanging suspended upside down on some amusement park rides. To reduce pressure from centrifugal force, you can retract your legs as you ski over a bump, so that your body is not pushed upward as much.

After skiing over the crest of a bump, the terrain falls away as

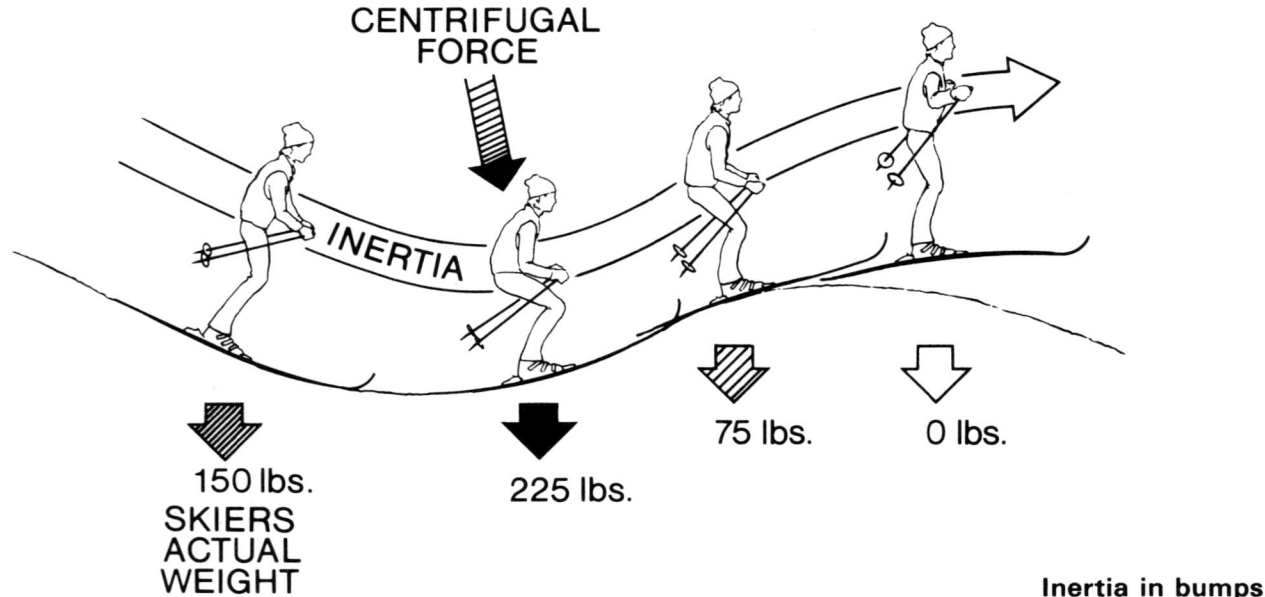

Inertia in bumps

your body continues in a straight line until gravity pulls you back down. This unweighting effect makes it easier to turn on a mogul crest than in the gulley between bumps. Of course, with enough speed inertia overcomes gravity and you become airborne. This momentary weightlessness is not always a desirable state of affairs, as what goes up. . . . You can maintain some pressure on the snow by extending your legs after passing the mogul crest. (Now aren't you glad you already retracted them skiing up the bump, so you have more leg length left to extend?)

Anytime you turn you are also changing direction and thus resisting inertia. Your body wants to go in a straight line, but your ski edges are digging into the snow and pulling you around. Centrifugal force tries to "push" you outward, so you must lean inward, toward the center of the turn, to avoid falling. This leaning is a dynamic position, one that won't work when you're standing still or in a traverse. You are now perfectly balanced against your feet, resisting both gravity and inertia. The centrifugal force helps your turn by increasing weight on the skis, putting them into more reverse camber. At slow speeds we often rely on skidding a ski's tail to force a turn, whereas at higher speeds we can thus rely on natural forces to carve a turn.

While bicycling or running you assume an inward lean automatically in a turn. Centrifugal force is the reason auto race tracks are frequently tilted inward on the corners. Without the banked turn the cars would skid out of control. Your skis will skid excessively also, unless you angle them against the snow. Higher speeds require extra edging. The most effective way to increase edging is through a low, flexed position, the same one racers use when rounding a gate. Standing straight in the knees eliminates lateral movement, and hence there can be no edging. As you flex more in the knees,

Inward lean against the centrifugal force of a turn

Knee and hip angulation
Sideways bending at the waist increases edge angle while maintaining balance over the feet.

the amount of possible edging increases. At high speed, bending sideways or angulating from your hip increases the ski edging while still keeping your center of mass acting through your feet. Use this low position combined with inward lean to maintain your balance toward the end of the turn, when centrifugal force is greatest. Extend to a more upright stance to maintain snow contact at the start of the next turn.

Whenever you turn, centrifugal force acts in a different direction. This means you must lean inward to your right for a right turn, or to your left for a left turn. Unless you step outward, your center of mass must move left or right to balance at the start of each turn. This lean or "incline" in the turn direction is called *inclination*. It can be a little scary at first, until you realize that centrifugal force will hold you up. As your speed increases, incline your body more toward the turn center. An early inclination will actually get you off your edges. Then, as you lean into the new turn, your skis are automatically put on their new edges, and centrifugal force takes over.

Let's forget about angulation and all that technical jazz for a moment, and learn an easy, fun turn by just leaning.

BANKED TURNS

Ski at moderate speed on a smooth slope. Stand fairly upright and start your turn by leaning your whole body sideways toward the inside of the turn. Stand square to your skis, riding with them the way they are pointed. As you accelerate, increase your inclination to balance centrifugal force. Return to an upright position and lean in the opposite direction to initiate a new turn. If you need to, use a small unweighting motion to help change edges, and a pole plant for balance. Also try stepping uphill to help start the turn.

Banking your body is a great way to relax tired thigh muscles, as you can stand quite upright. You'll feel as though you're becoming part of the terrain, flying down the mountain on autopilot. Don't confuse banking your body with banking just the ski bottoms, which can be done by angulation.

Banked turns
A relaxing way to ski easy terrain.

Inclination should be a part of each turn, but not necessarily from the upright stance you just used. Unfortunately, you don't get something for nothing, or everyone would totally bank each turn. You'll need wide open slopes to ski this way, as banked turns sacrifice control over turn radius. Normally you determine your path by steering the lower legs and by varying edge angle, both of which require the flexed knee position missing in pure banking. When you simply lean your skis onto an edge you rely on them to take you where they will. Their exact path will depend upon your speed, the slope pitch, and the length, side cut, and flex of your particular skis.

In pure banking you'll also need uniform slopes free of surprises to preserve your balance. When banking, your center of mass is quite a distance inward from your feet. A disturbance such as a bump or hidden icy patch could require greater edging than the lean angle supplies, causing your feet to slide outward. This disrupts the delicate balance of gravity, centrifugal force, and ski edge friction. In other words, you're about to execute a perfect nose plow. In normal, more strenuous skiing, you would incline into the turn, as a racer does, but also angulate with flexed knees and advanced hip for outward lean of the upper body. This places your center of mass lower and more directly over the feet. When additional edging is suddenly required a quick knee or hip thrust maintains balance.

At higher speeds you'll use more leverage to compensate for centrifugal force. When starting a turn this force is small. Place your weight on the soft forebody of the ski to put it in reverse camber

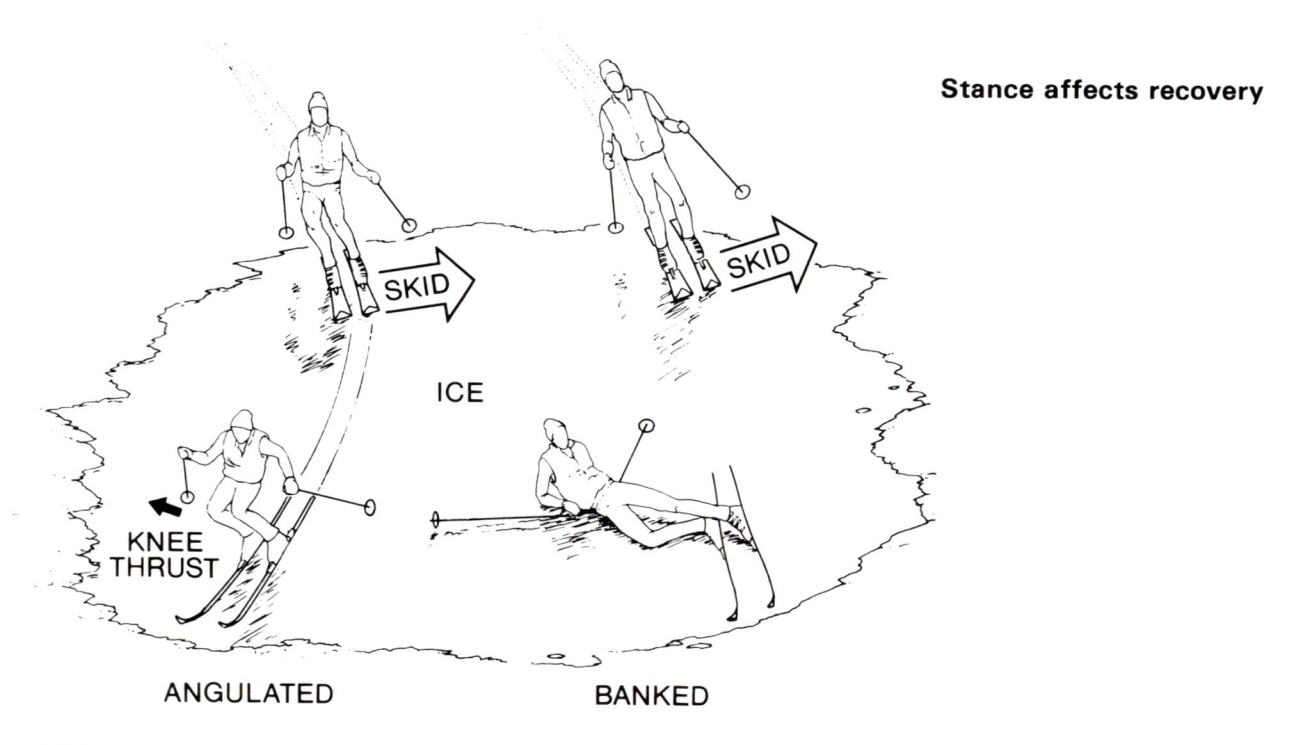

Stance affects recovery

ANGULATED   BANKED

170

Changing edges
A pure banked stance requires greater body motion to change edges than does an angulated stance.

and help determine the turning arc. Going into the fall line the centrifugal force has built up and weight should be evenly distributed along the whole ski length. Finishing the turn, centrifugal force and gravity act in about the same direction, and you should have weight back on the stiffer, straighter tail to complete the same arc turn. Placing weight on the wrong sections of the skis can cause them to chatter or to completely skid out of a turn.

Wind resistance greatly affects speed. Less surface area means less drag, which means more speed. This has led to the streamlined downhill racing position called the *tuck*. To appreciate the force of air, let's try one.

A TUCK POSITION

On a smooth, gentle slope, start down the fall line in an upright position. Then drop into a tuck, with the thighs parallel to skis and an extreme folding at the waist, so your back is also almost parallel to the skis. Hands are in front and poles close to the sides. To see where you are going crane your chin upward. Your speed will decrease immediately when you stand upright again.

Besides reducing wind resistance, stability at speed is increased with a tuck, since your center of gravity is lowered. Although the hips end up behind the boots, the upper body and hands counterbalance due to the folded waist, so your weight is still centered over the feet. Unfortunately the thigh muscles tire rapidly in this position and the knees have little additional shock absorbing capacity. Be sure to rise before riding up over a bump. Turns are made by driving the bent knees where you want to go. The tuck is fun once in a while, and will be useful to get you across long flat stretches of terrain. In case you get really enthralled with speed, you'll also need 220 cm skis, secret wax formulas, skintight slick suits, curved wraparound poles, a crash helmet, and good accident insurance.

Tuck position
In this recreational version of the racing tuck, the thighs are slightly upright for maximum endurance while still maintaining a streamlined shape.

section V
DYNAMIC ACTIONS

At this stage you're skiing all intermediate trails and occasionally an advanced one. You're looking for additional speed control and turning ability for steeper slopes, and you'd like to ski all snow conditions. In this section you'll discover that a dynamic edge set will unweight your skis with a rebound action. Coupling the rebound with a twisted torso, you'll learn to make an easy, rapid turn, one especially useful in the moguls. With increased speed you'll actively move your legs up and down to absorb the bumpy terrain. To ski more efficiently, you'll carve, fully utilizing the ski's design. You'll learn some racing step turns and finally apply all your technique to the pleasures of powder, and the technical demands of ice.

32

ANTICIPATION AND REBOUND UNWEIGHTING

Anticipation simply means a movement of part of the body in the direction of an intended turn, before the turn is made. Hence the body appears to "anticipate" a turn.

Now you know one reason I've emphasized the uphill ski ahead, and the upper body facing slightly downhill. This would be a good time to return to the chapter "Upper Body Position." There we exaggerated facing downhill, skiing the fall line while "serving a tray." You can also get a feeling of anticipation in a wider turn.

Ski at moderate speed on a smooth intermediate slope. To begin each turn, rotate your head, arms, chest and hips toward the direction of your turn, and also incline your body in that direction. As your skis flatten on the snow, your feet and lower legs will be drawn into the turn. Try these turns with an up-down motion to unweight the ski edges to initiate the edge change.

Anticipating should make your turns easier. Your feet follow your body into a turn. However, it's still work to unweight the skis, which is required for shorter radius turns. But you will shortly learn a magic turn which will both control your speed and make your skis turn by themselves. As a warm-up for this secret, practice hockey stops to control your speed and to set your edges.

As you ski steeper slopes, you must skid more to check your speed. Suppose you're driving a car down an icy road, a little faster than you should, and you see a curve ahead. When is the best time to slow down? Before the curve. Hit the brakes, steer around the curve, even accelerate around it to keep from spinning out, then hit the brakes again afterwards if necessary. The same principle applies to skiing, where your brakes are the edges. To control speed, you can skid prior to a turn. It may seem strange to turn your

ANTICIPATED PARALLEL TURN

Anticipated turn
The skis twist to line up with the body.

skis uphill to skid when you want to turn them downhill to cross the fall line. But it's not really extra work to turn from that position.

Imagine you're skiing along and decide to slow down with a skid or hockey stop motion. You sink down and twist the feet under you to point the skis across the fall line, letting your upper body remain quiet, facing downhill. But you didn't see a sheer cliff ahead and you ski off of it. There you are in midair, trying to skid, but it just doesn't work too well. Your body is all twisted, upper body one way, lower body another. As you fall, your body will untwist. Since there are no longer any frictional forces to resist the twisted muscles, your body can return to a normal position with upper and lower sections aligned. Now, do you think you'll generally face the way the upper or lower body was pointed when you land? Since most of the mass of the body is in the upper section (head, arms, chest, hips) you would land mostly facing that way. Now, further imagine that there is a slippery rope hanging alongside you in midair, which you grasp with one hand. The rope gives you enough stability so that your torso cannot untwist at all. Your lower body (legs and feet) will untwist completely to face the same way your upper body is pointing. Now, why does it have to be a cliff? How about a big bump, a small bump, or an imaginary bump? Now do you see what we're aiming at? That had to be an imaginary exercise (I kept losing students over cliffs), so now let's try a real one.

REBOUND GARLANDS

Traverse across a hill at moderate speed. Slow down by a hockey stop motion, or skid, sinking rapidly in the knees and steering the skis uphill. Make this motion dynamic and just long enough to "hit" the edges (a final uphill knee thrust) at the end of the down motion. Plant the downhill pole at this instant, and immediately straighten up to resume a traverse. Do a series of these in both directions, alternating edge set and traverse. Feel your skis automatically resume the traverse for you after the sharp edge set.

Rebound garlands
Skis automatically turn toward the fall line after an anticipated edge set.

It takes no effort at all to traverse again after a sharp edge set. In fact, if you are dynamic enough, you will find your traverse becomes a little steeper after each edge set. Your skis may even leave the snow momentarily to magically spring back into the traverse. This sharp edge set is known as a *check*. It is made most effectively by stopping your downward knee flex, causing the skis to be weighted and thus to bite into the snow better.

Remember the elements: upper body facing downhill, lower body twisting underneath to skid, and knee motion vertically downward and laterally uphill to set the edges. In more detail, you are winding up your body by turning your legs uphill underneath you. This turns you into a powerful coiled spring waiting to unwind. The more you wind up, the more violently or rapidly you can unwind. A cessation of downward knee movement in your skis will hit the edges or *create a platform*. The skid lasts as long as necessary but the final edge set or check is a rapid movement, perhaps one-tenth of a second, and is accompanied by a pole plant. This pole plant acts like the rope on the cliff: it stabilizes your upper body and prevents it from untwisting back up the hill to align with the legs. Additionally, the pole balances your body so weight can be transferred to the uphill ski for a turn.

You have previously been unweighting your skis by rising up before sinking down. Now you should feel your skis being automatically pushed off the snow. The final edge set has created a tremendous pressure. Your body is compressed and wants to spring upward in addition to wanting to untwist. You are now both a coiled and a compressed spring. The edge set puts pressure on your skis. They are in extreme reverse camber and are pushing back up like a leaf spring on a car. These dynamic forces thrust you upward, just as a mogul or a violent unweighting would. In short, all those words add up to *rebound unweighting*.

As soon as the final edge set occurs, let your knees roll into the fall line. This releases the edge pressure and your skis twist in the direction your body is facing. Go back and try the checking motion in the chapter on downstem turns. Do them until you really have the feeling of rebounding off the snow. Now try a pure parallel turn.

From a steep traverse, sink and twist the skis uphill under you. Skid to an abrupt edge set with a short, rapid down motion. Aid the rebound by flattening the skis with the knees, letting your skis turn into the fall line. Finish the turn out of the fall line with steering and edging. Repeat, starting your skis turning into the fall line immediately after the snow flies out from your skis in an edge set. Ski, making one turn after another down the fall line with a constant rhythm of pressure, release, pressure, release. Experiment with varying amounts of anticipation (twisting) and with amounts of pressure in an edge set to see how rapidly the skis turn. Exaggerate knee flex during edge set to create a more powerful rebound force.

The turn is started immediately after the final edge set, or greatest pressure. It requires knee movement downward to set the

REBOUND PARALLEL TURN

Rebound parallel turn
The edge set unweights and the anticipation twists the skis into an effortless turn. Notice how rapidly the rebound pushes the skier upward from the edge set.

FALL LINE

edges, and knee extension immediately after that platform phase so the knees can sink for the next edge set. All I'm really saying is make the snow fly up from your skidded edges, then start a turn.

Perhaps you are able to turn so rapidly that you have trouble keeping your balance. This is natural, as your skis have taken over some of the turning effort. Your skis may shoot or "jet" ahead of you as you start the turn. If so, besides inclining your body inward for the turn, also thrust your torso forward into that turn, to keep up with the skis. We'll talk more about this in the chapter titled "Weight Distribution and 'Sitting Back.'"

You may feel thrown into the air by the rebound force. Good! That means you're checking effectively. To keep your skis on the snow, relax your legs after the check. Let them extend from their flexed position. They have to stretch out to be able to flex again for the next check, and the start of the turn is the only time you'll have to extend them. At higher speeds and more dynamic edge sets, you can forcefully extend your legs after the check, to maintain snow contact. We'll explore this concept in detail in the chapter titled "Avalement."

This rebound turn with anticipation applies in all situations. With modifications, it is a turn for any slope or snow condition. The important aspect of it is winding up your body, causing your skis to turn uphill prior to changing edges for a new turn. Technically, this short radius uphill skid is known as a *pre-turn*. For a rapid turn on a steep slope, or in moguls, you must be very dynamic with a large ski displacement across your path of motion. This causes a greater twisted position of the lower to upper body, and a more violent rebound. For a wide radius turn on a gentle slope you can still turn with anticipation. However, since you don't need to slow down as much or to turn as sharply, you'll only need a small pre-turn, little checking action, and a lesser twisting of your body. Let's try one.

Traverse on a gentle smooth slope. Sink down to start a turn, steering your skis uphill slightly. During this gentle edge set, plant the lower pole. Then rise, transferring weight while changing edges to turn the skis in a wide arc toward the fall line.

TURNING WITH ANTICIPATION ON A GENTLE SLOPE

Whether on steep or gentle slopes, a pre-turn uphill precedes starting the actual turn into the fall line. The vertical knee actions are the same as for up unweighting (down, up, down), but now your skis rebound gently off the snow, and you don't have to hop or lift them. Your "S" turn tracks down the hill should show a skid at the junction of the upper and lower halves of the "S." The tighter the radius of the turn, the more pronounced the skid.

Skiing with anticipation, particularly in shorter radius mogul turns, relies heavily on a quiet upper body. Remind yourself to turn your skis from the knees and feet. Consider the uphill side of your torso as being ahead of the body, and the downhill side as being behind the body. Anytime your uphill hip, shoulder, or even hand

Turn on a gentle slope
Although little rebound is needed for a long radius turn, the skis still turn uphill slightly as you sink and anticipate a turn.

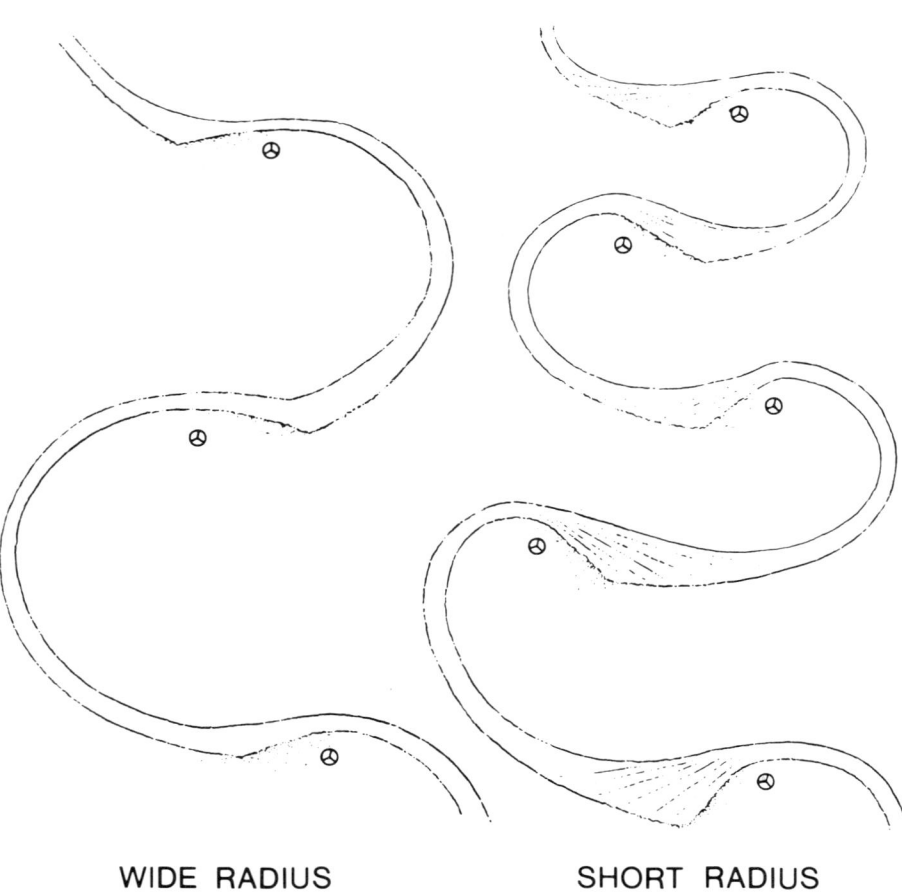

Anticipated tracks

WIDE RADIUS   SHORT RADIUS

drops behind your body, you are in trouble. That means that as you finish a turn your planted pole must come out of the snow before your body skis past it, to prevent twisting your torso back up the hill. Keep the hands where you can see them out of the corners of your eyes and you are always ready for the next turn.

Rebounding easily handles fall line skiing, so let's try some.

Ski the fall line with a rhythm of pressure, release, pressure, release. Keep the skis always turning, and make a definite edge set before turning into the fall line.

SHORTSWING

Shortswing
Anticipation and rebounds result in quick turns on this steep slope.

181

Look back at your tracks to verify you don't have any traverse sections. *Shortswing* is really the same wedel you have done several times. The more modern term generally applies to repeated round, parallel turns on steeper terrain, with a definite rebound action.

You've come to realize that steeper hills require more edge set and sharper turns to control speed. Make your turns more complete by skiing back up the hill. Plant your pole directly down the fall line for short turns. When the terrain changes you must vary the amount of anticipation and edge set.

SHORTSWING IN VARYING TERRAIN

Choose a hill with several changes in pitch. Pick a fifteen-foot-wide path, defined by imaginary boundaries down the fall line. Start straight downhill in this path until you reach a comfortable speed, then make one round rebound turn after another. Maintain your original speed all the way down the hill. This means frequent short radius turns on the steep terrain, and more relaxed wider turns on the flats.

If you enjoy these rebound turns on steep terrain, you may want to see how frequently you can turn. The number per second will depend on slope, ski length, and your reactions, but you may be able to make two turns per second. It's a good way to warm up on cold days.

Whether you make long or short radius turns, look frequently at your tracks. If they show a small radius pre-turn just before changing edges to start a new turn, you have anticipated the turn. Practice leaving tracks like these. They are the slope signature of a true expert who knows how to ski with anticipation, letting his skis work for him.

33

ANTICIPATION IN THE BUMPS

Moguls have grown in size and number as a result of shorter skis, better technique and more skiers. Anticipation provides the best way to both control speed and rapidly change direction in an ocean of bumps.

You've found that skiing with a check prior to a turn will both slow you down and rebound the legs in a rapid turn. Let's go back to our friendly local mogul and examine the anticipation effect on it.

Stand on the crest of a sharp mogul, with tips and tails off the snow. "Wind up" your body by facing your upper body straight downhill, and turning skis at a right angle to the fall line. Plant your lower pole on the downhill side of the crest of the bump, below the boots, and press on it. Sink very low in the knees, then spring straight up, still leaning on the pole. Let your skis turn across the bump as your lower body rapidly untwists. Steer your feet and flex to finish the turn, skidding down the back side of the mogul. Get the feeling that the skis turned by themselves into the fall line without having been forced.

STATIONARY ANTICIPATED TURN

You previously found many beneficial reasons to turn on the ridge of a mogul (see the chapter "Mogul Mastery"). Now your own body position makes a turn automatic. Instead of just skiing up to the crest of a mogul to turn, you can now check speed on a mogul, make the final edge set at the crest, and let your skis untwist into the turn. Let's practice skidding into the correct spot.

From a traverse, ski up a mogul, turning your skis under you uphill and skidding on the edges. End up on the crest with a sharp edge set and a pole plant on the ridge downhill of your boots.

CHECKING ON A MOGUL

Mogul turn from a standstill
Anticipating on a bump, leaning on the pole, and releasing edges results in a turn.

Checking on a mogul

Practice skidding to a stop on each mogul crest starting from the back (downhill) side of the next higher mogul.

This is simply a hockey stop ending up on the ridge of a bump. Now you can see why you planted a pole at the end of a hockey stop. Instead of a complete stop you'll be skidding almost to a stop, and then using the pole plant to aid the turn. Due to higher speed and the fact that the bump is rising beneath you, extensive knee flex is required to skid on it. You are both soaking up the bump and also down unweighting to pre-turn the skis and set the edges.

Once you can check stop on a mogul, use the motion just to slow down and set up your body for a turn.

Check your speed into a mogul with an uphill skidding action. Make a final sharp edge set and pole plant on the ridge. Let your skis turn across the ridge and skid down the back side up onto the next mogul, again making a final edge set on the ridge, turning and continuing through the mogul field in this way. Be dynamic and make the snow fly up from your edges.

During the rapid ski displacements your torso should face down the fall line constantly, without twisting motions. Your lower body only briefly aligns with your upper as the skis pivot from one edge set to another.

In learning the hockey stop, you skidded straight down a hill, turning from side to side. You're now doing the same thing in the moguls, with more emphasis on an edge set to create a platform and aid in rebounding. A skid before the turn and one after the turn in fact become one and the same.

As in all skids, your weight should end up on the lower ski, with your upper body angled over that ski. Weight is immediately transferred to the outer ski as you start the turn. It's all too easy to revert to hugging the hill when those monstrous bumps rear their ugly heads at you. Be a little aggressive and stay forward over your downhill foot.

TURNING ON A MOGUL WITH ANTICIPATION

Anticipated turn on a mogul
Check on the bumps and always face downhill.

Weight transfer in bumps
Transfer weight immediately at the turn point and stay forward over the skis.

WEIGHT TRANSFER IN BUMPS

In a gentle mogul field check your speed approaching the uphill ridge of a bump. Lift up your uphill ski so that you are balanced on the downhill one. With the final edge set, step to the unweighted ski which swings into the turn. Lift up your new uphill ski as you skid at the next bump, and continue in this fashion.

Normally two skis are needed on the snow for balance, but weight is still transferred from foot to foot, as this exercise exaggerates.

To keep an anticipated position, a good pole plant is essential. At higher speeds the pole plant must be placed ahead of the body, to a position even with where the edge set will occur. To do this, flick the wrist upwards, so the thumb rises and the basket goes ahead of the body. Little forearm movement is needed and your knuckles still point ahead the way your body is traveling. Good quality poles are well balanced for this motion, and they feel light in the basket area. Your elbows should still be somewhat away from your body, so that the pole plant goes in vertically and not at an angle.

Choosing a *line*, or path, through the bumps is important. A high line passes over the tops of the moguls. A line around the bumps will be faster. You'll probably want to choose a path that's a combination. From the top of the run, you shouldn't try to decide exactly where you will make each turn. Rather, fix a general idea of where you're headed and how fast you want to go. Choose only a first turning point, one directly down the fall line from your starting point. Great mogul skiers now take a deep breath and go into a relaxed concentration. Visualize yourself making a great run down your chosen line, push off, and do it.

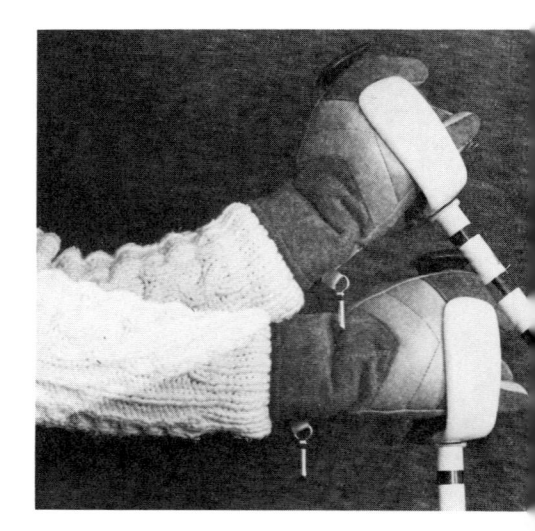

Efficient pole plant
Only the wrist and forearm are needed to flick out the pole for a plant.

As you gain confidence in the bumps you'll begin to express your own creativity and individuality. With more speed you may enjoy turning on a lower portion of a mogul and skiing around it to bank against the next one. When they are close together perhaps you will jump from the uphill side of one to the downhill side of the next. You may like to step your turns with a stem-like action for efficiency. Instead of skidding you may begin to ski rounder, carved turns. Whatever your style, you must be fluid and conservative of motion. A good mogul skier is so smooth and quiet you almost don't realize how fast he is going. Skiing with anticipation is a beautiful sight, particularly in soft snow with clouds of fluff billowing up from your edges at each mogul. The snow snakes will think twice about coming up to grab at your ankle when you're skiing this hot.

Versatility in the moguls
With increasing confidence you'll find moguls can be a playground in which to express your own personal style and inventiveness.

34

WEIGHT DISTRIBUTION AND "SITTING BACK"

I am going to destroy a myth. You may have cultivated it while admiring dramatic photos of expert skiers who are apparently balanced on the last inch and a quarter of their skis. There is no such thing as a useful sitting back position. Every accomplished skier strives to be balanced over his feet. Just as inward lean is only helpful while balancing against centrifugal force, sitting back is only useful while balancing against short-term dynamic forces. Neither position will work for continuous skiing.

Imagine riding a bus down the steepest hill in your town. Due to the rush hour crowd you must stand in the aisle, a package under each arm. Traveling at a constant 20 m.p.h. down the hill, you easily stand upright and balanced over your feet. Suddenly a pedestrian darts in front of the bus, and the driver slams on the brakes. Now you're no longer in balance. Your feet are slowing rapidly and you're in danger of tumbling headfirst onto your nose. You respond the only possible way, by flexing deeply in the knees and pushing your head, torso, and thighs backward. Once again you're balanced comfortably against your feet as the bus squeals to a stop. At this instant a friend glances out his second floor window and sees you apparently sitting way back. Knowing that you're one of the best bus riders in the county, he decides to imitate your style. Next day he "sits back" throughout his ride along the valley road, and arrives at work exhausted, covered with dust from numerous falls, and convinced he needs more practice to equal you.

Efficient skiing, like efficient bus riding, demands that you always stand on your feet balanced against all forces. However, rapid changes of speed create forces that can make you seemingly violate gravity. Take along a photographer friend and let's see how sitting back applies to your skiing.

Stand comfortably on the snow and have your friend snap the

Balance range
The feet support the body over a limited range of motion.

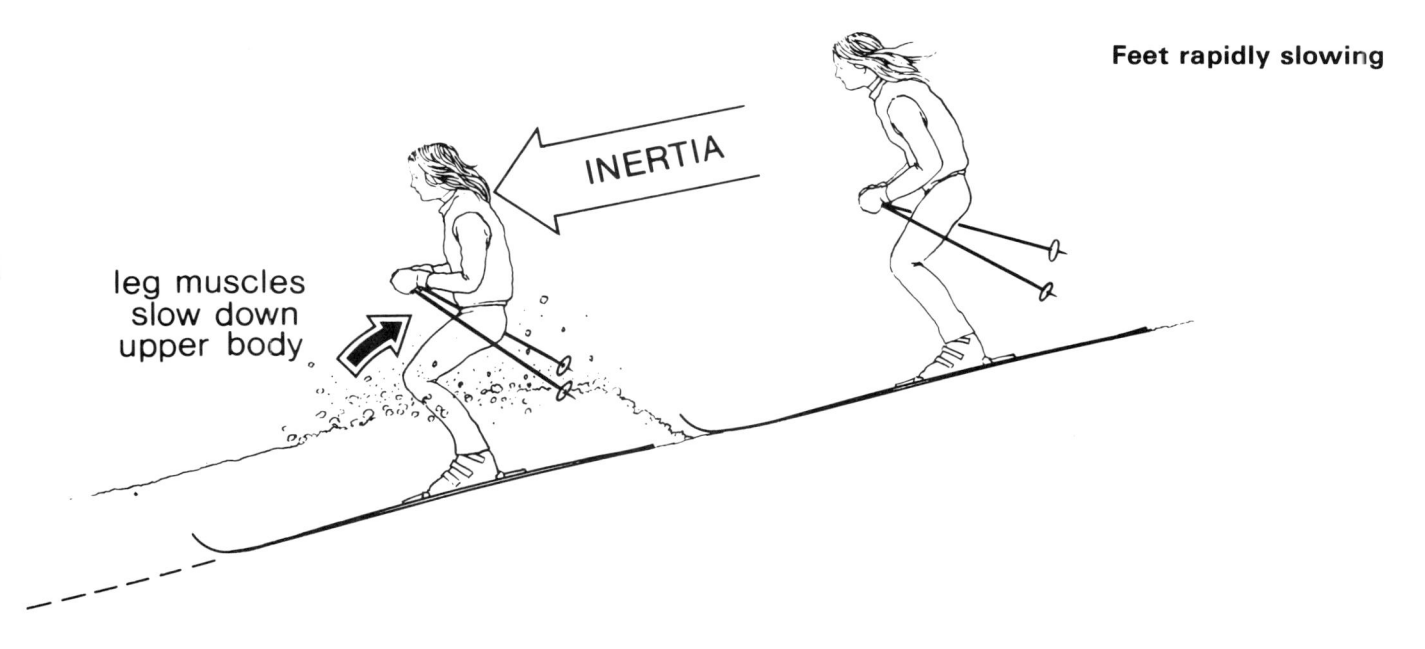

first photo. It will show you slightly flexed, shins against the boot tongues, and your upper body in a line over your feet. Your center of mass (located approximately behind the bellybutton) is pulled by gravity through the balls of the feet. Anytime you lean forward or backward more than about six inches, the center of mass is beyond the supporting area of the feet, your muscles become strained and you're in danger of falling.

You use the same balanced position in straight running down the hill at any speed. However, suddenly you slow down by skiing from ice into heavy untracked snow. That is, your feet slow down. Momentum of the rest of your body tries to throw you into a noseplow, but you resist this inertial force by flexing deeply in the knees and tensing calf, thigh, and trunk muscles to slow down your upper body. A photo at this instant shows you "back," but only because you are now resisting both gravity downward and inertia forward. The resultant total of these two forces is still balanced through your feet.

Feet rapidly slowing

189

Of course, more than changing snow conditions will rapidly slow down your feet. You could also have skidded on your edges, resulting in a back position. In any event, once you do either stop or reach a constant speed, the inertial forces disappear and you again stand upright, balanced against only gravity.

While skiing bumpy terrain your speed varies rapidly. Heading up a hill or mogul, centrifugal force presses you toward the snow, and you apparently defy gravity by being suspended "backward." This extra force also creates additional friction to slow down the skis, which you then resist by pushing the torso backward against the feet. Your friend snaps photos as you climb the bump near the crest, which show you sitting back even though you know by feel that you are perfectly balanced on your feet, with shins pressed forward against the boot tongues.

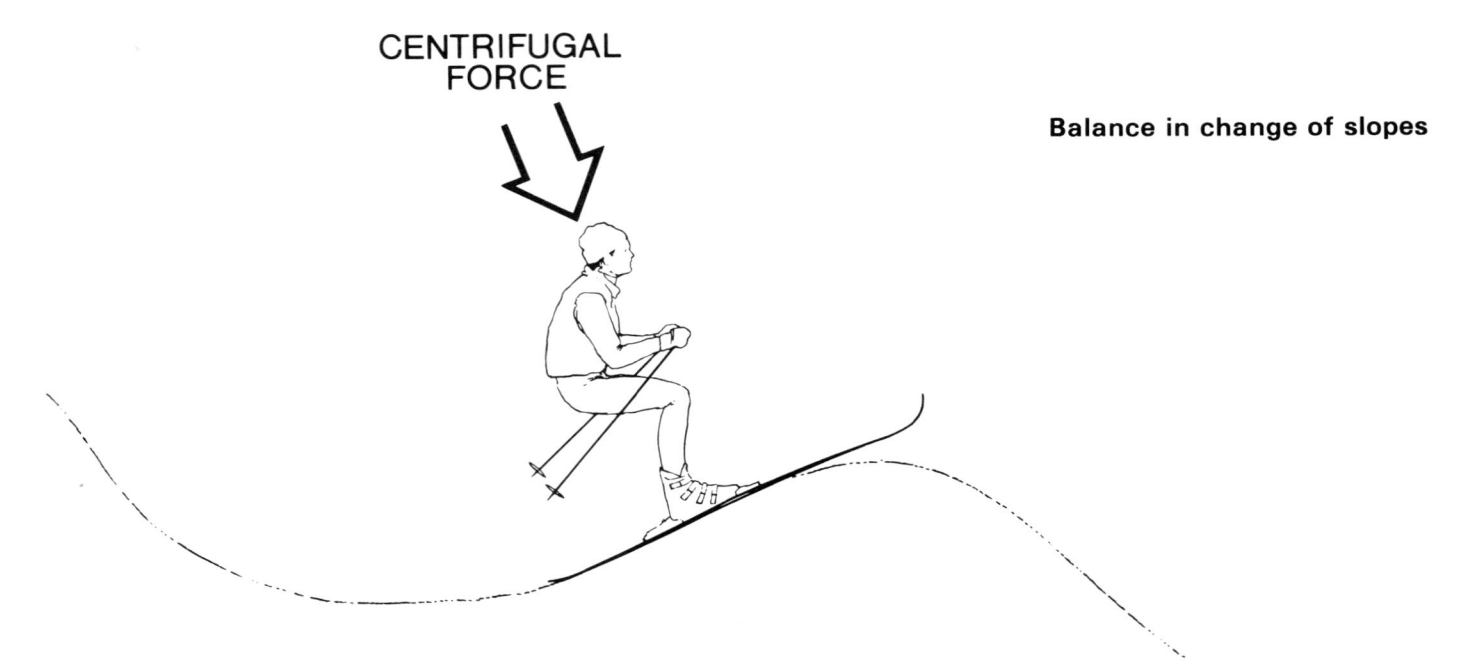

Balance in change of slopes

One other unusual phenomenon happens when skiing between short bumps or in tight turns—the feet travel a longer path than the head. Thus even if your skis magically did not slow down due to increased friction, your upper body would still attempt a head plant. Once again you must sit back to push against the feet, trying to slow down your trunk or speed up the skis. Flexing deeply to absorb the bump also adds to the illusion of being back.

In the finish of rounded turns, all the dynamic forces again try to push your upper body, which wants to go downhill, ahead of the feet, which are going uphill. The skis slow rapidly now, particularly in a skid or short radius pre-turn. You are in a low position to use maximum edging, resisting the centrifugal force which has increased friction. With the necessary inward lean during a short radius turn, your feet travel a longer path than your chest. In tight

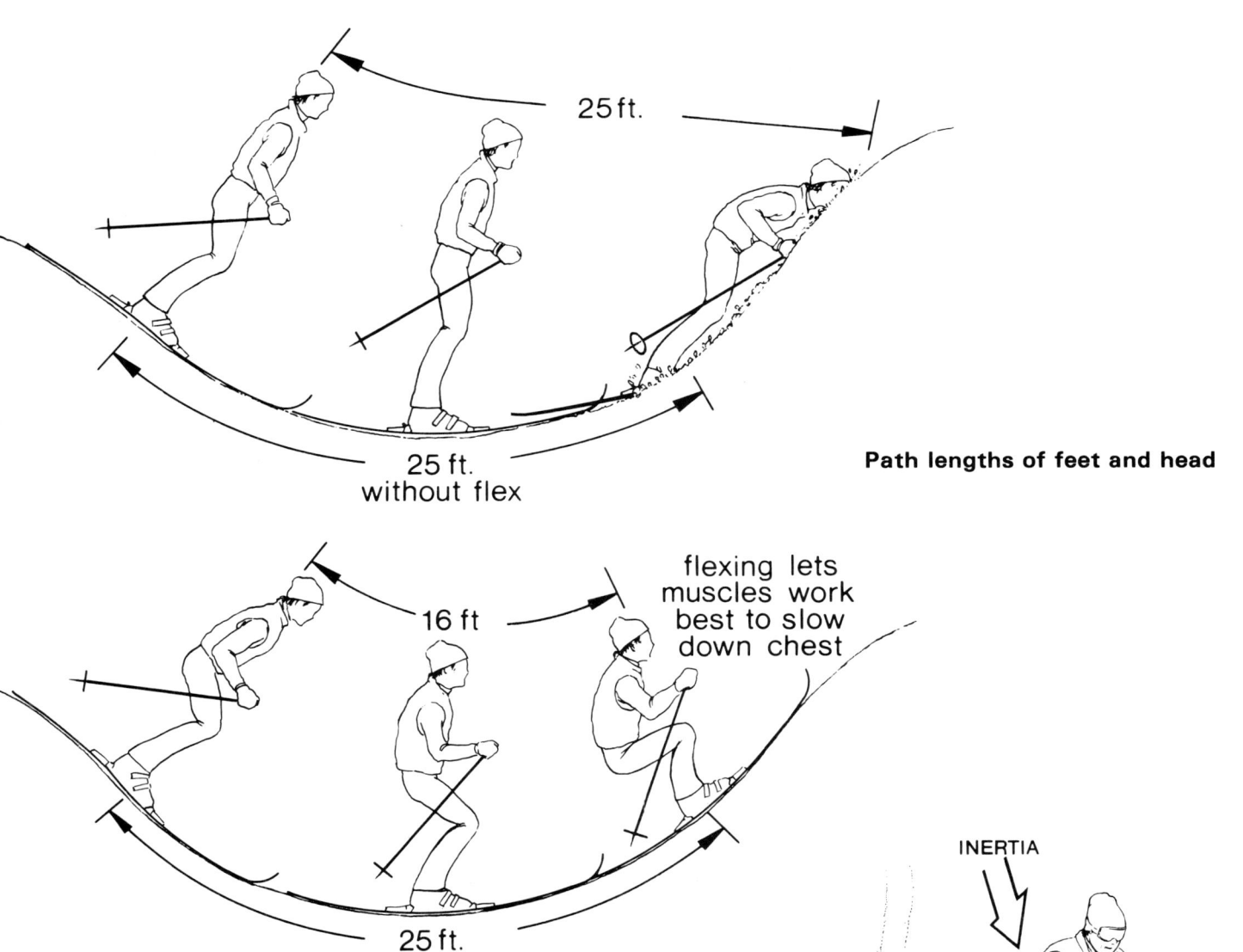

Path lengths of feet and head

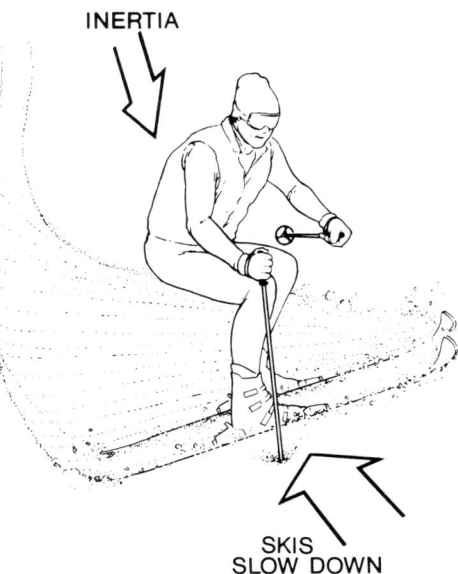

25 ft.
25 ft. without flex

flexing lets muscles work best to slow down chest
16 ft
25 ft. with flex

Balance at turn completion

INERTIA
SKIS SLOW DOWN

turns and at high speeds these factors require an exaggerated backward position, although all the short-term forces plus gravity are still balanced through your feet.

Perhaps by now you're convinced that on hard pack your weight is always balanced through your feet, but why do some skiers yell "Sit back!" when there's deep powder? Ski down the fall line in a foot of new snow. Your skis begin planing at an upward angle, and the powder exerts tremendous constant friction against the ski bottoms, your boots, and your shins. It's like sitting on the upstream side of a bridge and dangling your feet in the roaring stream below. You must push constantly on your feet to keep them from being swept backward. Similarly, your feet are being slowed down by deep snow, while your upper body is "free falling" down the steeper powder slopes. When you make turns you find a low flexed position gives you maximum knee drive to bank the whole ski

INERTIA

FRICTION AGAINST SKIS

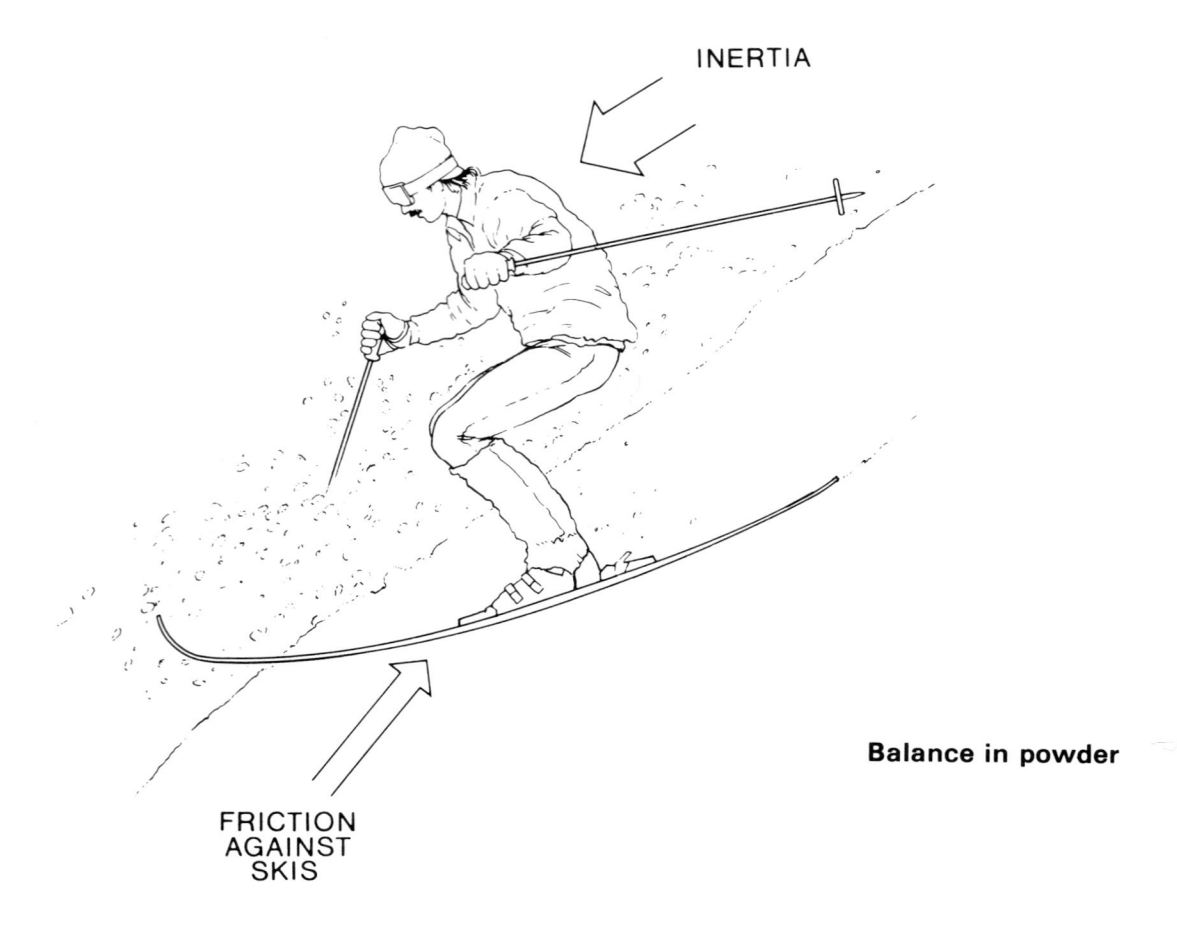

Balance in powder

bottom against the snow. All these factors make you appear seated with respect to the snow surface.

Let your camera toting friend snap his last photo to "prove" that you must sit back to ski powder. Then get some 8×10 blowups of your day's skiing to hang over the fireplace and impress friends. Just remember that the photos were static shots of dynamic skiing; throughout the day you were always balanced through your feet.

One situation occurs frequently where you can be back but also momentarily out of balance. After an edge set in rebound unweighting, your skis may suddenly shoot or "jet" ahead, as though they had a mind of their own. This jetting is not due to any esoteric mystical forces, but rather to a natural reaction.

Let's return to your downhill bus ride. You were standing in the aisle, braced backward against deceleration as the driver stomped on the brakes. Now imagine that he suddenly takes his foot off the brakes and applies full throttle to speed up. Inertia no longer "pulls" you forward, but instead backward, and you're drastically off balance as your feet speed ahead with the bus. To keep from falling on your derrière you tense leg and abdominal muscles to bring your chest forward and also drop the grocery bag to grab onto the seat frame for support.

In skiing, as in bus riding, forces change when you rapidly slow down or speed up. During a skid or during the finish of a turn your upper body is braced backward against your feet to resist inertia. When you reduce friction on the edges so that the skis are no longer slowing, this bracing position now acts to push or "jet" the skis ahead. The same thing would happen if you were roller skating down a sidewalk and came upon a short sandy stretch which retarded the wheels. You instinctively brace backward to balance your inertia against your decelerating feet. When the skates leave the slowing sand and once again roll on smooth pavement, they immediately shoot ahead because your tensed muscles are "pushing" your feet forward.

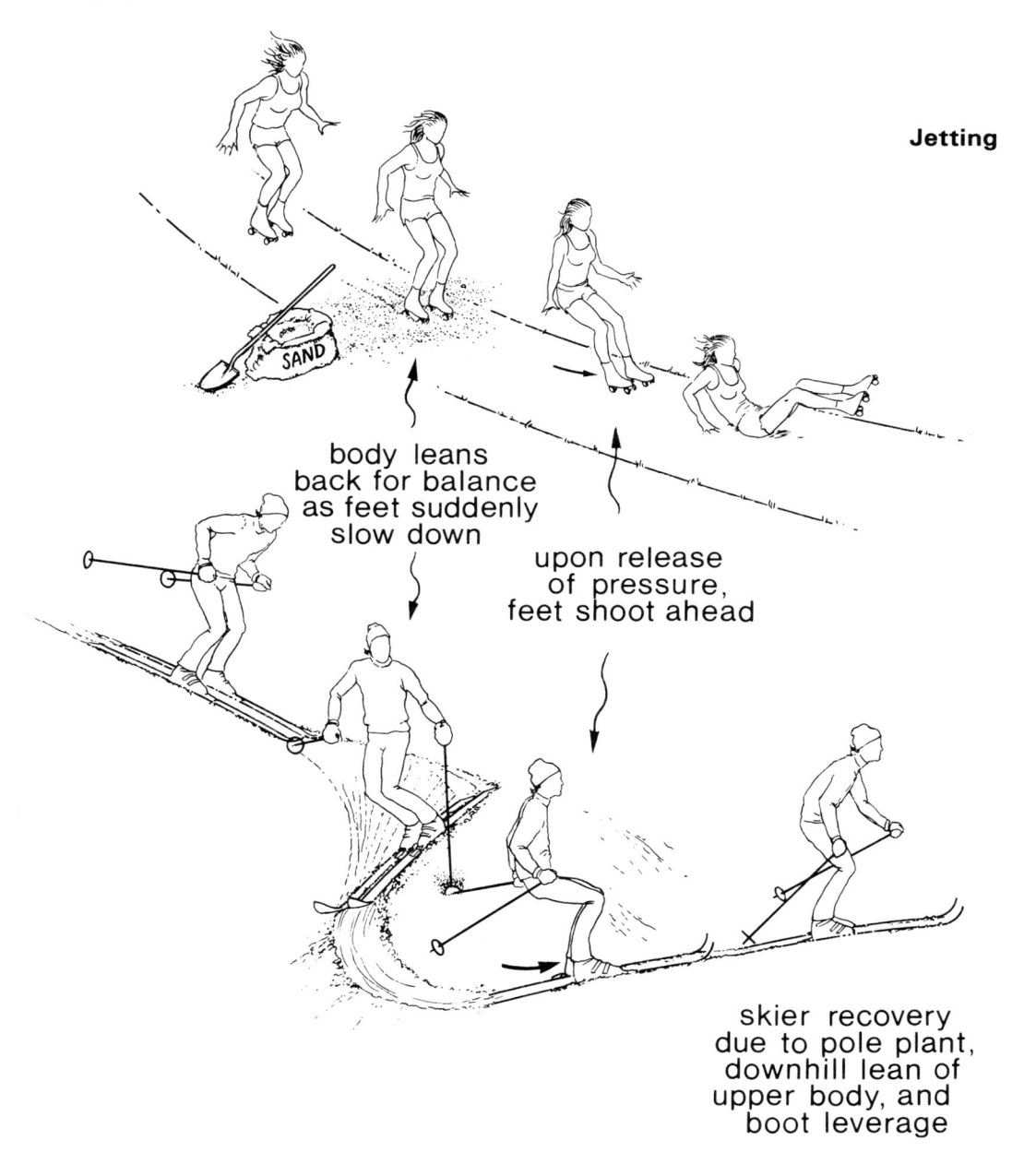

Jetting

body leans back for balance as feet suddenly slow down

upon release of pressure, feet shoot ahead

skier recovery due to pole plant, downhill lean of upper body, and boot leverage

To start the skis jetting, pressure must be relieved from the edges. This can be accomplished by many methods. Terrain can do it for you, as in turning on a mogul where the bump simply drops away. Perhaps the easiest way you can release edge pressure and initiate the new turn is with knee drive. From an angulated position you simply "crank" the knees toward the new turn to change edges and away they jet. An excellent way to release edges is by a step turn, stepping first the inside ski uphill onto its new edge, and then the outside ski. Unweighting will also release edge bite. This can be down or up-down, perhaps aided by the pole plant. Generally you won't need excessive active unweighting. At the higher speeds we're talking about there is a helping natural rebound unweighting due to the skis being pressed into reverse camber. Usually once the turn is initiated you must concentrate on pressing the skis back onto the snow, rather than trying to lift them into the air.

The big trick in a jet turn is how to play "catch-up" with your feet, which have been pushed farther ahead. This is a precarious moment when forces are no longer balanced through your feet. Now you must get your center of mass back over the feet, pressuring the ski tips into the new turn. The best aid here is the ski pole. Planted at the moment of edge change and weight transfer, it gives you a support point from which to move your torso forward. Highspeed, short-turn skiing is virtually impossible without pole plants, much as recovering your balance on an accelerating bus depends upon grabbing a support. Through this stabilizing pole contact with the snow you can more easily realign your body, using muscular action to bring the chest forward and the feet backward.

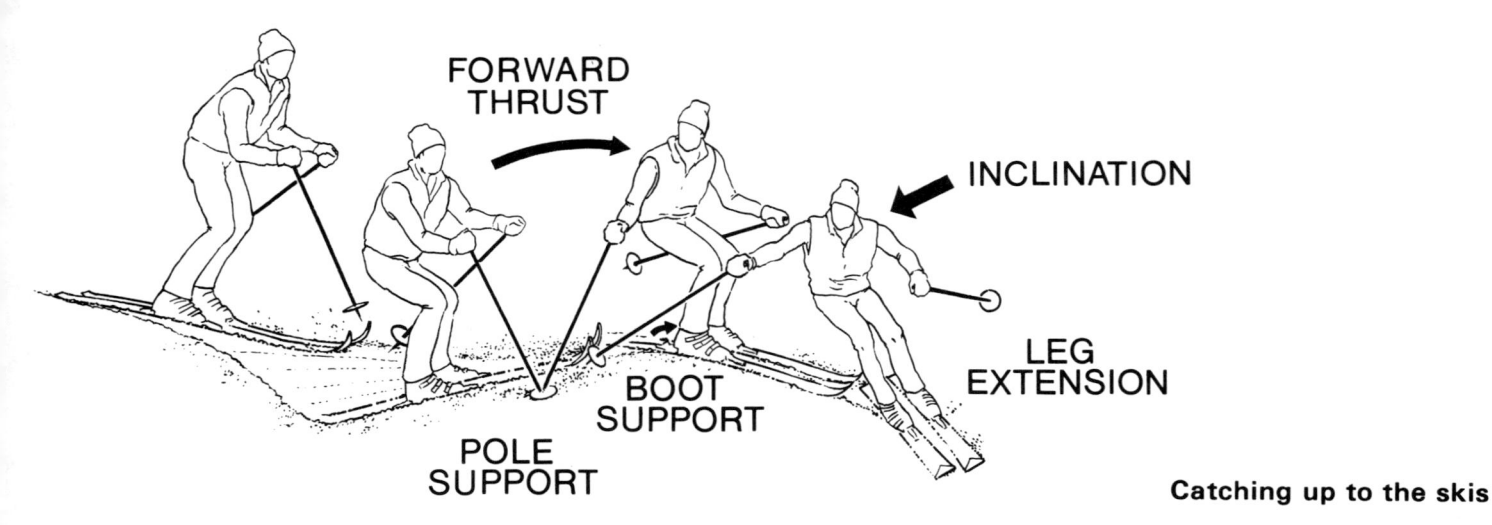

Catching up to the skis

High back boots aid this catch-up process. Upon jetting, your calves make contact with the rear of the boot. This firm section positively prevents your lower leg from bending backward and gives you a momentary mechanical advantage. The boots now provide upward support from the ski tail. Most importantly, once your leg muscles have switched from pushing on the feet to pulling them back under you, the boots efficiently transfer this motion to the skis.

Whenever the skis are in contact with the snow you can control your balance better by moving your body's center of mass to the desired position. Thus, after a jetting action, try to pressure the skis immediately by extending your legs to press the new edges into the snow. Edging early in the turn creates centrifugal force early, which then increases the weight on the skis and thus increases the chance to regain balance.

Centrifugal force requires that you must always lean into the turn. This means that the feet follow the longest path, while your chest is running a straighter line down the slope. Thus your upper body has a shorter path to follow, helping it to catch up to the feet. You can aid this by leaning into the new turn with your upper body as you change edges. On a mogul, or on the steeps, this means putting your head well out over the outside ski and reaching directly down the fall line with a pole plant. Admittedly, it takes extreme mental discipline to give up the false security of hugging the hill and launching yourself into space. However, without this forward position, catching up to the feet will be almost impossible.

Step turns provide a good catch-up method, since they edge and pressure the skis immediately. Stepping automatically banks the body into the new turn by moving the feet away. This is easier than having to project the upper body, and helps reduce the dependence on an accurate pole plant. We'll explore step turns further in the chapter titled "Lateral Projection."

Not all high speed turns need be jet turns, of course. Wide radius turns don't generate such sudden forces. In short turns you could stop resisting inertia an instant before releasing pressure from the ski edges. This would thrust your upper body into the new turn and eliminate the jetting action. Now your pole plant might even need to momentarily retard your upper body. This method keeps you over your skis all the time, but requires split second timing.

High speeds are dynamic, so don't lock yourself into one static position. Adjust your stance to balance against forces, but make it easy on yourself by always pressing your "weight" through your skeletal structure to your feet. Your muscles will thank you as you ski efficiently and fluidly like the best.

35

AVALEMENT

This chapter should rightfully be titled "Extension-Retraction." But I think avalement, the French term, sounds much more exciting. In translation, it means "swallowing," and indeed it does just that. Avalement is simply an active folding movement of the body which absorbs the pressures generated by bumpy terrain and high speed turns. Perhaps you are already skiing with avalement without consciously knowing it (which is, after all, the best way to do anything).

To understand avalement, let's consider skiing over a large bump. At very slow speed there is no problem, and you don't mind riding up and over it. At a more moderate speed, unless you relax and let your legs absorb it, this bump could throw you into the air. However, at higher speeds, the legs take too long to passively ride up and down, and you must actively help them.

Find a series of rounded bumps. Ski over them in a high speed traverse, keeping your skis constantly in contact with the snow. To do this, actively retract your legs with the thigh and stomach muscles when going up the bump, and forcefully extend your legs on the far side of the bump, pushing on the skis to keep them on the snow.

Now you see why this is also known as retraction-extension. Avalement results in a folding movement of the body to swallow terrain. In gymnastics this is called a jacknife move, where the legs are pulled forward and upward at the same time the trunk is pulled forward and downward. It is a dynamic motion and not a stance to be held continually or used at slow speed. This folded position may create an appearance of "being back." Combine this with the extreme pressures of sharp pre-turns or decelerations on large bumps

AVALEMENT IN STRAIGHT RUN

High speed without absorption

Avalement in straight runs

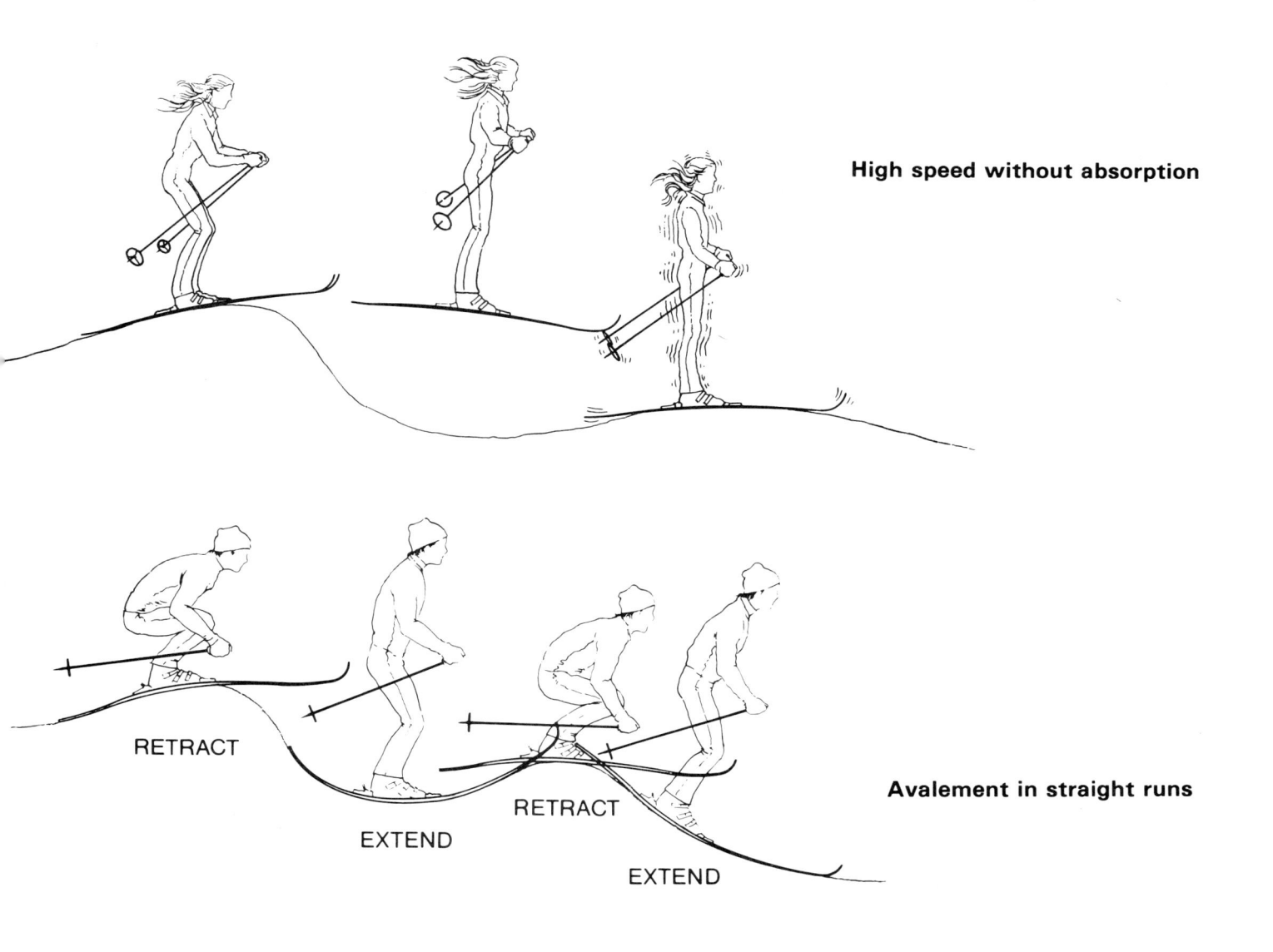

RETRACT
EXTEND
RETRACT
EXTEND

and the illusion is heightened. However, from the chapter on weight distribution you know you must always remain balanced against the feet, with pressure on the tongues of your boots.

Besides the thigh muscles, retraction uses the abdominal muscles, just as if you were doing sit-ups. Of course, with larger bumps or more speed you will reach a point where your body cannot completely absorb the terrain. For best results, go into the bump from as high a position as possible to allow for more flexing. Also, lower your hands toward your boots for additional absorption.

Extending after the bump requires a strong pushing movement downward on the skis. You must feel with your feet how much pressure is required to keep them on the snow. Too little will result in your skis becoming airborne. Too much pressure will push your torso upward, decreasing the distance your legs can continue to extend downward. Once you understand the principle, you can have some fun with it.

Momentary extreme absorption of a bump at high speed

Find a single large bump, the lip of a catwalk, or similar terrain. On one run approach it from a crouched position. Push upward as you climb the bump so that you become airborne. On your next run, approach the bump from a high stance. Retract your legs sharply as you ski up it, and extend them forcefully immediately after the crest, so that your skis always stay on the snow.

As you discovered in the chapters on rebound unweighting, a hard edge set or a sharp pre-turn can actually lift your skis off the snow. Extension can keep you from flying low.

On a steep smooth slope finish a high speed, wide radius turn using a very sharp pre-turn with a hard edge set. Release the edge pressure suddenly. As your skis jet forward, maintain snow contact by extending your feet. Finish the turn by driving the knees and sinking into the next pre-turn.

In this absorption, your feet shoot ahead and the skis flatten on the snow. During this phase the edges are changed, and weight is transferred to the outer ski. Even though the untwisting action of anticipation is as rapid as ever, due to your high speed the unweighted portion of your track is elongated. In the "S" tracks this should appear as a very short, narrow, and essentially straight section between the two halves of the "S." It is the area of change from one set of edges to the other.

Skiing in the bumps requires absorbing the pressure of the terrain, as you did in a straight run, only now with turns added. This is the goal of most skiers and the primary use of avalement.

Approach a bump at moderate speed and choose a spot just before the crest on which you will turn. While skiing up the bump

JUMPING OR SWALLOWING BUMPS

ABSORBING REBOUND FORCES

AVALEMENT IN MOGULS

Jumping or swallowing bumps

In the top sequence the skier sinks before the bump, then pushes upward against it (using poles to help push) to jump into the air. In the bottom sequence the skier soaks up the bump by retracting his knees to his chest (lowering the hands for maximum absorption) and then pushing after the bump to maintain snow contact. Each series of photos takes place in about one second.

extend legs to maintain snow contact

Absorbing rebound forces

SKIDDED EDGE CHANGE

"S" tracks

FALL LINE

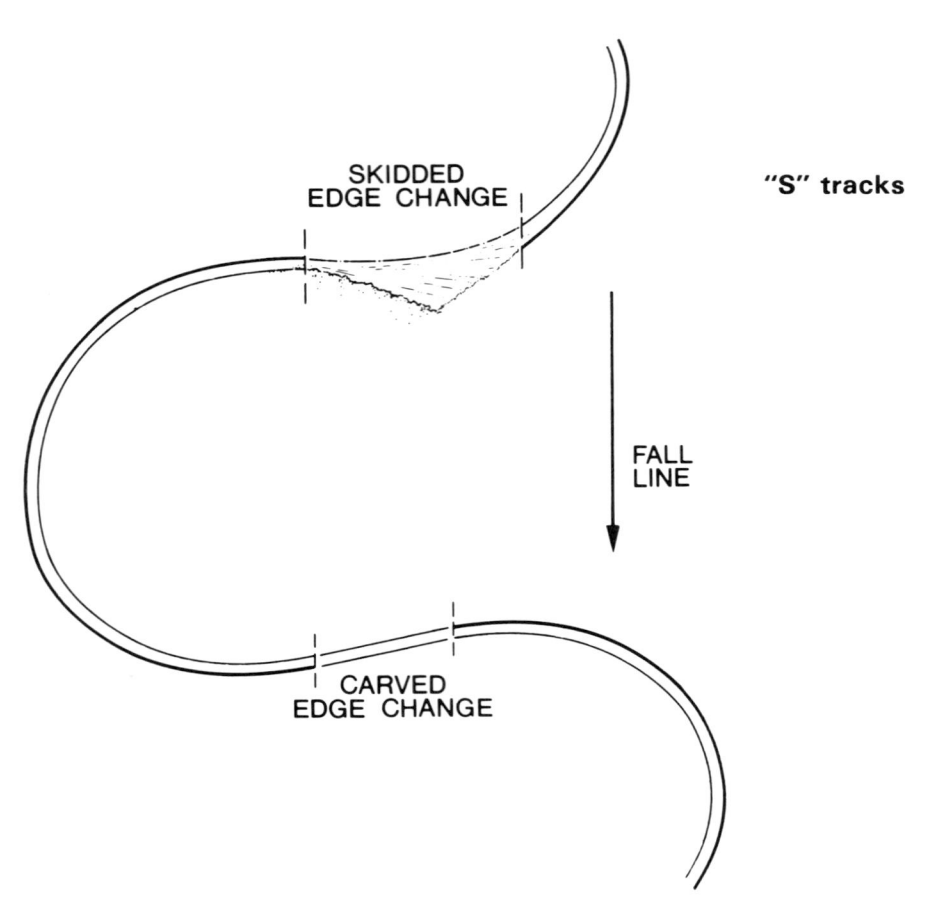

CARVED EDGE CHANGE

retract your legs, plant the pole below the turn spot, and pre-turn with a sharp check. Skidding to the turn spot, release edge pressure, feel the skis go forward, transfer weight to the outside ski as it starts to turn, and extend your legs to keep contact with the snow. Carve across a trough and up onto the next mogul.

Avalement in moguls
Active leg flexion and extension during the turn erases the bump to maintain snow contact.

Don't be overwhelmed by the words. This is simply a check to slow down, anticipation to aid your turn, and active knee motions to compensate for terrain.

Changing edges does take time, and at higher speeds going through a flat ski phase on the back of a mogul before edging can cause excessive skidding, besides losing valuable terrain on which to carve toward the next bump. This means that the crest might be too late a spot to pivot. Instead, release edge pressure as you are going up the bump. Because the bump is still rising, continue to retract your legs to absorb the terrain. Your feet now appear ahead of your body, and the skis are momentarily flat on the snow. (With the snow still flying from the edge set, the seat back, and the tips in midair, this is a great time for a magazine cover shot.) By the time

High speed mogul turn
An early edge change allows the skier to carve down the back side of the mogul and be ready for the next one. The total time of this sequence is just over one second.

you have reached the highest part of the bump your skis are edging into the new turn. You now extend and carve down the back side. Remember that you must extend to a normal position in order to be able to absorb the next mogul, and also that your weight must quickly be balanced over the skis after the pivot point.

You may be worried about balance during these higher speed turns in bumps. Your weight is still on the heels to finish a turn, and moves onto the toes to start a new one. You must project your upper body forward into the new turn. Lean on a pole plant down the fall line for balancing adjustment. The extension and inward lean into the new turn provide a shorter, quicker path for your upper body. Finally, the high boot backs provide a mechanical advantage to regain balance. If you fail to use these techniques to get forward you will lose tip control and your skis will pick up speed straight downhill. I'll spare you the sad details of what happens then.

Your choice of turning point will be dictated by your speed and by the size of the bumps. Changing edges on or near a crest may be easiest, but also may make it impossible to keep your skis on the snow. Frequently a turn can be made prior to the crest, snaking around the side of a bump, across a trough, and up the side of the next. Carving a pre-turn is ideal, but modern moguls may demand a series of skids. In some cases you may have to ski a turn or two in the troughs, particularly around huge moguls which have miniature sheer cliffs on their downhill side. When in doubt, turn. Be alert, smooth, and completely flexible. Once you relax and have a hot run with avalement, you'll go looking for bigger and better bumps.

Upper body projection into the turn
A pole plant maintains balance during inward lean into the new turn.

36
CARVING

Racers and expert recreational skiers ski effortlessly at high speed. The secret is their ability to carve. *Carving* means eliminating skidding and instead using the ski's design to turn efficiently. In a skid, the skis move sideways and friction slows them. In a carve, the skis move only forward, making a sharp track. There's a time and place for each technique. You'll find carving particularly helpful for control on ice, for speed on a race course, and for ease of turning in general skiing. If eliminating your fun-type skid bothers you, think of a carve as a skid so small it can't be seen.

Carving utilizes ski design to its fullest. We'll review some things you've already done, and apply them to carving. The principles you'll need will be edging, pressure, and leverage.

Skis are designed with sidecut. That is, they are narrower in the middle than at the tip and tail. When a ski is pressed into the snow and put on edge, it forms a curve. Snow resistance all along the edge forces the ski to carve in this arc. Skiers complicate matters by flattening the ski and twisting it, causing a skid. When starting a new turn, the skis go through a flat phase as they change edges. To avoid "washing out" of the turn, you must edge early and weight that edge immediately to get the skis tracking. At the completion of one turn, crank your knees into the new turn and step on the outside ski.

To emphasize edging and weight transfer, let's modify an exercise you've done before while skiing on one foot.

Start off on flat skis down a wide gentle slope. As you begin to move, stand on the inside edge of one foot. As that ski carries you to the side of the trail, transfer your weight to the inside edge of the other ski. Stand only on one ski or the other, and only on a

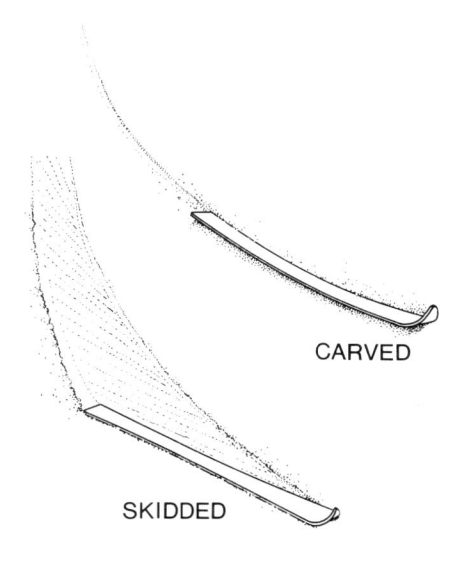

Skidded versus carved skis

NATURAL CARVES

Natural carves
Ride an edge to carve.

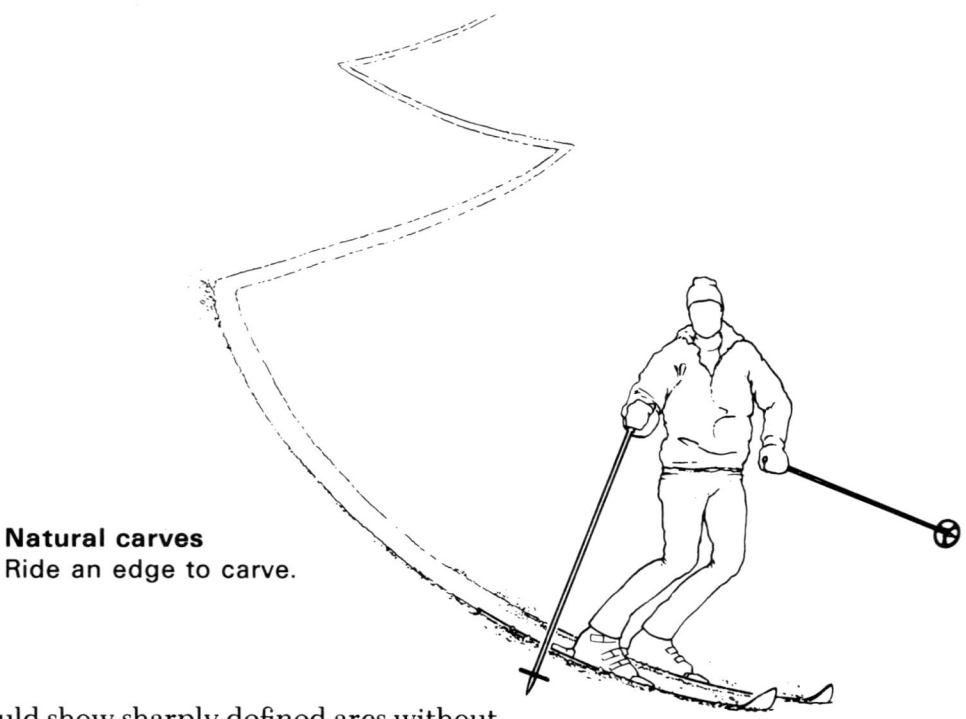

definite edge. Your tracks should show sharply defined arcs without skids.

It's a good thing you did the carves on a gentle slope, because it's amazing how much speed you can attain when you don't skid. The trick to speed control while carving is to *finish your turns.* That means to keep standing on the edge until it carries you back up the hill, slowing your speed. Your tracks will have the characteristic "S" shape to them.

The actual arc you carve can be controlled in several ways. In the natural carves exercise you found that as your speed increased, your turns became sharper. This is due to our old friend, centrifugal force. As your speed increases, so does the centrifugal force in a turn. This puts more "weight" onto the ski, which then bends more in the middle. Technically, it has a greater reverse camber. This larger bend is part of a shorter radius arc, and hence a tighter turn. You may have noticed this effect while traversing.

Find a steep hill with soft snow. Traverse across it with equal weight on both feet. Then stand entirely on the downhill foot, and see how your track takes on a gradual curve. Step back and forth from two skis to one ski.

WEIGHT EFFECT ON CARVES

You can vary the amount of body weight on the outside ski to help turn. This is particularly useful at the start of a turn, where you can extend your outer leg to maintain snow contact. Put all your weight on that one ski as it begins to turn. If you up unweight excessively you'll delay the ski weighting, and hence slow down the turn. Think of stepping your weight sideways, not up, and pushing against the skis as soon as you change edges.

The edge angle also controls the ski arc. This is an easy one to see.

Traverse across a hill in a high stance. Then drop to a low stance, pointing your knees up the hill to increase your edge angle. Your skis will immediately turn up the hill.

Your skis' sidecut, combined with their camber, caused your skis to turn. To visualize this, cut a modified hourglass shape from construction paper. Place this paper ski flat on another sheet of paper and trace the curve of one edge. Now lift the other edge of the paper ski, so it is angled to the paper. Only the tip and tail touch now, but in real life you'd be standing on the ski bending it into reverse camber. Press the paper ski's center until it touches also, and again trace the curve of the edge. You'll find the greater the edge angle, the sharper the curve.

You must increase your edge angle to make a tighter turn. If you like, think of it as showing more of your ski bottoms to the onlookers at each side of the trail. Of course, to edge more you must be in a low position to increase knee flex. (Now your see why racers finish a high speed turn in such a low stance.) At the start of your turn, inward lean toward the turn center will also increase edge angle.

Now that you're aware of edging and weighting, you can try a fun exercise to demonstrate them.

EDGE ANGLE EFFECT ON CARVES

Edge effect on carving
Increasing edging tightens the turn radius.

Edge angle and sidecut determine a turn's arc

LESSER EDGE ANGLE MAKES MORE GRADUAL TURN

GREATER ANGLE MAKES SHARPER TURN

Ski down a slope in a wedge. Stand entirely on the inside of one foot. Quickly switch weight entirely onto the inside edge of your other foot. You will immediately zip off in the direction that that ski is pointing. Continue back and forth down the hill. Roll out the ankle of your unweighted foot to flatten that ski so it doesn't hinder sideways motion. Make sure you leave sharp tracks in the snow without skid marks.

This is also called the crab walk, because with a wide wedge you travel forward and sideways with instantaneous changes of direction.

Where you place your weight on the ski, or the *leverage,* also affects the radius of a carve.

EDGE LOCKS

Edge locks
Carve from foot to foot without skidding.

Traverse across a hill in an upright stance, with your weight rocked back to your heels. Then flex forward at the ankles to place weight on your toes. Your skis will immediately turn up the hill.

LEVERAGE EFFECTS ON CARVES

Leverage aids carving
Weight forward initiates a rapid turn.

The flex pattern of a ski is not uniform. Rather, the tip area bends more readily than the tail. When you apply forward leverage the section from foot to tip bends in considerable reverse camber, causing a sharp turn. This effect is heightened by the greater width of the tip as compared to the tail, resulting in a sharper arc.

Thus to start your turn your weight should be pressed forward. This can sometimes be a formidable mental barrier to overcome. As your skis start toward the fall line your brain says "Look out!" and directs you to hug the hill. With weight on the tails your turn is delayed while you accelerate downhill.

Like red pepper, leverage is good in moderation. Changing your weight distribution is a subtle maneuver, best done by varying knee and ankle flex. Generally the ball of the foot is centered over the running surface of the ski, so that a neutral stance utilizes the entire ski length. Just a small displacement of your body puts pressure onto either tip or tail. Once a turn has been initiated your weight should return from the toes to the neutral point. Using the whole ski length now avoids tip chatter and tail skid. Near the finish of a turn centrifugal force has greatly increased your weight. Now you should weight your heels slightly so that the tail will maintain the chosen path.

Carving can be a powerful force. If you enjoy tug-of-war at summer picnics, find a partner of equal size and try this.

CARVED TUG-OF-WAR

On a gentle slope ski side by side in the fall line with a partner. Each person should hold on to one end of a shared set of ski poles. At the start signal, each person tries to pull the other to his side of the slope. Edge your skis with a large knee flex. See if you can

207

Leverage in a turn

FALL LINE

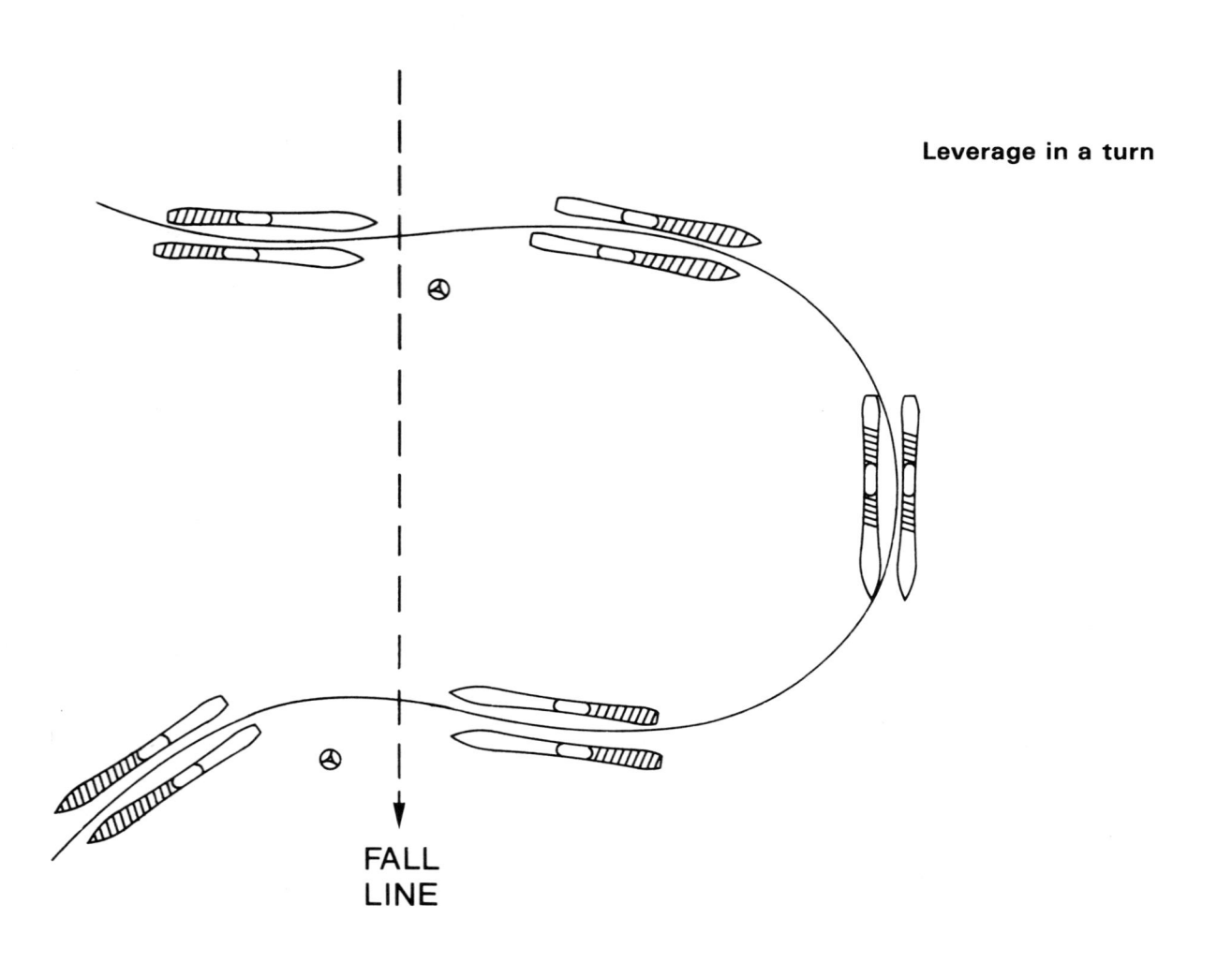

Carved tug-of-war
The skier with the best edging and least skidding will win.

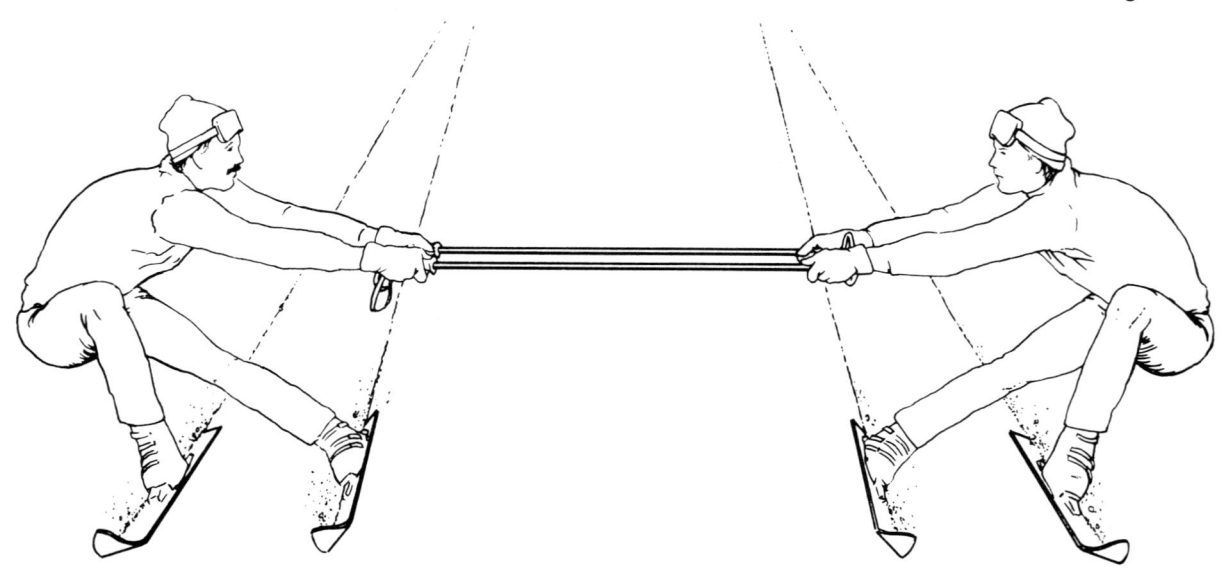

increase your pull by standing only on your outer ski, then by increasing your edge, then by varying leverage.

It's fun, and you can learn something. Think of your partner as the centrifugal force. Just don't let go of the poles or you'll both probably slingshot into the trees.

Your tracks never lie. Always look at them to see if they leave crisp, rounded arcs in the snow. Actually, carving feels so good you'll know when you're doing it. You'll fly down the slopes in perfect control. The skis even sound good as they slice through the snow. You'll also be happy to know that after spending so much money on a pair of skis, you're finally putting them to work for you.

37

LATERAL PROJECTION

When you began skiing, you moved each leg independently as, for example, in a stem. As you progressed, you found that it was possible to move them simultaneously, in parallel. Not too long ago this was the mark of an accomplished skier. Nowadays, we find that an advanced independent leg movement is the signature of an expert. *Lateral projection* is simply a movement of the body or skis to the left or right; it's easily done by a stepping motion. Sometimes these steps will be called racing turns, as they were perfected on courses to ski more efficiently.

Actually you've projected laterally several times already. (Sounds like some new Zen mind trip, doesn't it?) Stepping skis uphill to change a traverse, or transferring weight from the downhill to uphill ski are sideways movements. Frequently the pole plant helps push your center of mass to the uphill ski. Rebound unweighting also can project your body laterally uphill.

Perhaps you wonder why you want to step sideways. Imagine you're schussing straight down the hill and a three-foot-diameter Douglas fir pops up directly in front of you. A sideways step and you've avoided it. That could also have been a racing gate or a mogul. Combine the lateral action with a turn and you have an extremely efficient way to get down the hill.

Let's go back to skiing on one ski, only now with the modification of stepping a ski outward. Just standing on the snow, pick up the uphill ski and move it an additional twelve inches up the slope, but still parallel to the downhill ski. Now step onto the uphill ski, moving your body sideways, in a lateral projection. This leads to a neat turn.

At moderate speed on a smooth slope, initiate a wide turn by stepping the unweighted uphill ski farther uphill and parallel to the

STEP TURN TO AN INSIDE EDGE

Step turn to an inside edge

downhill ski. Smoothly transfer your weight forward to the inside edge of that uphill ski and start driving the uphill knee into a new turn. Pick up the lower ski and step it next to the weighted outside ski. Use a pole plant for balance when you transfer weight.

The motions are the same ones you already used in skating on the flats. In fact, these turns are often called *skating turns*. This step turn is especially fun when cruising on a wide open slope at high speed. You may find it's so smooth you won't even need a pole plant. Because you're moving your feet rather than your center of mass, your balance is not very critical.

If you're a little lazy about stepping, here's an excellent practice exercise.

STEPPING

Borrow some ski poles and lay them in the fall line. (Or use marks in the snow, a long ridge crest, or snowballs.) Step over the obstacles to the left and right as you ski down. Next offset them, so you make a short turn before stepping over each one. Finally, set up an actual slalom course and step around each gate.

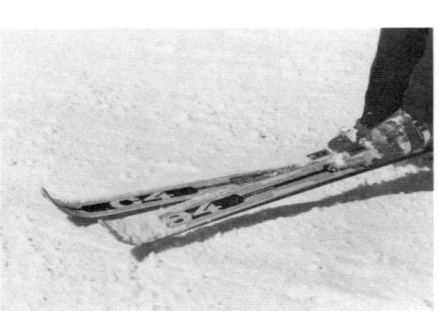

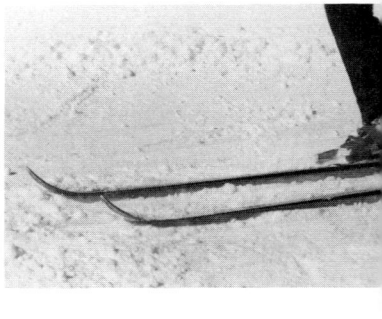

Close-up of skis in a step turn

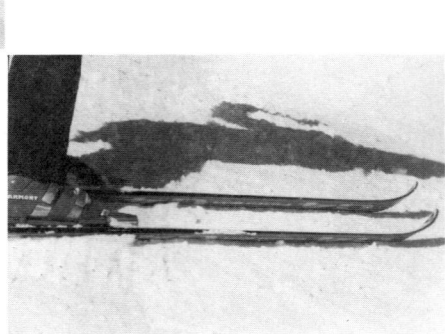

Stepping practice

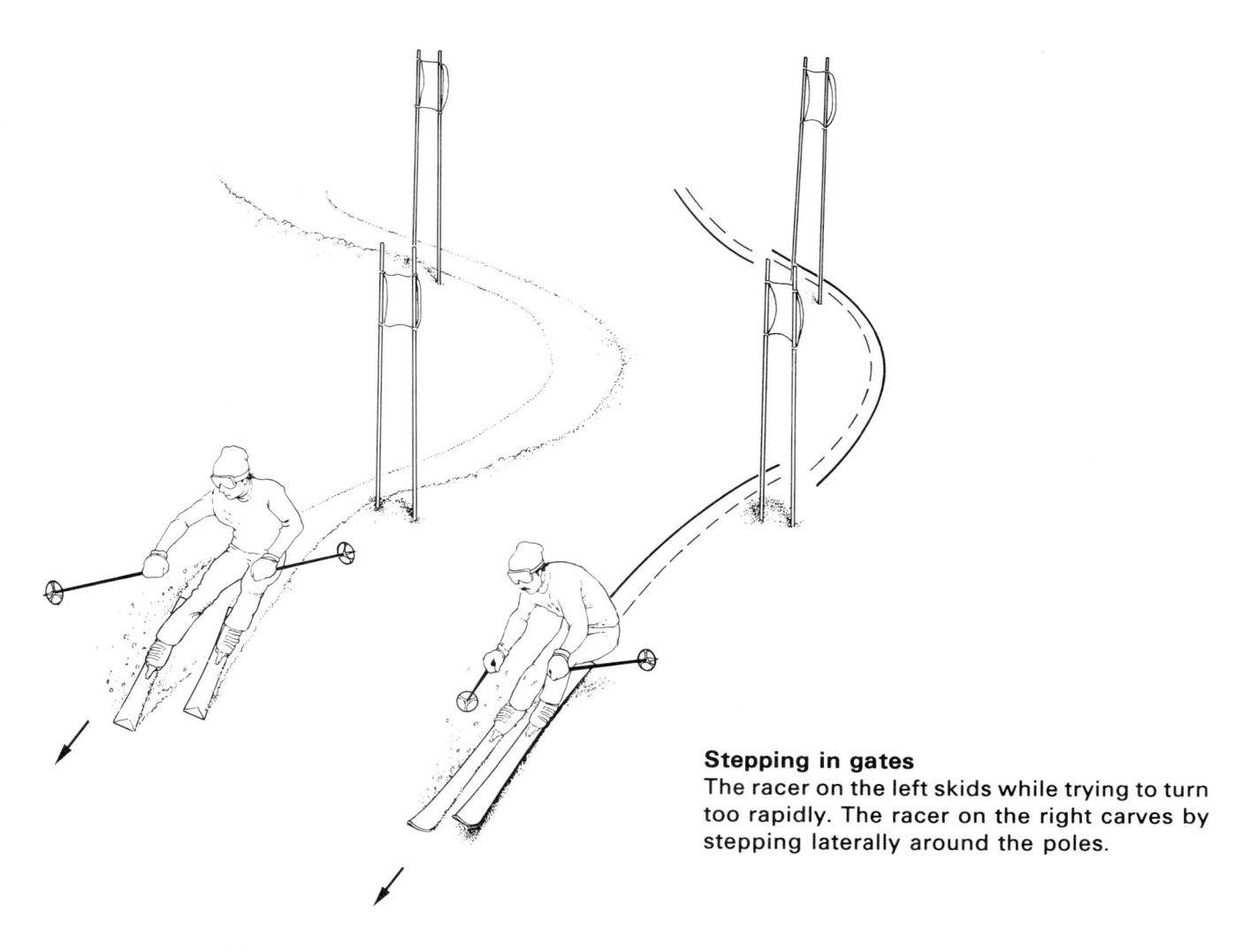

Stepping in gates
The racer on the left skids while trying to turn too rapidly. The racer on the right carves by stepping laterally around the poles.

You can readily see the advantage of stepping, as the effective radius of the turn is increased. Due to the sideways step, the ski track is discontinuous, so the turns do not have to be as sharp. This is particularly useful in racing, since a skier may come straighter down a slalom course stepping around gates. It eliminates lost speed and skidding in tight turns and saves time due to its shorter path down the fall line. With the skating "push," you can actually increase your downhill speed.

Just as in skating, you should feel yourself push off from the toe area. Your weight will be back slightly on the heel after you cross the fall line. Therefore you must also project it forward as you step sideways. The pole plant will give you the necessary thrust to do this. Another method to weight your toes is to drive your hands far forward as your step begins.

There is no reason the step has to be parallel. It could also be stemmed, to initiate a turn sooner. This is a common racing turn. Be cautious on too wide a stem, as too large a change in direction can start a skid.

So far you've been stepping to an inside edge. You guessed the next one.

213

Step turn by stemming
A quick way to turn.

At moderate speed on a smooth slope, initiate a wide turn by stepping the unweighted uphill ski farther uphill and parallel to the downhill ski. Smoothly weight the outside edge of that uphill ski. As you step the lower ski uphill, flatten the upper ski and then put it on its inside edge. Leave your weight there as you drive your knees into the turn.

STEP TURN TO AN OUTSIDE EDGE

FALL LINE

Stepping to an outside edge
When stepping to an outside edge, the skier moves laterally (2 and 3). However, the new turn is delayed until the ski edge is changed (4 and 5).

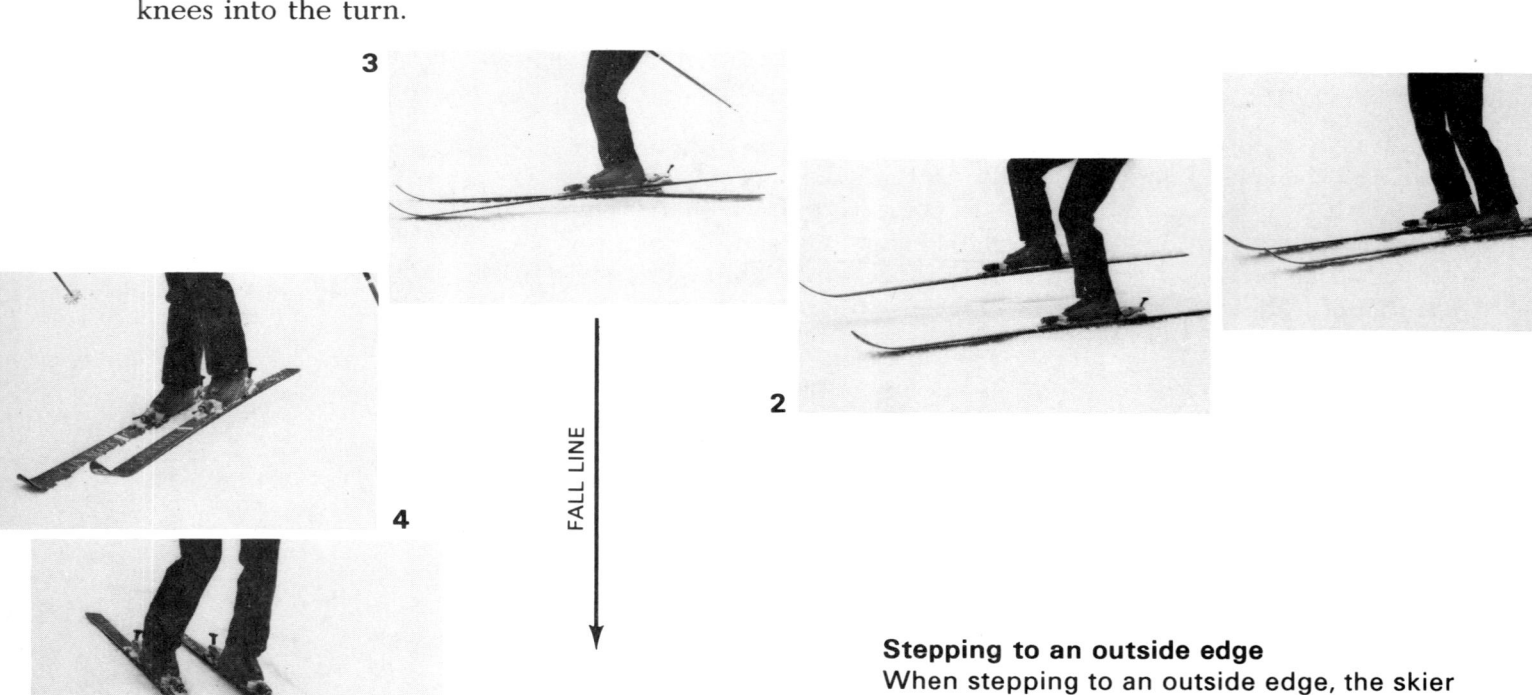

This probably felt a little strange, as you stepped to the "wrong" edge. Weight on the uphill ski's outside edge is a starting point for much of trick skiing. It's also useful for a lateral movement with a delay before starting the new turn, enabling you to move to a higher line.

Weighting the outside edge of the upper ski can also be done without actually stepping.

Near the finish of a turn, put some weight on your inside ski, particularly toward the tip. The inside ski will climb away from the lower ski. Help it by steering the inside foot and edging it more from the uphill knee. When the tips are separated by about two feet, step to the uphill ski. Change edges by driving that knee into a new turn. At the same time, pick up the lower ski to match it beside the upper.

Due to the spreading action of the tips this turn is sometimes called a scissors turn. It also uses lateral projection, only here you have allowed the inside ski to carve uphill, rather than stepping it up to start the turn. Your center of mass transfers smoothly to the uphill ski in this *cramponnage* or "holding on" maneuver. It can be used for tight racing turns, as the inner ski travels a smaller radius turn. Anyone who is bowlegged and is not canted will find this turn extremely easy. His inside ski will be edged more naturally than the outside one.

CRAMPONNAGE TURN

Cramponnage turn
Let your uphill ski climb higher, step to it, and start a turn.

FALL LINE →

Stepping can be quite effective when combined with jet turns, avalement, and rebound.

From a steep traverse, make a sharp check, sinking in the knees while pivoting the skis uphill. Step the upper ski out and forward onto its inside edge to absorb the upward rebound motion. Immediately pick up the inside ski and match it to the outer one, continuing the turn with knee drive. Do short radius turns in the fall line, checking on one ski and projecting to the other.

You can use lateral projection when turning in the bumps, to check on one side of a mogul and step around to the lower side. It will allow you to step over a rut or pile of snow left by a grooming machine. You'll sing its praises on ice when you eliminate skidding. If you enter a NASTAR or similar race, you'll find it especially helpful for shaving seconds from your time. On the ten scale, lateral projection turns rate at least a 9.8. Try them.

STEPPING FROM A REBOUND

Stepping from a rebound

38

POWDER PASSION

Powder has been described as "the ultimate sensual experience." Some floundering skiers, unaccustomed to the light snow, may feel it will be their final experience. However, once you learn to handle powder you'll never be completely happy with packed snow again.

Powder comes in various forms, starting with a fluff so light you can compress a handful down to almost nothing, to a nasty wet variety known by various regional names, including "Sierra Cement." It can be "cheater's powder," 3 to 6 inches over a packed base, or the "deep stuff"— 8 inches or more where you actually float. The best powder skiing is found during a snowstorm, while it is still light and untracked. This is when the true "powder hounds" are out, waiting in line early for the lifts to open.

If the new powder is only a dusting, any old technique will work, since your skis sink to the packed surface. But skiing the deep snow requires a smooth refinement of your present technique. An apt powder expression goes "You can't bluff in the fluff." This means you may be able to somehow force your skis around on the packed snow, but in the deep you must have balance, economy of motion, and the confidence that comes with really knowing how to turn the skis.

Ask one hundred skiers how they ski powder and you'll get one hundred different "techniques." More than any other snow condition, powder brings out the individuality of each skier. Powder adds another dimension to movement, as now your skis can also sink down or float up. This leads to great confusion in technical jargon, since when you do things such as extend your legs to rise up, your skis will sink down. Powder does not require a new technique, but rather a refinement of your present one. I'll concentrate on the common principles of powder and let you expand on them.

Any ski will work in powder, but to make it easier, a soft flexing one is best. Most newer skis are designed with enough flex to float in powder. Specialized racing skis or old stiff boards will sometimes imitate a submarine in a crash dive, and you'll work harder with them. Shorter lengths perform beautifully, as they have less resistance to twisting into turns. I prefer safety retention straps rather than ski brakes; they save me an hour's digging in search of a buried ski.

Your basic stance for powder will remain the same, with the weight balanced between heels and toes. A more erect back may help your balance if you feel the tips dive on you. Although powder can be skied with a stem, most people prefer a parallel method. *Put your feet together.* Whenever they are apart, snow pushes them every which way. Most importantly, *weight each foot equally.* Otherwise the heavier ski will sink out of sight. Think of the two skis as being one big one and you'll be in good shape. Now let's take a first run.

FIRST MOTIONS IN POWDER

On a gentle slope find a patch of untracked powder. Keeping your feet together and equally weighted, let your skis run straight down the fall line. Feel yourself float in the snow. Make a series of smooth, unhurried down and up unweighting motions, exaggerating knee bend and alternating pole plants. Your skis will rise toward the surface as you flex (or retract) your knees. Now make small turns left and right of the fall line with the same rhythm. Start the skis into each turn as the tips near the surface. Come to a stop through a long sweeping uphill arc in a flexed position. Repeat the turns by changing the rhythm of your unweighting and also the amplitude of your up and down motions. Look back uphill to admire your tracks!

You'll notice immediately that skis travel more slowly in powder than on packed snow. You feel the slowing effect radically if you ski into the powder from a packed slope; you'll have to lean back momentarily to maintain balance. Conversely, when skiing onto the packed from the powder your skis accelerate. The slower speed is due partly to the snow crystal structure, but primarily due to the extra resistance of your boots and lower legs pushing against the snow. Your skis plane in powder much like water skis. This increased angle of attack presents a broad resisting surface to decrease speed. Here's where a wide soft tip comes in handy, as it more easily flexes upward to keep the ski from diving.

Everyone takes a spill in powder now and then. The soft snow will cushion you, so just relax when it happens and make a perfect angel in the snow. Getting up with no solid support can be an exhausting problem, however. If the pole baskets sink in deeply, try crossing the poles in the shape of an "X." With the crossed poles flat on the snow, you have a large supporting surface and can put your hand in the middle of the "X" to get up. If a ski has come off, stamp out a firm platform in the snow on which to stand for better balance.

Unweighting motions in powder

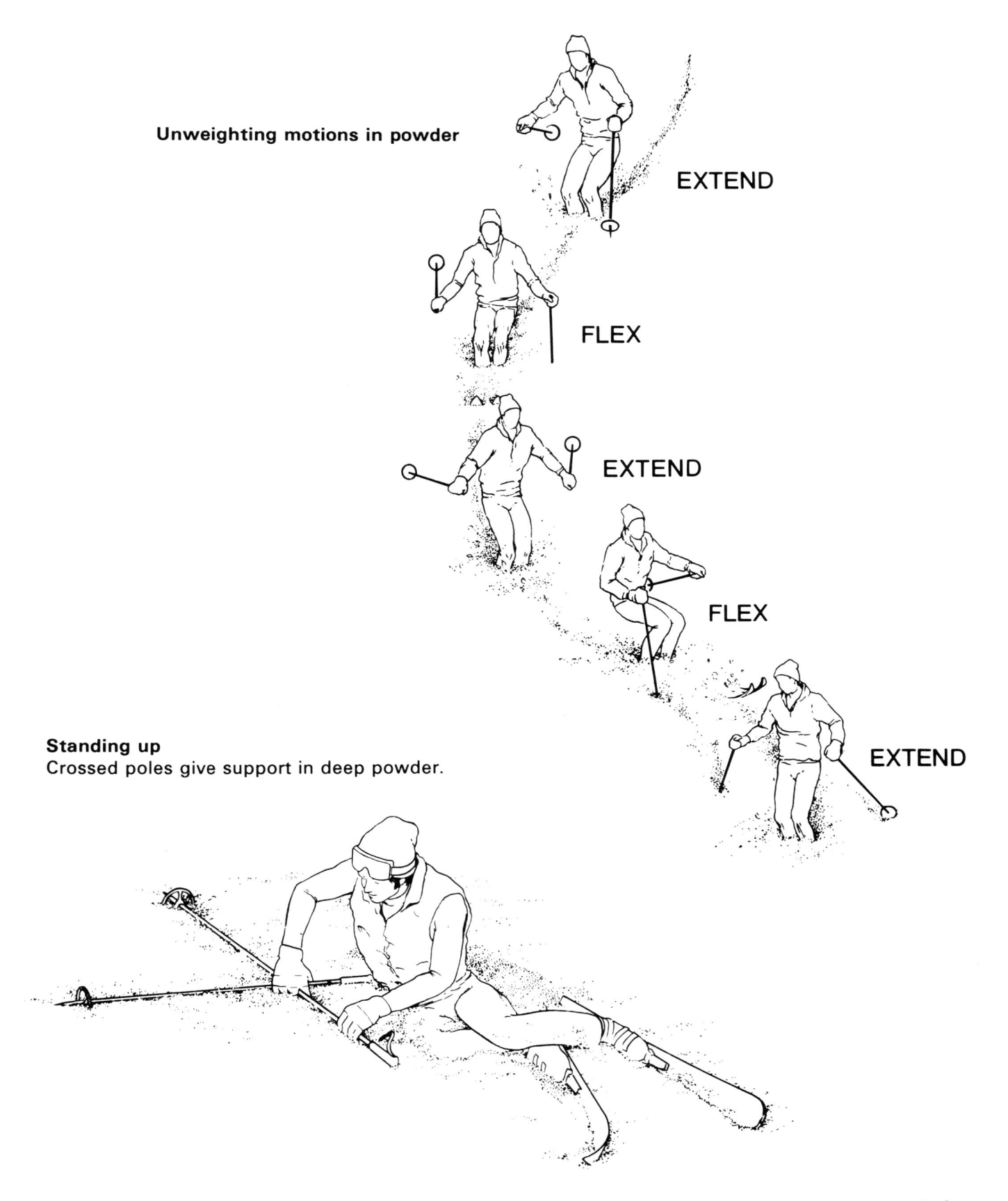

EXTEND

FLEX

EXTEND

FLEX

EXTEND

Standing up
Crossed poles give support in deep powder.

Finally, if you can get your skiing partner to stop laughing, ask him for a hand up.

You can discover the resistance of powder to motion in this unique turn.

CANOE TURN

Ski powder in the fall line on a gentle slope. To turn, push one pole basket into the snow beside you and drag it forcefully along. You will gradually turn to that side. Remove the pole from the snow and drag the opposite one to turn the other way.

It's not very elegant or refined, but it works.

The large resistance from powder makes most skidding techniques useless. If your skis are below the surface and flat with respect to the surface, they may slice sideways all right, but your feet won't. The snow will grab them and flip you downhill. If you attempt to stop in an upright stance you will prove this to yourself. A carving technique is needed in powder. You cannot use your

Canoe turn
Dragging a pole causes a turn to that side.

220

edges, but you can consider the whole bottom surface as one large edge. The same resistance against the bottom which supports you in a straight run in the deep also provides the resistance necessary for a turn. The flex properties of your skis determine the turn radius. As the skis are forced in reverse camber by snow pressure they are bent in an arc, and they travel in this curve. Your ski bottoms must be banked into the snow against the direction of travel for the maximum resistance and turning force. You can experience this quite easily.

Ski down the fall line in powder. Lower your hips to sink in the knees. Drive both knees in one direction. Your skis will immediately bank against the snow and turn. To increase the turn sharpness, drive the knees farther up the hill, increasing the skis' banking angle.

BANKING SKI BOTTOMS

Banking ski bottoms to turn

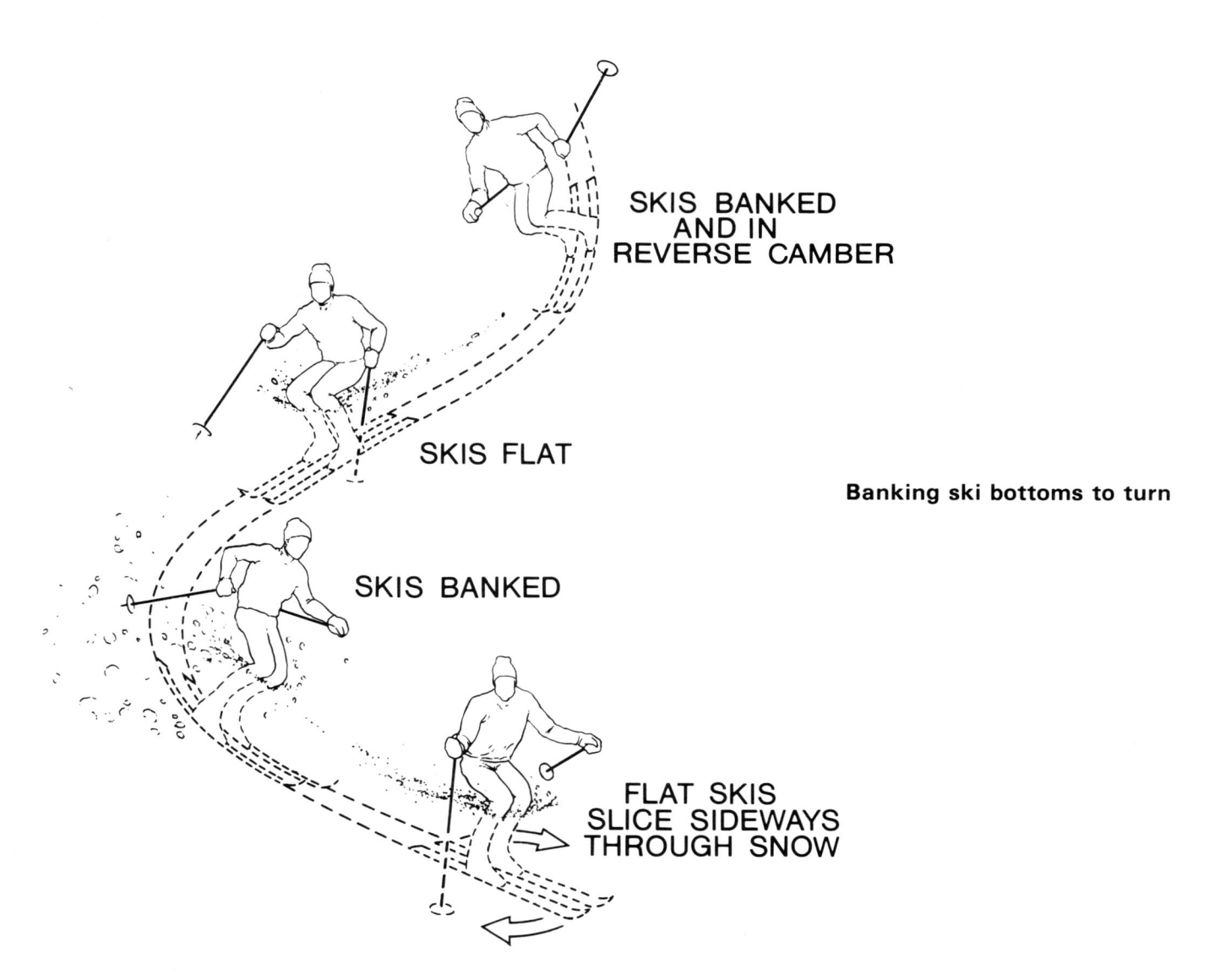

Because of the need to bank the ski bottoms, you will need to lower your hips over your feet to achieve a low stance. Remember, the lower you are the more lateral knee motion you have available. You can aid the angle by also banking your whole body into a turn.

The lower stance also helps balance against the snow resistance. Snow pressing against the skis and lower legs slows them down, and your center of mass would go headfirst over the tips if you did not continually hold your upper body back. This restraining is done by constantly pushing the feet forward to balance. Once again, imagine yourself sitting on a bridge facing upstream, dangling your feet with swim fins into the rapid brook. To keep your feet under you requires constantly pushing the toes forward, which soon tires your thigh muscles. Expect burning thigh muscles after long stretches in the deep.

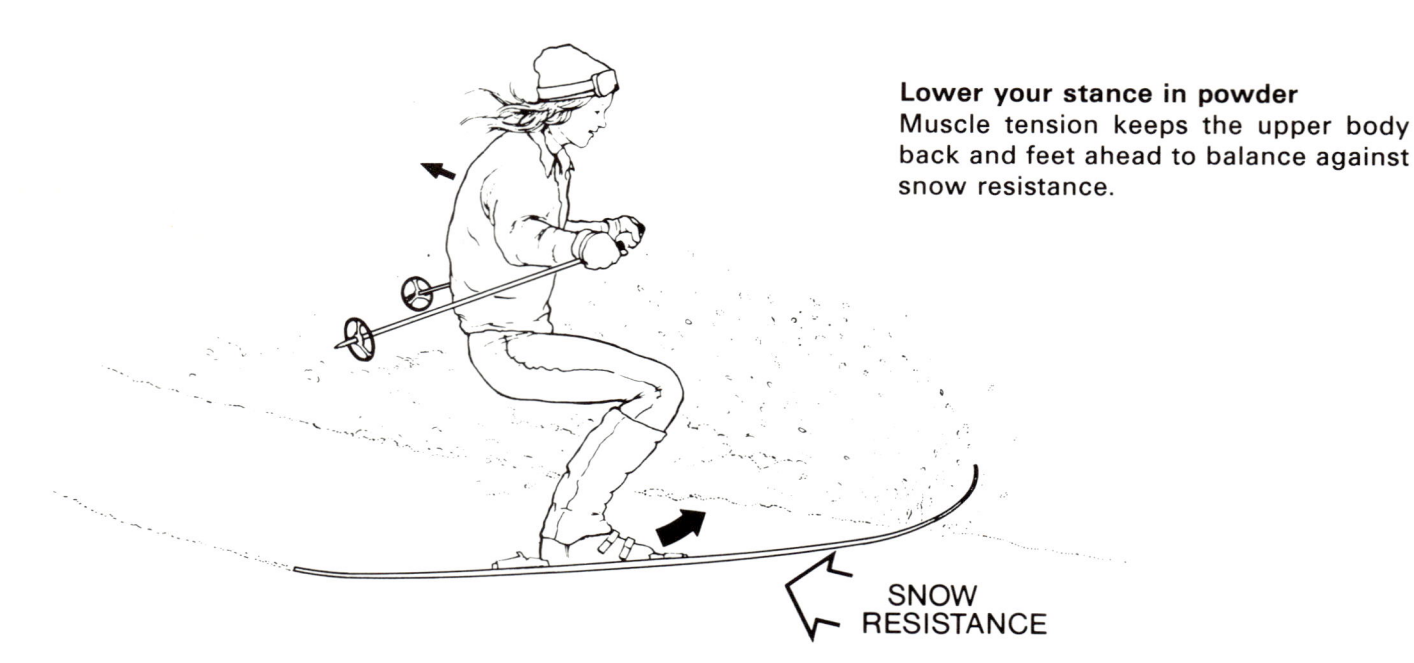

Lower your stance in powder
Muscle tension keeps the upper body back and feet ahead to balance against snow resistance.

SNOW RESISTANCE

Banking the ski bottoms from one direction to another in a turn means the ski must be flat when changing arcs, just as on hard pack an edge change requires passing through a flat ski phase.

Flat skis slice sideways easily through the snow to steer into the turn. If you become a real powder fanatic, you'll buy the softest, thinnest skis available and wax the side walls for even less friction. The big trick is to get the skis near enough to the surface that snow resistance to the boots and legs is minimized. To be technically correct, when you take a header in the fluff don't say "I caught an edge" but rather "I caught a boot and shin."

In very light powder the resistance is small, and you may be able to ski with knee cranks left and right. In any other snow consistency, you'll need unweighting.

While skiing the fall line, flex the legs smoothly and then extend up forcefully. At the end of the leg extension, flex down again and let the skis plane toward the surface. Drive your flexed knees into the new turn. Complete the turn by extending your legs, then flex again and drive the surfacing skis into the next turn with your knees. You'll feel as though you are pulling the feet upward and slightly forward as you flex. Use a pole plant to time the start of the knee flexion and turn.

TURNING IN POWDER WITH UP UNWEIGHTING

Up unweighting in powder
A definite unweighting motion can start the skis into a turn.

That was a lot of words to say "Down, up, down, up . . ." As you reduce weight on the skis they rise and are easier to start into the new turn. You may actively help them rise by an avalement motion, pulling up on your feet. With speed, your skis are in considerable reverse camber near the end of a turn. Combined with the snow resiliency this can give you a nice rebound to help unweight. If you need extra unweighting, throw your arms higher up into the air with each turn. In extremely heavy snow you may even have to break the rules and momentarily sit on the tails to push your feet ahead so the tips surface. During the turning phase use foot steering and knee drive to twist the skis into the new direction. I prefer to ski powder with a great deal of anticipation, keeping my upper body facing down the fall line. This gives me a large twisting force to initiate a turn. Some skiers will use less anticipation, but will drive the outside hand around to help rotate their skis into the turn.

Another way to aid the twisting is by projecting your hips directly outward. This is not a rotation movement, but a type of lateral projection. It causes your skis to pivot about the tip area by more forcefully displacing the tails into the new turn. You can also start the skis banking during this motion by projecting your upper body forward into the turn. You'll feel as though your chest area is launched outward into the fall line. Leaning on the pole provides a pivoting aid. Use large baskets in powder to get more support for a firm pole plant.

Rebound unweighting in powder

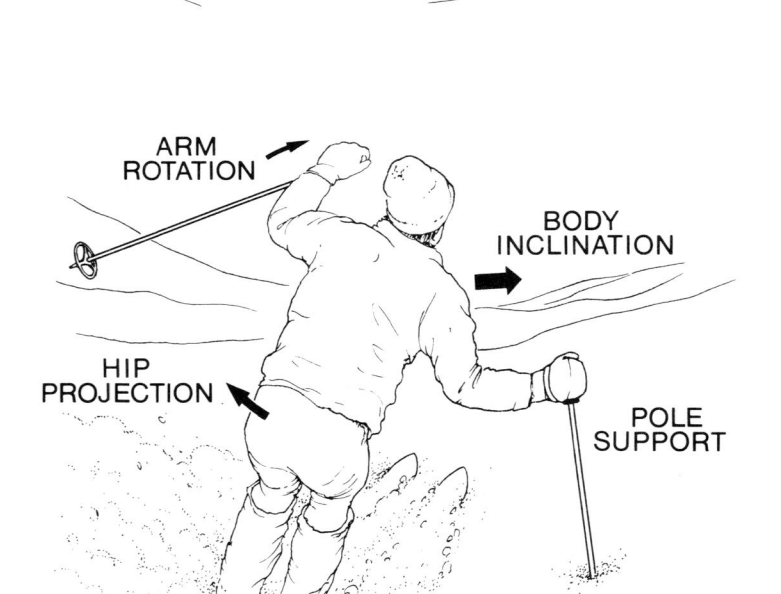

Aids to powder turns

The secret is to be smooth and rhythmic. Jerky motions won't do anything. Keep your skis continually turning in the fall line, as radical solitary turns from a traverse are difficult to make. Due to the slowing effect of powder, and the need for speed to keep the skis planing, you'll be skiing steeper slopes than normal. You will gain speed staying in the fall line, but continual turns will control your descent.

When you start a run, head directly down the fall line rather than traversing. That way you will pick up the necessary speed and also will only have to make half a turn for your first turn. From a stop, turn one ski and then the other straight down the hill, remove your poles, and go. If you're ambitious, jump straight up from your stopped position, turn your skis in midair to point downhill, give a yodel and you're off.

Head for the untracked snow whenever you can find it. Stop at the bottom of a slope and look back at your tracks. This is where one round symmetrical turn after another should really show. Stay loose in the knees to soak up any hidden bumps. Skiing a steep mogul field is fun on a powder day, as your speed is less than it would be on a hard packed day and you have additional time to plan your line.

Once you learn to like powder, you'll cringe when skiers traverse across a slope before you've had a chance to ski it. The best powder is untracked, partly for esthetic reasons but mainly because it's more fun. In cut up snow the skis alternately speed up and slow down, making balance difficult. Ski tips are also easily deflected by hitting piles of disturbed snow. Look for large drifts or untracked piles of snow to ski through to help control your speed. Avoid hitting clumps of snow while skidding sideways, so you don't get thrown over. Just take them straight on. They will slow you down, and also amaze onlookers as you explode a snow pile into a cloud of flakes.

If you head into a tree area to find the last unravaged snow, remember to remove your pole straps. That way if a basket snags on anything you won't dislocate your arm. Wear goggles to protect your eyes from unseen branches, and ski with a friend for safety. It's a good rule anytime you venture off the patrolled trails.

Unfortunately, all new snow isn't light and fluffy. For the lightest snow, stick to steep north facing slopes, or tree shaded areas. With warm temperatures or sun exposure the powder can be like mashed potatoes. With a freeze the surface can become hard, while still soft underneath, a condition known as "breakable crust." With the addition of wind even to dry snow the surface can also become packed and rippled, resulting in "wind pack." Any of these complications can call for additional unweighting efforts, exaggerating an up motion to surface your skis to start them into the turn. You must be balanced over the skis, and be sensitive to rapid changes in snow condition. For extreme conditions you can always hop the skis up out of the snow to turn, or stop by skiing uphill, make a kick turn, and proceed.

Skiing untracked snow can be an exhilarating experience. Don't worry too much about how, just get out and do it. Powder is really 90 percent in the head and 10 percent in the technique. If you think smooth and graceful, you'll ski that way and enjoy it. This is a chance to express yourself, to adapt to the snow and to become one with it.

The joy of powder

39
INTRIGUE ON ICE

Too often ice becomes a skier's last stand. Problems caused by ice are inability to hold an edge, excessive skidding without control, and general apprehension. The very sight of sun reflecting off a shiny patch sends far too many skiers heading for the bar to stare at ice in their drinks instead. However, look at the bright side of things. Fewer skiers will be on the slopes, and skiing ice will make you a better skier for other conditions. There's even a special breed of skier who enjoy the extra challenge ice provides.

Ice is formed when the individual snowflakes start to melt and refreeze together. The crystal formations are destroyed due to temperature from the sun, wind or rain, and also due to pressure from skis forcing them together. Several categories of snow are lumped under the general category of "ice." Hard pack is white and sometimes smooth looking. However, you can still get a good edge and throw sprays of snow from your edges. Frozen granular, a typical spring condition, is a rough icy surface. You'll see a diffused glare from the sun reflect off it. Luckily, with warmth, frozen granular softens into corn and then a slushy surface. Real ice has lost its white color and may be "gray" or, even worse, "blue." The sun glints sharply when reflecting from its surface.

Thankfully, hills are seldom solidly covered with one type of snow. Choose a trail carefully to avoid the worst ice. Loose snow crystals blow off exposed surfaces, leaving a hard pack surface underneath. If you find a spot sheltered from the wind, the snow will be better. For example, the lee side of a stand of trees will protect snow. You might even find a bonanza of soft snow by skiing trails on the lee side of a ridge. A fierce wind blowing up and over that ridge could drop all its airborne snow just past the crest.

Since skiers pack out snow, causing it to harden, choose trails which normally have less skier traffic. On well-traveled runs, stay to the side of the trail. All rules have exceptions, so look at the snow. If it was slushy the previous day the trail edges could have frozen into ruts, forcing you to stay in the center. Remember that the tops of moguls have softer snow, since most people ski around them. Find where the snow cats are grooming, so you can ski the slopes they have softened and manicured. In frozen granular, follow the sun around, starting with east facing slopes. With judicious planning you may be able to enjoy corn snow all day, rather than ice or slush.

Proper equipment always aids skiing, and this is especially true on ice. A longer ski gives you more gripping edge. Your ski will hold better on ice if it maintains contact with the surface and doesn't chatter. A highly damped ski is best. Most racing skis distribute more of your weight to the tips and tails, which will aid your hold on ice. Torsional resistance should also be on the high side, so the ski isn't as easily deflected from its arced course. Most importantly, the edges must be sharp. A piece of steel with a perfect right angle and a sharp edge bites into the snow far better than a rounded, nicked edge. To ensure that this edge carves efficiently, use cants if you need them. I keep my feet apart to increase my edging

Aids for ice

capacity on ice. Any free play between your leg and the ski can induce vibration. This means the boot should fit well and transmit lateral knee motions instantly. Any slop in the bindings caused by maladjustment should be removed. If the bindings are worn and "give" a little, they should be replaced. Missing a pole plant destroys a turn. If your pole tips are dull and slide on the ice, replace them. Special ice points which grip well on hard snow can be inserted.

Technically, ice poses no problems in starting turns. The difficulties arise from the lack of friction, consequent high speed, and large amount of edging required. You're going to move fast, so start out on slopes with half the pitch you normally ski. Ideally, you should carve continually on ice, to cause the ski edge to always bite into the surface. When a skid begins, control is sacrificed, as skidding skis are very difficult to direct. Therefore, a stance that enables you to stand balanced on an edge is quite important. Let's reexamine some concepts of angulation.

Stand sideways on a very steep short patch of ice. Plant your downhill pole an extra foot downhill and remove the uphill pole basket from the snow. Now sidestep down toward the pole with your lower leg. Lift the upper leg and bring it under the body, but keep it slightly in the air. You should be balanced in this position. Remove the downhill pole from the snow to verify balance. Feel all your weight press straight down on the uphill edge of your foot. Your uphill shoulder will be higher than the downhill one, making a shoulder "slope" greater than the snow slope.

ANGULATED POSITION ON ICE

This stance will give you optimum edging on ice. Keep your body mostly square to the skis. Turns will be easy enough to start, so you won't need anticipation to twist the skis. Obviously, the steeper the slope, the more you must angulate for balance. This means also angling the knees inward and bending sideways outward at the waist. This is sometimes called a comma position. It's an aggressive stance, with your upper body out over your downhill ski, and you'll have to remind your brain that it's okay. A lower body position gives you greater knee flex for increased angulation. The important point is that the ski be edged enough to bite into the ice.

Now try this stance with a little action.

Find a short but steep patch of hard snow or ice. Traverse in a straight line across it at slow to moderate speed. Lift the uphill ski so that you are carving on one ski. If your ski skids, vary your body position until you can maintain a single track across the hill. Try to distribute your weight over the whole ski. Taking several runs, see how easily a skid is caused by any of these motions: leaning your torso up the hill; straightening to a high stance; rotating your downhill hand, shoulder, or hip "ahead" of your body; leaning too far forward. As your lower ski slides out in each case, regain balance

ANGULATION FOR CARVING ON ICE

Angulation on ice
For maximum edging keep feet apart and angle sideways at the waist so your shoulders form a greater angle than the slope.

Verifying stance for carving

by lowering your uphill ski onto the surface. Once you have a confident stance, start skiing in a series of increasingly steeper arcs across the ice, until you end up starting down the fall line. Keep two skis on the snow, apart for balance, but put your weight mainly on the outside ski. Leave smooth rounded tracks.

As you've discovered, body position is crucial to staying on maximum edge and avoiding a flat ski. If you're used to lazy, upright, banking turns you'll be in trouble. Stay low, balanced, and angulated with your weight primarily on your outside ski.

Keeping contact with the snow facilitates carving. Whenever this contact is lost the skis may start to chatter or skid. Rough motions or small errors are magnified on ice, so very little unweighting is really necessary or desirable. Sudden down or up motions can result in a skid, as can any sudden changes in direction. You'll need smooth, rounded turns as much as possible without a lot of rotary or twisting motions.

In a "normal" parallel turn, both skis are momentarily flat on the snow. This is a no-no for efficient ice skiing. Transferring weight to a flat ski may cause it to skid. You should always be on an edge, which requires a step turn.

Finish a turn in a low stance, with your feet apart and weight almost entirely on the downhill ski. Step out your unweighted uphill ski onto its inside edge, keeping it parallel. Transfer your weight smoothly sideways to the upper ski. Carve into the fall line pressing against the turning ski with knee extension to weight it. Step the inner ski parallel, but still separated from the outer. As centrifugal force adds to your weight, flex to increase edging and then step to start a new turn.

STEP TURN ON ICE

Step turn on ice
Step to always maintain a carving edge on the snow.

In summary, edge early and weight early. Imagine you're as stealthy and lithe as a tiger as you ski the ice this way. Feel surefooted, using quiet, refined and effortless motions.

Of course, we can't always ski ideal rounded turns, and skids do happen. Try to recover by simply stepping to the uphill ski. Another possibility is to flatten your lower ski and twist it in the direction of the skid. Then re-edge it and carve again. The best alternative is simply to start a new turn. Step out your uphill ski onto its inner edge, but this time stem it, to point more downhill, in the direction of the skid. Transfer weight to it and you'll turn easily. Interestingly, one of the simplest early turns is also one of the most advanced.

In fall line or mogul skiing, rapid turns may cause skids. Your edges will still bite, so set them for short, sharp edge sets. Keep turning to control speed. Where you might normally make one turn on a mogul, make two, throwing in an extra turn on the back side of the bump. Keep the feet apart for balance, but still feel as though you are on only one ski at a time.

Admittedly, ice is more demanding than packed powder. It requires precise edging and smooth motions. But once you gain confidence, ice can actually be a fun experience, and it certainly beats skiing on mud and rocks.

EPILOGUE
WHERE TO FROM HERE?

To be reading this epilogue, either you have a bad case of insomnia or you have really applied yourself to learning the sport. By now you know how to move your knees left and right and up and down, and how to balance with your upper body. If there's snow on a slope you are ready to ski it. Your movements are fluid, refined and subtle. Other skiers may turn their heads to watch as you ski by. Everything you do on skis feels good and therefore looks good.

But you're only at a new beginning. Maybe you'll want to tackle racing or ballet skiing. Perhaps you'd like to patrol or instruct. How about that last run you took? Was it really as good as it could have been? Could you ski that trail on ice or in a white-out? What about that steep run waiting on the next mountain, where the powder is so deep everyone claims you'll need a snorkel to ski it? There really is no final limit. Just by being on skis you've been finding and surpassing personal limitations, and discovering a little about yourself on the way. Perhaps, all along, without realizing it, you have truly been a master of the mountain.

GLOSSARY

ANGULATION: a laterally balanced stance on the uphill edges, where the lower body edges the skis and the upper body must compensate by angling down the fall line over the edged skis.

ANTICIPATION: a movement of the upper body in the direction of an intended turn before edges are changed for the actual turn initiation. This can also be accomplished by a quiet upper body with the skis turning away from the intended turn direction. The net result either way is a twisted body position which can powerfully "unwind" the skis into a turn.

ATHLETIC STANCE: a relaxed, balanced, ready position common to many sports. It's characterized by feet somewhat apart, flexed ankles and knees, hips over the feet, torso bent slightly forward, hands in front, and head up.

AVALEMENT: an active retraction and extension of the legs, combined with a folding and unfolding at the waist, to swallow changes in terrain. This keeps a skier from being thrown into the air. It's especially useful at higher speeds in the moguls.

BALANCING: remaining upright over the feet without muscular strain, despite changes in terrain or speed.

BANKED TURNS: turns in which the ski edges are controlled by leaning the whole body from an upright stance.

BRAQUAGE: a powerful foot and leg steering action, aided by knee thrust, done from a wide stance.

CAMBER: the built-in bow-like arch shape of the ski; this serves to distribute a skier's weight throughout the skis' length.

CANT: a mechanical compensation in boots or on the skis to correct any natural misalignment of the knees and feet. It permits easier edging without requiring a change in the skier's basic stance.

CARVED TURN: a turn in which the skis' edge engagement prevents sideways motion (skidding). This results in an efficient forward motion with good control and maximum speed. Carved tracks show a narrow, smooth, and distinct arc.

CENTRIFUGAL FORCE: the inertial force which tries to throw a skier to the outside of a turn, requiring a compensating inward lean to balance over the feet.

CHECK: a dynamic rapid skid to slow down, ending with an abrupt edge set.

CHRISTIE (CHRISTY): a turn which is finished by skidding on both uphill edges.

COMPLETING A TURN: finishing a turn by continuing to ski in a round track back up the hill until speed has been controlled enough to start the next turn.

COUNTER ROTATION: when skis are unweighted, twisting the upper body in one direction will cause the skis to twist in the opposite direction.

DOWN UNWEIGHTING: flexing in the knees to momentarily reduce weight on the skis and make the start of a turn easier.

EDGE SET: abruptly increasing the edge angle or edge weighting during a skid or sharp turn.

EDGING: placing a ski's base at an angle to the snow. The amount of edge can be controlled by angling the ankle, knee or hip, or by leaning the body.

FALL LINE: the downhill path a snowball would follow if released at a skier's feet.

FLEX (KNEES): the bending of the knees. "To flex" means to contract the legs, bringing the feet closer to the body.

FLEX (SKIS): the amount a ski will temporarily bend when a force is applied against its camber (longitudinal flex) or the amount it will twist when a rotary force is applied around its long axis (torsional flex).

FLOW: a viscous boot liner material which slowly conforms to the foot's shape.

FORWARD LEAN (IN BOOTS): a built-in angle thrusting the lower leg toward the toes, resulting in a bent ankle and flexed knee.

GARLAND: any repeated maneuver which doesn't cause a turn, resulting in a garland-like track across the hill.

GRADUATED LENGTH METHOD (GLM): a learning program which emphasizes starting on very short skis and progressing in ski length as ability improves.

HIP PROJECTION: a motion of the hip sideways (not rotated) away from the intended turn direction to aid in displacing the skis into the turn.

HOCKEY STOP: a rapid parallel stop accomplished by twisting the skis across the direction of travel and skidding on the edges.

INCLINATION: a body lean in the direction of the new turn.

INDEPENDENT LEG ACTION: allowing each leg to bend or twist as terrain or turns require, instead of locking both legs together into one unit.

INSIDE EDGE: the ski edge which is on the inside (big toe side) of the foot.

INSIDE SKI: that ski in a turn which takes the inside (and hence shorter) path.

JETTING: a sudden forward ski thrust occurring after the release of edge pressure in some high speed turns. It's caused by the body having been balanced against a rapid slowing, and it may result in a temporary off-balance stance.

KICK TURN (KT): a standing 180 degree change of direction initiated by kicking the lower ski upward.

KNEE CRANK: driving the knees forcefully left or right from a flexed position.

LATERAL PROJECTION: a sideways motion (usually stepped) of first the uphill and then the downhill ski. This can efficiently change a course, maintain a constant edge contact, and eliminate having to lean the upper body excessively into a turn.

LEVERAGE: the application of body weight to the fore, middle, or aft portions of the skis.

NASTAR: the National Standard Race, in which amateur skiers compete to see how close they can come to a pacesetter's time.

ORTHOTIC: a device to support the foot and improve edging capability.

OUTSIDE EDGE: the ski edge which is on the outside (little toe side) of the foot.

OUTSIDE SKI: the ski in a turn which takes the outside (and hence longer) path.

PARALLEL: both skis continuously lined up in the same direction, but not necessarily touching each other.

PIVOTING: twisting the skis. This foot swivel is most easily done on a flat ski or on a bump.

PLATFORM (as in "creating a platform"): a sharp edging at the end of a turn which sets up the skier for a step or rebound.

POLEPLANT: placing the downhill pole into the snow at the start of the arc of a new turn. This pole action may aid in timing, unweighting, balancing for the weight transfer, deflecting the skis, accelerating, or stabilizing upper body motion.

PRESSURE CONTROL: varying the amount of weight applied to or reduced from the skis.

PRE-TURN: a tightened radius uphill turn (or skid) prior to starting a new turn across the fall line.

PRONATION: a common foot rotation which reduces the effectiveness of an edging movement from the lower leg.

QUIET UPPER BODY: keeping the chest area facing somewhat down the fall line and turning the skis from the feet and legs.

REBOUND: an unweighting which results when forces are removed which have pushed the skis into reverse camber and which have compressed leg muscles. This results in a strong upward spring off the snow.

REPLOIEMENT: letting the knees freely flex and extend to soak up bumps.

RETRACTION-EXTENSION: the flexing and straightening of the legs.

REVERSE CAMBER: a ski under pressure flexes into this shape, which is opposite its normal arch.

ROTATION: twisting the upper body, arms, or hips in the direction of a turn. If the skis are weighted while twisting, this motion can cause the skis to follow, although it's inefficient and results in an off-balance position for the next turn.

ROUND TURNS: turns which make a continuous arc, in an "S" shape, without straight traverse sections.

SCHUSS: a downhill run without turns.

SHORTSWING: repeated round turns in steeper fall lines with a definite edgeset and rebound.

SIDECUT: the hourglass shape of a ski, with the waist being narrower than the tip or tail. It functions to cause a turn.

SIDESLIP: a downward slide at right angles to the direction the skis point. It is started by reducing the edge angle, and stopped by increasing the edging.

SIDESTEPPING: walking sideways up or down a slope, using uphill edges to keep from sliding down the fall line.

SKID: a sideways slide of the ski at the same time it is going forward.

SNOWPLOW: a wide V-shaped stance with the skis on edge.

STEM: the displacement of one ski from a parallel stance to form a wedge position, where the tips are close and the tails spread apart.

STEM, DOWNHILL (ABSTEM): moving the downhill ski into a braking wedge to slow down.

STEM, UPHILL: moving the uphill ski into a wedge to initiate a turn.

STEERING: a rotary motion applied to the skis. This twisting around the axis of the legs aids a turn.

STEP TURN: a turn in which the uphill ski is stepped laterally sideways to change edges for a turn (see "Lateral Projection"). The step may be parallel or stemmed.

TERRAIN UNWEIGHTING: a lightening or removal of weight on the skis by skiing over a bump or other convex terrain.

TRAVERSE: a straight run on two uphill edges across the fall line.

UNWEIGHTING: reducing pressure of the skis to the snow. This is used to more easily twist the skis into a new direction.

UP UNWEIGHTING: a flexing of the knees which has been preceded by a leg extension, giving an upward motion to greatly increase the period of weight reduction on the skis.

VERTICAL DROP: the elevation difference between the top and bottom of a ski area or a particular ski lift.

WEDEL: continuous turns in the fall line without traversing.

WEDGE: a V-shaped stance with ski tips near each other and tails apart. When ski bases are essentially flat on the snow it is a "gliding" wedge, and when skis are riding their inside edges it is a "braking" wedge.

WEIGHTING: increasing pressure of the skis on the snow. This is useful to maintain snow contact, or to increase reverse camber for a tighter turn or more rebound. It happens while extending upward, stepping to a ski, stopping a downward flex, tightening a turn rapidly, checking, or suddenly skiing uphill, as on a bump.

WEIGHT TRANSFER: the changing of weight from one ski to another, generally to the outside ski of a new turn.

WIDE TRACK: a feet apart stance for better lateral balance and a more powerful steering force.

WIND CHILL FACTOR: the still air temperature which would be equivalent in coldness to a warmth robbing wind at a higher actual thermometer reading.